GLOBAL INSTABILITY

Social Indicators Research Series

Volume 13

This new series aims to provide a public forum for single treatises and collections of papers on social indicators research that are too long to be published in our journal *Social Indicators Research*. Like the journal, the book series deals with statistical assessments of the quality of life from a broad perspective. It welcomes the research on a wide variety of substantive areas, including health, crime, housing, education, family life, leisure activities, transportation, mobility, economics, work, religion and environmental issues. These areas of research will focus on the impact of key issues such as health on the overall quality of life and vice versa. An international review board, consisting of Ruut Veenhoven, Joachim Vogel, Ed Diener, Torbjorn Moum, Mirjam A.G. Sprangers and Wolfgang Glatzer, will ensure the high quality of the series as a whole.

The titles published in this series are listed at the end of this volume.

GLOBAL INSTABILITY

Uncertainty and new visions in political economy

Edited by

STEPHEN MCBRIDE
Simon Fraser University,
Burnaby, B.C., Canada

LAURENT DOBUZINSKIS
Simon Fraser University,
Burnaby, B.C., Canada

MARJORIE GRIFFIN COHEN
Simon Fraser University,
Burnaby, B.C., Canada

and

JAMES BUSUMTWI-SAM
Simon Fraser University,
Burnaby, B.C., Canada

Springer-Science+Business Media, B.V.

A C.I.P. Catalogue record for this book is available from the Library of Congress.

ISBN 978-94-010-3947-5 ISBN 978-94-010-0251-6 (eBook)
DOI 10.1007/978-94-010-0251-6

Printed on acid-free paper

TABLE OF CONTENTS

LIST OF TABLES

LIST OF CONTRIBUTORS

Bradley Bowden is Head of the School of Management at Queensland's Griffith University, Australia.

James Busumtwi-Sam teaches political science at Simon Fraser University, specializing in international relations and comparative development.

Duncan Cameron teaches political science at the University of Ottawa, Ontario.

Benjamin J. Cohen is Louis G. Lancaster Professor of International Political Economy at the University of California, Santa Barbara.

Marjorie Griffin Cohen is an economist who is a professor of political science and women's studies at Simon Fraser University.

Gus diZerega teaches political science at Whitman College, Walla Walla.

Laurent Dobuzinskis teaches political science at Simon Fraser University.

Daniel Drache is Director of the Robarts Centre for Canadian Studies, York University.

Marc Lee is a research economist with the Canadian Centre for Policy Alternatives, British Columbia office.

Stephen McBride teaches political science at Simon Fraser University, specializing in political economy.

Andrea Migone is a Ph.D. candidate in political science at Simon Fraser University.

Andrew Molloy teaches political science at the University College of Cape Breton, Nova Scotia.

Maureen Appel Molot is Director of The Norman Paterson School of International Affairs at Carleton University.

José G. Vargas Hernández is Professor in the Social Sciences and Humanities Department at the Centro Universitario del Sur Universidad de Guadalajara, Mexico.

Russell A. Williams is a Ph.D. candidate in political science at Simon Fraser University.

John Wiseman is Associate Professor in the School of Social Science and Planning at RMIT University, Melbourne, Australia.

S. McBride et al. (eds.), Global Instability, viii.

ACKNOWLEDGEMENTS

Most of the chapters in this book were originally presented at a conference on Global Turbulence: Instability in National and International Political Economy held at Simon Fraser University (SFU) in July 2001, sponsored by the Department of Political Science at SFU. The conference brought together scholars from four continents with diverse disciplinary backgrounds to examine some of the key theoretical and policy issues arising from the study and practice of political economy, with a central focus on the theme of "turbulence" and "instability" in the new global era. This collection publishes a selection of the best papers from this conference, which have since been reviewed and revised. We would like to thank all those who made the conference possible including, Daniel Cohn, Theodore Cohn, Anil Hira, Michael Howlett, Allen Seager, Jen Chang, Sherry Lloyd, Roxanne Jantzi, Marlie Murphy, Eliza So, Libardo Amaya, Tim Came, Scott Matthews, Fiona MacDonald, Johnna Montgomerie, and Paul Weaver. We are particularly grateful to Margaret Manery for her diligent editorial assistance in preparing this volume.

Financial support for the conference was received from the Boag Foundation, the Social Sciences and Humanities Research Council of Canada, and Simon Fraser University.

S. McBride et al. (eds.), Global Instability, ix–x.

Chapter 1

GLOBAL INSTABILITY: UNCERTAINTY AND NEW VISIONS IN POLITICAL ECONOMY

Stephen McBride
Simon Fraser University

Laurent Dobuzinskis
Simon Fraser University

Marjorie Griffin Cohen
Simon Fraser University

James Busumtwi-Sam
Simon Fraser University

INTRODUCTION

Unprecedented levels of instability and uncertainty have been generated by the complexity of events and trends in the contemporary global political economy. To a large extent, at the crux of this instability is the growing political salience of various forces and activities that appear to transcend and impinge not only upon existing political boundaries and forms of economic production and distribution, but also on the values that underpin social institutions and existing modes of social and cultural differentiation. These activities include, but are not limited to, the phenomenal growth in global trade and private capital flows, increased pressures for financial liberalization and the growing instability of national currencies, increased cross-border flows of people and ideas, and the growth of transnational social movements as well as in various illicit activities associated with transnational organized crime.

While the precise meanings and implications of these trends and phenomena remain unclear, in different ways, they serve to reinforce the fact that the "international" and "domestic" cannot be isolated from each other, analytically or in practice. They also create a pressing need to question the assumptions and values underpinning actual forms of globalization, and of taking a moral/ethical stance on its effects. This book presents a collection of papers that undertake these tasks. The essays examine the political consequences of existing forms of globalization for states and their populations, and explore the issue of alternatives to the dominant model of globalization we are presently experiencing. The various chapters attempt to ground their analysis of instability, uncertainty and change in the real

S. McBride et al. (eds.), Global Instability, 1–6.

problems that globalization creates for states and peoples, and for those who might attempt to devise alternatives.

The opening four chapters explore the operation of and alternatives to the existing trade regime centred around the World Trade Organization (WTO), the challenges posed by currency instability in an environment of financial deregulation, the rights conferred on investors by the North American Free Trade Agreement (NAFTA), and the progressive liberalization of trade in services built into the General Agreement on Trade in Services(GATS). The theme then shifts to the analysis of the national and sub-national dilemmas that are posed by attempting to manage a set of global developments within a given territory. The difficulties faced by states in managing these dilemmas are examined in four chapters that address various industrial, social, and development policy issues. A final sequence of four chapters explore some theoretical alternatives to a globalized world, as well as some of the normative and ethical exigencies that create a need for alternatives. Responses at the level of institutions and ideas are canvassed in these chapters, and the urgency of the problems generated are highlighted.

The initial chapter, by Daniel Drache, explores a still-born post-war international organization, the International Trade Organization (ITO), that offers a different vision of how a globally integrated economy might operate. On the basis of his investigation of the post-war concept of an ITO, Drache concludes that the WTO is a truncated version of the original concept of an international governing body to supervise world trade. He argues that the WTO model privileges the interests of capital, and that an international institution with a wider mandate that takes into account the goals of other social forces, like full employment, is needed in this field. As Drache shows, the case for this exists not only theoretically, but also in an actual example, the ITO, the characteristics of which are worth recalling. The chapter concludes by noting that if it was once possible to envisage a broader globalization regime it is possible to do so again – and there is a pressing need to do this.

The problems created by accelerating cross-border competition among currencies and the resultant turbulence in the international monetary environment is the focus of Benjamin Cohen's chapter. In addressing the question of whether national currencies are becoming obsolete, Cohen argues that currency competition compels governments to choose from among a limited number of strategies, only one of which involves preservation of a traditional territorial money. His analysis suggests that many national currencies may disappear, leading to an increasing number of regional currencies of one kind or another – a distinctly new geography of money. But there is no sure way to predict what that new geography of money will ultimately look like. The chapter concludes with the observation that while we have a fairly good idea of the principal factors that are likely to influence state preferences, many actual configurations are possible and even probable. The chapter by Maureen Molot shifts the lens back to international trade through an examination of the negotiation and evolution of Chapter 11 (the investment chapter) of the North America Free Trade Agreement (NAFTA). The basic question posed is that of regime evolution: has the experience of the signatories met their expectations and what are the processes for regime evolution or change? Molot analyzes the demands and expectations of the NAFTA parties around the investment chapter, outlines the norms and procedures established by the regime, reviews the cases brought thus far under Chapter 11, and then examines demands for changes in the regime.

Russell Williams continues the examination of trade issues. He sets out to show that an understanding of the history of the General Agreement on Trade in Services (GATS) requires an account of how international norms or "ideas" altered policymakers' conceptions of service industries. Beginning in the early 1970s, several private sector think tanks and industry associations succeeded in convincing national trade negotiators, that services could be traded like goods and consequently, barriers should be liberalized to promote efficiency. As a result, leading multinational service conglomerates were successful in getting the GATS included in the WTO. The importance of ideas in this story poses lessons for both structurally-based theories of International Political Economy, which focus exclusively on actors' materially-determined interests, and for popular political debate. Here, globalization of service industries was not technologically inevitable, but rather was the product of changing understandings of trade in services.

The next four chapters examine a number of sectoral, industrial, and social policy issues that illustrate the dilemmas confronting national and sub-national actors and groups as they seek to cope with globalization's challenges. In chapter five, Bradley Bowden and Andrew Molloy compare the evolution of the coal mining industry in the Cape Breton area of Nova Scotia in Canada and the Queensland coal mining industry in Australia, highlighting the different responses to crises produced by changing markets, alternative energy sources and new mining techniques. Their analysis shows that while the term "globalization" is a relatively recent addition to scholarly discourse, exposure to the vagaries of the international market is hardly a new experience to those in the natural resource sector. Trade in such commodities as timber, animal furs and minerals became the "staples" upon which "New World" economies were built. And for the mining communities of both Cape Breton and Queensland the experience of the last 100 years indicates the continued vulnerability of the natural resource sector to market forces, whether or not the industry is in public or private hands. Marc Lee addresses the past, present and future of active industrial policy. In the first part of his analysis, Lee surveys the historical development of today's industrialized nations, and finds legacies of government involvement to channel resources into strategic sectors, protect emerging industries and offset market forces. In the second part he shows how industrial policy has been constrained by WTO rules. Finally, Lee considers what is left of industrial policy in a WTO world and the remaining options available to countries. He argues for a renewed public sector as an anchor for industrial policy in the future.

The next two chapters provide an interesting contrast of state responses to globalization pressures in Australia and Mexico. John Wiseman provides a critical, grounded discussion of policy options that are beginning to be explored by governments seeking alternatives to neoliberal political and economic directions. The discussion combines an overview of relevant international trends and dilemmas with lessons to be learned from the experience of a state government in Australia – the Bracks Labor Government in Victoria. Noting that the critique of extreme forms of neoliberalism is increasingly influential, Wiseman traces the emergence of an alternative political and policy paradigm that strives for a more balanced and integrated relationship between economic, social and environmental values and goals. Wiseman concedes that the shift from neoliberal policy directions is slow, uneven and contested. However emerging spaces for exploring new policy directions provide important opportunities for linking alternative policy ideas to new approaches to political engagement and policy implementation.

The role of the state in Mexico is the focus of the chapter by José G. Vargas Hernández. This role is analyzed as one of transition from an "entrepreneurial state" toward a state of entrepreneurs. He argues that the era of the presidential Mexican entrepreneurial state, protectionist and populist with some emphasis on a welfare state model, was followed by presidential reinvention of the state based on neoliberal premises. This was the result of several factors including the economic and political impact of globalization and its pervasive effects on unequal income distribution, weak governance, political instability and lack of property security. It also reflected a new relationship between government and business enterprises. The new regime has achieved some impressive results in terms of economic growth and development. But this has been accompanied by an increase in poverty, declines in real incomes, increased unemployment, and a widening gap between the rich and the poor, leading to fissures in society and fuelling guerrilla warfare and crime waves. Vargas argues that only a turn to democratic legitimation of the regime could produce an ability to manage such problems.

The final four essays examine possible alternatives to existing forms of globalization and take up some important ethical issues and dilemmas raised by its effects, which centre on the kinds of values that do, or should, underpin political and social institutions. The section begins with an examination of ecological issues that are among the most contentious with growing globalization. Gus diZerega shows that traditional political institutions have done poorly in protecting these ecological values and the advent of global economic integration threatens them even further. Forestlands are poorly suited for either traditional political management and oversight or traditional privatization. Using temperate forests, particularly

U.S. National Forests, as his case study, diZirega explores more promising alternatives. He argues that geographically defined governments do not handle such public interests well. In the case of the U.S., traditional bureaucratic management, congressional oversight, and interest group politics have done a poor job. The public record elsewhere is often no better, and privatization also tends to ignore important values served by these public lands. diZerega shows that the model of a democratically governed trust holds great promise for solving or ameliorating many issues. Based on experience with the National Trust of England, Wales, and Northern Ireland, public forests would be better and more democratically governed by forest trusts than by traditional democratic institutions. They would also be more attentive to the complexity of values served by each forest than would privatization.

Laurent Dobuzinskis examines the contemporary renewal of interest in the rhetoric of civic republicanism, which is particularly evident in France and the United States but is by no means limited to these countries, as possibly pointing the way toward new creative responses to the challenges of globalism. Liberal democracies are pulled between the neoliberal logic of increasingly global market forces and the democratic aspirations of citizens. And it is often argued that the social democratic consensus of the post-war years no longer provides adequate answers to this dilemma. Dobuzinskis argues that civic republicanism has been used both as a means of ineffectively invoking a nostalgic past and as a source of inspiration for the articulation of a new cosmopolitan political project. While this chapter underlines the merits of the latter, it also argues that civic republicanism is an ambiguous ideology within which both retrograde and emancipating ideas are inextricably meshed.

Andrea Migone contends that the current approach to globalization suffers from a dual problem. On the one hand, many of the definitions of globalization are unduly simplistic and often fail to capture the multi-layered complexity of current changes especially the cultural and institutional elements. He also addresses a second shortcoming of the debate on globalization – the lack of an explicit ethical background, with the exception of some vague notion of market fairness, for what amounts to a highly comprehensive and wide-ranging set of changes and interventions. To correct this situation, Migone assesses the possibilities of the re-emerging field of Economic Personalism. Drawn mainly, but not uniquely, from the tradition of Catholic ethics, Economic Personalism represents a coherent attempt at bringing together economic theory and moral ethics and at applying them to the concrete realities of today's economy.

In the chapter by Duncan Cameron, analytical categories developed by the noted political theorist, C.B. Macpherson, are brought to bear on the need to revisit and update our conceptual thinking about democracy in the age of global instability. Cameron argues that the ascendancy of neoliberalism represents the extension of investor's rights (property rights) to a point where they now trump civic or democratic rights. But what happens when the investors' interests conflict with workers and with the rest of society over the distribution of wealth and income? Does the greatest number win out through democratic government in action? Neoliberalism holds that only the market is productive, and that the public sector represents a burden on society. From there it is just a short step to urging the elimination of public services and arguing for tax cuts. Cameron attributes the deterioration in Canadian democracy, hence his assertion that the country is really a "quasi democracy," to a dynamic whereby the desire of owners of capital to protect the accumulation process has led to basic political rights of representation being overwhelmed by the combined political intervention of foreign and domestic investors to protect their perceived interests. Consequently, he argues that Canada needs a reinvigoration of its democracy amounting to a peaceful democratic revolution.

PART I INTERNATIONAL PRESSURES

Chapter 2

WHEN LABOUR AND INVESTMENT STANDARDS ALMOST MATTERED: A PUTATIVE HISTORY LESSON IN TRADE POLITICS THAT OUGHT NOT TO BE FORGOTTEN

Daniel Drache
York University

INTRODUCTION

When the international order was redesigned from scratch in the late 1940s, policy makers had to decide whether a global trade organization could extend beyond trade and address issues like labour standards, developmental needs and human rights. Like today they needed a rules-based system to organize the world economy. Indeed they had to find the optimum structure for such a body in which liberalism, in the words of the *Economist*, would be "freed from theology"[1] and effect a compromise between market forces and the democratic aspirations of people.

Along with the World Bank and the International Monetary Fund (IMF), the International Trade Organization (ITO) formed the centrepiece of a new kind of international organization. What was particularly novel about the International Trade Organization, proposed in the Havana Charter of 1948, was that it was not simply or mainly a trade organization like the WTO, its latter day descendent. The countries of the world rejected the idea that it was possible to maintain firewalls between trade, development, employment standards and domestic policy. The ITO's most distinctive feature was the integration of an ambitious and successful program to reduce traditional trade barriers with a wide-angled agreement that addressed investment, employment standards, development needs, business monopolies and the like. It pioneered the idea that trade disputes had to be settled by consultation and mediation rather than with legal clout. Further it established an institutional linkage between trade and labour standards that would effect a major advance in global governance. Finally it embedded the full employment obligation,

S. McBride et al. (eds.), Global Instability, 9–28.

along with "a commitment to free markets" as the cornerstone of multilateralism.

Despite its bold vision, the U.S. Congress refused to ratify the Havana Charter, even though the U.S. government had signed it. In the end, the Charter's demise had long lasting effects on the world trading system. General Agreement on Tariffs and Trade (GATT), not the ITO, was left in charge and this was to make possible the return of the free trade canon in all international organizations, and in the practice of multi-lateralism over the next four decades.

The global economy of the twenty-first century is strikingly different from the heady-days of the ITO and it would be foolish to believe that the ITO can serve as a template for reforming the WTO. There are, however, some striking parallels. The ITO created a rules based system as did the WTO when it was created. The ITO had to find ways to rescue trade liberalization from the inter-war crisis that had discredited laissez-faire free trade. It spent a lot of time wrestling with the north-south divide that was as divisive then as now. The final dimension of its agenda was the issue of global governance, again much like our own time. Faced by similar issues, the ITO was more ambitious and visionary than the WTO. The ITO founding fathers found a way to link it to the other Bretton Woods institutions. This meant that trade was not beholden to financial markets and it was possible to create linkages to non-trade issues. The ITO accepted the proposition that as a governance structure it would have a place for civil society actors and other organizations such as the International Labour Organization (ILO).

This chapter examines of the historical case of the ITO and, in the process, presents an important argument. Unlike the ITO, the WTO is a truncated version of the original concept of an international governance body responsible for overseeing world trade the WTO model privileges the interests of capital at the expense of public need. As we shall see, there is an emerging consensus about the need for a different kind of international institution in this field that has a wider mandate and appeal, one that takes into account the goals of other social forces, including full employment and development. As well as there being a theoretical case for preserving the social bond, the characteristics of the ITO are worth recalling as a bold experiment in governance in a period when the world community was able to envisage a broader globalization regime. This kind of hinge moment may come again should states begin to address the systemic needs of the world trading system rather than merely look for new ways to boost investment rights. When such a moment occurs, the ITO may remind us that international governance can take a different path, and that the world trading system can look strikingly different than the way it does in our own times. Thus the ITO represents a lesson that ought not to be idly forgotten.

Why A History Lesson?

The ITO highlights the efficacy of policy ideas, both in changing statecraft and in "their practical value in solving political dilemmas that gives them a force in history."[2] The steps taken to create the ITO represented an occasion when the needs of international civil society and modern statecraft coincided, when ordinary people demanded that trade, employment goals and development should reinforce each other in the world trading system. The final Havana text is worth looking at because it is authoritative and comprehensive and because all countries of the globe signed on to it.

The rebuilding of the world's trading system took place in the context of the Keynesian revolution that transformed economic thinking and state practice. The full employment obligation also explains the many linkages that were drawn between trade and non-trade issues. Ideas that transform a discipline or an era or the collective psychology of a period are a relatively rare occurrence. Those that succeed only do so because, at the time the existing orthodoxy is discredited, a powerful and an alternative conceptual framework exists that is compelling and meets popular and elite expectations.

There was a consensus that the ITO, or any similar body, would have to be more than a set of principles. It could not survive on generalities alone. It had to be an effective organization, one that enabled countries to maintain their exports, compete internationally for markets, safeguard their exchange rates and fulfill their employment obligations. All of these factors created the demand for new international rules to organize the world's trading system as a practical exercise in statecraft. In Meade's (1951) words, the ITO had to find the optimum way to internationally maximize production and optimize trade,[3] a formulation which continues to have much contemporary relevance for southern countries.

Of course not everything included in the ITO Charter was innovative; indeed much that was contained in it reflected the conventional wisdom of the period. However, it wanted to modernize liberal free trade values and practices and make them compatible with a Keynesian age. And, in addition, it did have a new vision of political economy that suggested that a trade and investment regime had to be more than an abstract set of rigid legal principles with which to defend investors' rights at any price. Along with the World Bank and the IMF, it formed the centrepiece of new kind of international organization, which in the words of Richard Gardner, "sought to make finance the servant, not the master of human desires internationally."[4]

Recently, a new generation of researchers is beginning to take a second look at the ITO and its larger role in the restructuring of the postwar world. A unique set of conditions pushed full employment onto centre-stage and laissez-faire free trade on to the back burner. For many years, leading international political economy scholars have neglected the complex set of relationships of the ITO and other postwar bodies charged with the functioning of a multilateral international economic order. Their accounts tend to give pride of place both to the IMF and the World Bank in their first decade of operation and generally have little to say about the putative role of the still-born International Trade Organization other than to note that it disappeared from centre stage, a victim of U.S. trade politics. Yet, there is more to those dramatic events than has been acknowledged. Political will, ideas and expectations dramatically converged for a brief critical period to create a different kind of international governance system.

Present at Creation: The Hinge Moment

Created to oversee the world trading system in the immediate postwar period along with the World Bank and the IMF, the ITO was the model for a new kind of international organization. Stamped by the powerful idea that people mattered even more than export opportunities, it embodied the radical ideal that liberal trade principles had to serve the full employment agenda that every industrial country began to adopt in the closing years of the war. With all industrial countries placing "a high and stable level of employment" at the top of their policy agendas, there was no turning back to pre-war arrangements. Along with the principles of multilateralism and trade liberalization, the full employment revolution in economic thought had arrived and a coalition of social forces demanded that the employment and developmental needs of nations be addressed by the countries of the world once peace was restored.

The ITO was established by fifty-three countries at Havana as the Final Act of the UN Conference on Trade and Employment and spanned more than five years of intense international activity in wartime and peacetime.[5] Its over-arching mandate for the regulation of trade included tariff reduction, business cartels, commodity agreements, economic development and foreign direct investment. Hundreds of officials were involved in its creation and there are 100 volumes of transcribed minutes of its deliberations. It was to be, in Truman's words, "the solid foundation of continuous co-operation in economic affairs." A small group of U.S. and U.K. experts had begun to prepare a draft treaty in 1943 outlining the principles, objectives, rules and constitution for an organization responsible for world trade and a draft was ready that explicitly linked trade and employment in the title. *Proposals for the Expansion of World Trade and Employment* were presented in London in 1945 for debate, discussion and revision. This document was subsequently revised at the Geneva meeting and the final text of the treaty, *Suggested Charter for an International Trade Organization of the United Nations* was finalized in Havana in 1948 during the UN Conference on Trade and

Employment. The ITO was to be the third "essential" pillar of the international economic organization of the postwar world.[6]

At the time that the ITO was organized, the notion of giving equal weight to employment considerations and to establishing new multilateral trade rules had become part of mainstream thinking. Traditional methods of liberal trade policy could not be relied on to dismantle trade barriers. The ITO can be understood as a major break from prewar arrangements when all governments believed that international monetary policy alone was "the glue that binds national economies together."[7] Jacob Viner, the doyen of international trade theory and a leading advocate of liberal principles of trade dismissed the outmoded views of the free trader in his influential 1947 article in *Foreign Affairs*: "There are so few free traders in the present-day world, no one pays any attention to their views and no person in authority anywhere advocates free trade."[8] Exchange rate stability, that elusive ideal of classic liberalism, had meant employment losses and falling wages when Central Banks defended the gold standard with a high interest rate policy. The consensus in London, Washington, Paris, Rome, Ottawa, New Delhi and Canberra was that in the new world order state-market relations had to be put on a new footing so that governments would be insulated from market pressures in order to pursue more important goals than commercial gain.

World leaders had learned from the experience of the 1930s, and the failure of the League of Nations, that solving economic problems required practical solutions to complex trade, technical and international questions. In an international economic organization designed to uphold the new world order, the ITO or any similar body would have to be an effective organization, one that covered many complex issues and enabled countries to maintain their exports, compete internationally for markets, safeguard their exchange rates and fulfill their employment obligations. All this demanded new international rules to organize the world's trading system as a practical exercise in statecraft.

In retrospect, linking the objective of a much-broadened concept of trade liberalization with an unequivocal commitment to the goal of full employment is not all that startling. Mass unemployment was the scourge of the interwar period. It overshadowed all other issues and concerns, affected the lives of millions of people and was the social problem that finally destroyed the last remaining vestiges of legitimacy of the gold standard and laissez-faire free trade. Unemployment policy as well as tariff, credit and exchange rate policies were properly regarded as the individual concern of each country. But the experience of the 1930s taught another equally important lesson, namely, that employment was linked in a variety of ways "with the outside world."[9] No country on its own could solve these problems without addressing its international relations with other states.

Still, the reconstruction of a universal expansionist trading system met with well-deserved scepticism from many quarters so long as there was no answer to the question of how "the iron framework of wages, profits, state claims and international payments," could be first eased and then recast?[10] On this fundamental issue Anglo-American diplomacy was of one mind that the postwar order had to be designed from scratch and not simply tinkered with.[11] The idealist anchor of liberal internationalism, "the abnormal laissez-faire interlude of the nineteenth century," would have to be abandoned.[12] In its place countries had to find new ways to maintain exports, compete internationally, preserve their exchange rates and fulfill their employment obligations.

The *Economist* came as close to the truth as anyone in June 1944 when it identified the principal challenge facing postwar policy-makers. As the historic advocate of free trade, it claimed boldly "the greatest need of all was to rescue trade from the atmosphere of theology." If that step was taken then the principles of trade could indeed be recast. The re-establishment of an "expansionist, universal and multilateral trade" had to be the long-term goal of British and American policy. All governments were willing to look at "less than universal and less than completely orthodox alternatives" that could form a "natural starting point for a restructured international order." For the *Economist* understood as well as any government that imposing import controls that reduce living standards was not acceptable when the war ended. The only conclusion to be drawn was that "no country could afford to go back to the gold standard" where international trade was controlled by rigid monetary principles. How did they intend to maintain economies in balance "without a great excess of imports or exports" of the self-regulating market? If the full employment standard replaced the gold standard, what would this mean practically? How would a multilateral, non-discriminatory trading regime embody the idea of the full employment obligation at the international level?

Provisions of the Havana Charter

If the old principles did not work, the thinking in elite circles was that new ones were needed. The nations of the world could not suspend trade policy because the world was such a disorderly place. Instead they had to define an international division of labour that permitted countries to maximize their production and optimize trade.[13] In practice, they needed an economic model premised on high exports and high imports of member states so that they were not required to choose – as they had been forced to in the past – between their international obligations and their national priorities.

In the rear-view mirror of history, two ideas stand out. Firstly, as the framework agreement for a new age, the ITO could not be a system of pure commercial gain designed primarily to advance the free enterprise principle.

Instead, investment rights had to accommodate the full employment obligation that all states accepted as the cornerstone of the world trading system. The deal-making trade-off was that all signatory countries had to make an equal commitment to eliminate all forms of arbitrary and discriminatory barriers that the state and market actors routinely erected for public or private profit.

Secondly, the theoretical understanding behind the Havana Charter was that countries would make national adjustments to international forces when international trade was expanding rather than contracting. Integration into the world trading system was its non-negotiable principle. This made impeccable economic sense as well as smart statecraft. If economic growth stalled, few countries would accept the dictates of crude market logic to open their economies. Thus, the signatories settled not for the abstract doctrines of free trade but for the more powerful notion of trade liberalization that required the nations of the world to dismantle their tariff walls while restructuring their economies.

In the imperfect world of the late 1940s, much like our own, countries everywhere employed export subsidies, quantitative restrictions such as those used currently in the Softwood Lumber Dispute and commodity agreements for protectionist ends. For instance, the U.S. had its special deal in agricultural products and the U.K. relied on the Imperial Trading Preferences and other "special" relationships. Both undermined the world's trading system. So the challenge of five decades ago was to adopt principles of conduct such that countries would be able to "establish a system of balanced mutual advantage" that also required regulation of investment rights to be part of the package.

How Good Was the Template? The Criteria of Success

What was needed was a framework for a new investment regime with a strong pro-active capacity to hold foreign direct investors and multinational corporations accountable internationally. The ITO's provisions in the key areas of labour standards, international development, investment and international regulation are outlined below.

In terms of *labour standards and full employment guarantees,* the ITO was bold and innovative for an international organization. In addition to the principles already discussed, it recognized that labour standards belong in a trade agreement. More specifically, Article 7 of the Charter recognized that there were links between core labour standards and trade, as well as foreign direct investment and employment. It stated, "the Members recognize that unfair labour conditions, particularly in production for export, create difficulties in international trade."[14] It also included a provision that ILO (International Labour Organization) and ITO members "shall cooperate with that organization in giving effect to that undertaking."[15] Its most innovative feature was to provide grounds that required unfair labour conditions to be subject to a nullification and impairment complaint within the ITO's dispute settlement procedures.[16]

While the ITO did not define a core group of labour standards, it did provide an all-important institutional mechanism within the ITO for members and its Executive Board to consider such issues. Social dumping, the practice of selling exports below what the costs of production would be if international labour standards were followed, had received attention at the UN Conference on Trade and Employment, as well as at the World Trade Union Conference held in London in 1945. The ITO called for making long-term loans for economic and social development to colonial countries "conditional on observance of internationally agreed to working conditions."[17]

The Charter provided that the ILO and the ITO should "act in close cooperation with each other and consult [with] each other regularly in regard to matters of common interest." Where violations of labour standards occurred, countries could bring their complaints to the Executive Board for remedy. To underscore the importance accorded the ILO, by the ITO Charter, the ILO was allowed the right to participate in ITO meetings. This partially fulfilled Roosevelt's wartime promise that the ILO would have an essential part to play in rebuilding a "stable international system of social justice for all peoples."[18] The provisions concerning employment-creation were put in very general terms creating a "high standard" without a formal legal obligation.[19]

In the area of international *economic regulation*, the ITO provided for a dispute resolution system that would become a standard feature of a modern trade regime to promote stability by means of an international trade tribunal. Beyond this, its jurisdictional scope included power to make recommendations and to promote agreements "to facilitate an equitable distribution of skills, arts, technology, materials and equipment" to assure just and equitable treatment for the enterprise, skills, capital, arts and technology brought from one Member country to another" and to "avoid double taxation."[20] It included a chapter requiring states to prevent enterprises from engaging in practices restraining competition, limiting access to markets, or fostering monopolistic control, and it set up a procedure for investigating and reporting on specific complaints about such practices.

Another group of trade norms and principles were addressed under the category of *special circumstances*, that is, times when a country could not implement the principles of the Charter due to a "drastic and sudden change in existing trade practices." At such times, countries were entitled to relief though negotiation or a transitional period, after which conformity was required. Here too, the Charter could hardly be considered radical in permitting this kind of escape clause. It had already been agreed to at Geneva when the GATT was negotiated. More importantly, U.S. trade law recognized that its trade authorities had discretionary power to "suspend, withdraw or prevent the application of concessions to carry out a trade agreement" which was interpreted to be discriminatory, restrictive or burdensome for U.S. commerce.

For developing countries, new ground was broken with respect to *marketing of primary commodities* such as mining and agricultural products. Both developing and industrialized countries agreed to establish procedures for temporary intergovernmental commodity agreements based on a regulation of price and production though excluding buffer stocks (Chapter 6). The aim was to bring price and revenue stability for primary producers and consumers. At the time this provision was path breaking. The collapse of primary products had affected all countries severely in the interwar period and the Charter attempted to provide a practical alternative that would permit and encourage marketing boards and other market-limiting institutions. In addition, special provisions were designed to guarantee effective support for the agricultural sector through subsidies and quantitative restrictions.[21]

Finally, the *investment provisions* of the Charter recognized the right of expropriation of host countries and entitled them to impose specific requirements on foreign direct investment even though the far-reaching issue of host rights vs. investor obligations was not resolved. Host countries could take any "appropriate important measures" to prevent foreign direct investment from interfering in their domestic policy. Countries would be entitled to permit or refuse future investment and, regarding nationalization, the host country's right was implicitly recognized and payment of compensation was acknowledged.[22] These special provisions to promote economic development were designed "particularly for those countries which (were) in the early stage of industrial development" (Chapter 3). At the insistence of developing countries this principle was given a very broad reading including, tariff preferences, quantitative restrictions and limitation of investors' rights.[23]

If much was left to be worked out with its sister organizations, the Fund and the Bank, the ITO nonetheless was a remarkable organization. It pioneered the idea of an integrated trade, employment and development organization, not a specialized one like the WTO today. Despite its brief existence it showed that politics and economics could not be treated as separate watertight compartments. The governments of the time gave it a mandate to legislate and make rules for the global trading system and not be only a commercial court to hear disputes between countries. It explicitly recognized that its members had the authority to make legal and binding changes to its Charter that would enable the ITO to grow and adapt to the changing international environment.

In other domains too the ITO brought an air of realism to the private world of commercial trade. For example, the Havana Charter not only applied to governments but also to the actions of private firms whose restrictive trade practices threatened to undermine the liberal goals of open trade.[24]

Looking Back to Look Forward

The key question posed by our history lesson is what does this forgotten and ill-understood organization have to do with the present?

As states everywhere feel the adaptive pressures from the new international agenda for deep integration, they would do well to take a long hard look again at the Havana Charter for both its strengths and its shortcomings. It was a highly normative exercise in trade politics that attempted to redefine the public sphere internationally by deepening and extending it.

The global trading system has always been a contested site for citizens and elites alike. The world of the public has always been pervaded by hierarchies of status that gave rights to some, while excluding others. In theory, all are to have universal civil, political, social and economic rights as the seedbed of citizenship. Frequently in the past, however, it was the spread of the market and the arrival of international commerce that tied communities, regions and countries together and freed many from the strictures of feudal hierarchies, absolute religions and monarchist states. The market has always been part of the emergent public sphere in which people could act on their own interests. Since the publication of Karl Polanyi's *Great Transformation*, the consensus amongst political economists is that the market needs regulation and people require collective goods that the market cannot be expected to deliver.

If the Washington Consensus has taught a basic lesson in the last three decades, it is that the common good cannot be subordinated to the private good. In the post-Washington, post-Seattle, post-MAI world, societies everywhere are seeking to strike a new balance between public and private and are struggling to reassert the common good as a benchmark of governance. So far success has been partial and uneven. The liberal idea of the public in a post-Keynesian world has strongly influenced political elites. Its message equates the public interest with the rent-seeking activities of powerful interests, most often corporations.

Yet the public domain that furnishes us with our public goods, spaces, places and practices has always been a site of policy contest. This is why the notion of the public domain, even a poorly defined and protected one, is highly relevant. It is both a strategic concept, a benchmark and a goal. The public domain is an area of social life with its own rules, norms and practices that cuts across the primacy of state authority and market power. It furnishes civil society with much needed resources to function effectively by creating sanctuaries where the price mechanism does not operate. It emerges out of the constant clash between the predatory aspects of the price system and the bureaucratic top-down practices of the state. It supplies civil society actors with a powerful lever against a purely economic discourse.[25]

In the past, the public domain in its Keynesian incarnation included many policy areas, including social policy, housing and autonomous public spaces that became facts of national life and were essential to the institutions of liberal democracy. Citizenship rights, rather than the market, guaranteed the allocation of social goods. In many Southern countries these policy spaces were carved out from adjacent private and market domains at different times. In all democratic societies the public domain contributed to the mutual obligations of common purpose, the provision of collective goods and other non-income objectives.

The Global Public Domain: An Elusive or Incipient Standard?

Today the basic problem in terms of global governance is that there is no provision for elementary social justice, the provision of social goods globally, and other non-market objectives. At a time when the disjuncture between the economic side of globalization and its social impacts has reached its outer limits, the need to limit market intrusiveness in all its many forms is high on the agenda of global civil society.[26] Certainly business is not shy about asking government assistance to restructure. For instance, U.S. Steel believes that government action is essential to any effort to restructure the industry including state subsidies to pay for health and pension liabilities. The question is whether this world of "single instances" will lead to a general reassessment of the role of public authority more broadly?

Past trade rounds have been narrowly focussed on enhancing investment and property rights, promoting trade and services and broadening market access. Industrialized countries have promised poorer countries a more equitable world trading system. Even in terms of market access, the poor and developing countries face tariff barriers that are four times higher for poor countries than for industrialized ones. The WTO has no legal or other kinds of capacity to create a world trading system that enables developing countries to gain a fairer share of global wealth. They are forced to support a trade system that effectively skews the benefits of world trade against their common interest. In textiles, food products and investment rules, the industrialized countries and the WTO continue to discriminate against southern countries, a practice which has continued since the end of the Uruguay Round.[27]

Sylvia Ostry (1997) makes the important argument that it is a utopian fantasy to launch a drive to build a single global market with a minimal governance structure like that of the WTO. The only recognition in the WTO of the existence of a social deficit is in the area of technical barriers in the trade agreement, which Ostry describes as a mind-boggling WTO instrument. It allows the countries of the world to deal with product standards, environmental regulation, standards for food and potentially even labour standards, but only as a "technical" matter. In all of these critical areas, there is a need for public supervision, social regulation and collective goods globally.

Conventially-minded economists and trade experts have shown remarkable little sympathy for, or inclination to address the social deficit arising from a narrowly cast set of trade rules. Only recently have advocates of global free trade acknowledged that societal losses from open market and regional trade pacts often exceed the gains. Losers in the global trade wars are never compensated and most losers are the poor and the marginal whose labour-intensive products are excluded from Northern markets. Since 1994, pressure from corporate lobbyists in the U.S. and the EU has pushed governments to launch almost 250 anti-dumping cases against developing countries. Northern countries prefer the anti-dumping route to protect their industries from countries with much lower labour costs and regulatory standards. Neither the Uruguay Round nor the new Millennial trade negotiations have curbed the new protectionist sentiment. So a different framework for the world trade regime is needed that will require substantive rewriting of trade rules and first principles.

How should the line between trade investment and the social dimension of markets be redrawn so that the global commons is not turned into a global commodity for export and the social bond protected? It is this question above all that has moved from the edge of the envelope to occupy front and centre stage, not only among political and economic elites but, most importantly, in the public's mind.

Towards a Global Reconnect: Confronting the Fire Walls

Traditional trade rules of the WTO are supposed to be only about commerce, trade and other strictly economic matters. As the WTO millennium trade round gathers steam, post-Doha, non-trade issues have become part of its agenda particularly in the area of public health and affordable drugs (TRIPS), the environment as well as public services (GATS). Little progress has been made in addressing the social deficit of markets. This is because the World Trade Organization has constructed real and imaginary fire-walls between the social and the purely commercial. In the global economy not everything is for sale but everything is potentially a future commodity to be exported for one country or another. So no-go preserves are needed to ensure a more balanced approach to trade – those areas of national and international life that need to be preserved as part of the global public domain. High on the agenda are those public spaces, places, goods and services needed for an interdependent world. While this list is meant to be illustrative and not inclusive, the Millennium round of WTO negotiations has to protect global public space from powerful market actors. Some of the key areas where trade rules and principles need to be rethought are:

Food – Intellectual property rights to the world's genetic heritage has redefined the role of agriculture. Much of the world's food could be genetically engineered. A new kind of code is required to protect the right of nations to manage their food supply according to their best practice.

Water – Water is another part of the global commons that can be sold and traded in the open market. Water is one of the last untapped frontiers of global resources and if water is included in the service agreement of the WTO, then it will be put on the open market for sale. In order to protect the basic needs of people everywhere, a new global agreement is required to prohibit the trade in water as a commercial service.

Labour Standards – So far the attempt to link labour standards and trade has been stalemated. As incomes and living standards have fallen in many southern countries a narrow focus on core labour standards needs to be rethought. The question that needs to be addressed is: what kind of measures are needed to eradicate global poverty?

Social Services – The fastest growing sectors in international trade are in health and education services. In many countries these are provided publicly for the majority and privately for the elites. With global expenditures on education and health targeted to rise above the $2.5 trillion mark, new rules of international competition and discipline are required to protect public health and education programs from for-profit corporations.

Culture – Already there have been seven complaints concerning culture in the first five years of the WTO's brief existence. From a trade perspective the question is: is culture simply an entertainment industry with its many-sided services to be bought and sold, or are these cultural industries part of a country's identity and heritage? If the latter, what rules are needed to protect the diversity of nations from the monoculture of commercial ends? The need for states to protect their cultural industries from largely U.S. dominance has become one of the flashpoints of the world's trading order.

Pharmaceutical drugs – Huge pharmaceutical companies control the supply and cost of miracle drugs, as well as drugs needed to restore health to the planet's billions. Many drugs that the poor of the world require cost pennies to produce but sell at often fifty-to sixty-times the cost of production. Here too, intellectual and patent protection are at the core because it is no longer clear that what is so essential for public health and safety should be patented only for profit. For people desperate to gain access to life-saving medicine, social need must be a determining factor. The commercial criteria give primary access to the wealthy parts of the world that are able to afford them. New rules and new conventions are required that will guarantee generic affordable drugs for all who are in need of them.

Corporate Rights – In the area of investment and corporate behaviour there is little in the WTO about the obligations and responsibilities of private corporate actors. The OECD recognizes the need for full transparency in corporate financial reporting and many of the most offensive kinds of tax loopholes, which legitimate corporate tax avoidance behaviour, are likely to be closed in the coming period. Yet the largest legal deficit still exists because WTO trade rules are too intrusive on national laws and social regulation designed to protect health, human security and human rights.

In the forthcoming Millennial trade round post-Doha,[28] global governance requires different solutions than the template of increasing market access and entrenching trade openness. Even if goods can be produced in sites around the world, the place of manufacture is not all that arbitrary. In a global age, the distribution of fabricated resources matters more than ever and differences in social capital are crucial in understanding the outcomes of the world trading system.

What is evident is that each new round of trade liberalization has exacerbated and accelerated the asymmetrical gains of trade openness. This is disturbing because it explains the deepening fault line between North and South in the last decade. As well, the absence of an adequate supply of global public goods, particularly health, clean water, adequate housing and agreement on food standards poses the most serious threat to the world trading order. Addressing the democratic deficit globally requires an international public authority with a different mandate, one capable of establishing what is public and what will be private.

A FINAL WORD

This brings us back to our history lesson. Just like the WTO, the ITO wrestled with the question of a rules-based system. It had to find ways to rescue trade liberalization from the inter-war crisis that discredited laissez-faire free trade. Its project was to modernize trade liberalism and not abolish it. As well, it had to devise a new architecture that went beyond trade by creating linkages to non-trade issues; and it needed a democratic and representative governance structure that gave civil society actors access to it. Its founders also spent a lot of time wrestling with the North-South divide that was as much in evidence then as now. It faced difficult global governance issues just as we do today. Its founding fathers linked the ITO to the other Bretton Woods institutions so that world trading system to avoid subjection to financial markets.

With capital more mobile than ever and domestic economic growth at a standstill or negative for most of the world's countries, there is a parallel between our times and those of more than fifty years ago. Building counterweights was one of the central ideas that lead to the Havana Charter and the ITO and it has lost none of its relevance since then. The advanced countries of the world have always favoured national controls over their own resources and strategic sectors and have never abandoned state aids and subsidies to support their home industries. Yet the public domain, the commonweal, public interest, public goods and national interest in Geoffrey Underhill's words "those busybodies through the ages" have not been able to protect the wider collective interest from individual investor choice. If these busy bodies are to strike a different balance between "the public" as a whole and the selfish pursuit of private material gain, the long-term strategy to expand trade requires strengthening market-constraining institutions such as unemployment insurance, education, training and social policy. Internationally a world trading order needs to establish a full set of mechanisms to promote development and ensure equity in trade.

It should be recalled that despite its short but significant life, and whatever its shortcomings, the ITO was a remarkable organization that pioneered the idea of a broad integrated trade and employment organization. It pioneered the notion that trade had to serve the broader purpose of development and social need. The ITO can be considered as the high water mark of an incipient world trade regime premised on different principles to those embodied in the WTO.

If there is a common understanding forming after the Quebec summit and after the massive anti- globalization protests in Genoa, it is that unfettered global market forces have produced a large and dangerous social deficit. The basic problem is that there is no explicitly ethical commitment to building a socially inclusive global economy. Despite all the soul-searching, collective action is at a standstill and global public goods, ranging from the environment to sustainable human rights, labour and health standards are in short supply. There is an urgent need to conceptualize the global, re-connect and develop a viable and sustainable notion of the public domain that gives authority everywhere a choice between it and the market.

The polity needs to be governed and the post-Washington Consensus world is about building institutions internationally, as much as nationally, by political means for public ends. Commercial organizations are by intent rigid and rule-driven by their institutional culture and framework, do not adapt readily to change, are suspicious of non-trade issues and are important vehicles for protecting the rights and interests of large private actors. The WTO presents itself as a strictly commercial organization but it is increasingly involved in domestic regulation and sovereignty. Its trade agenda and disputes system affects many leading edge non-trade issues from public services to generic anti-viral drugs. Increasingly post-Doha its weak point is its over-reach with a small governance capacity. Added to this is the non-representation of civil society in its deliberations. Decisions are arrived at by arm-twisting and late night phone-calls. Not surprisingly the trade-offs and deal-breakers are unequal and problematic for international civil society. Southern nations are going to feel cheated that the development round has no substance but is largely rhetorical. The concept, idea and goal of the public domain is surely a very large part of the new policy agenda. Time seems to be on the side of civil society and the angels of hope – or is it?

THE RISE AND FALL OF THE ITO

1941 Atlantic Charter Articles IV - VI set the stage for future international negotiations on the links between national recovery, the international economic order and security. The fifth principle called for "the fullest collaboration between all nations in the economic field with the object of securing for all improved labour standards, economic advancement and social security." The sixth proclaimed the hope of establishing a peace "which will afford assurance that all men in all lands may live out their lives in freedom from want and fear." Article VII, Lend-Lease, commits U.S. and U.K. to begin to search for new principles for rebuilding the world's trading system.

1942 James Meade writes a *Proposal for an International Commercial Union* calling for "far-reaching and imaginative proposals for the reduction of restrictions to international commerce"; top civil servants are preoccupied with working on the proposal.

1943 Interdepartmental and inter-agency committees meet continuously in Washington from the spring of 1943 to summer of 1945 chaired successively by Acheson and Clayton; also talks with Canadian officials.

1943 "New Dealers" in Department of State begin to prepare the draft treaty proposing the ITO; eventually they lose control of the agenda.

1943 First U.K./U.S. postwar planning negotiation related to Article VII in Washington.

1944 U.K. White Paper on Full Employment followed by Canadian and Australian White Papers on Employment.

1944 *Economist,* "Restructuring the World Trading System," a series of six articles on trade, employment and the design of the commercial order.

1944 Schumacher publishes a major statement on trade and employment as Fabian pamphlet; Hayek's book *Road to Serfdom* appears in print.

1944 ILO Philadelphia Convention on full employment policies.

1944 Finance Ministers at Bretton Woods meetings establish the IMF and the World Bank including full employment obligation to be included in their original mandates. The ITO was to be established later as the "essential" third pillar to the new trading system for the world.

1944 Brynes replaces Hull as Secretary of State; free trader Clayton nominated Under-Secretary of State for Economic Affairs.

1945 Alvin Hansen, key economic advisor to the President, publishes influential volume, *America's Role in the World Economy.*

1945 U.K. Labour victory.

1945 Australia elects a labour government under Chifley, a strong advocate of the tariff for national development and of the ITO, World Bank and full employment goal internationally.

1946	First meeting of the Preparatory Committee of the ITO, October 15 to November 26 in London; representatives of 18 countries have exploratory talks on the ITO and on U.S. *Proposals for the Expansion of World Trade and Employment.*
1946	France establishes national planning under Jean Monnet.
1947	Joint GATT/ITO meetings at Geneva; successful tariff negotiations make possible non-tariff measures to be included in Havana Charter.
1947	U.S. initiates Marshall Plan to support European reconstruction and a rival agenda to the ITO.
1947	India becomes the world's largest democracy independent from Britain.
1947	Jacob Viner, leading U.S. trade authority, declares support for the ITO in *Foreign Affairs*, a leading U.S. forum of opinion and expert advice.
1947	UN Conference on Trade and Employment is opened in Havana, November 18; 56 nations send delegations. A great deal of criticism of Geneva text that it was one-sided and served the interests of the major industrial powers and not the developing countries.
1948	The U.S. sponsors the creation of the Organization for European Economic Co-operation (OEEC) to promote trade liberalization and the further reduction of barriers.
1948	U.S. Congressional elections return a Republican Congress hostile to many ITO provisions.
1948	Havana Conference, final text is signed by 53 countries on 24 March. Includes major chapters on trade policy, cartels, commodity agreements, employment, economic development and international investment and the constitution of a new UN institution for international trade.
1949	*Report on National and International Measures To Achieve Full Employment* published by the UN's Economic and Social Council Group of Experts, among them Kaldor.
1949	ITO Treaty is submitted to Congress, not voted on.
1950	U.S. abandon the ITO. A coalition of protectionists and perfectionists, critics of the Charter, convinces Truman to withdraw the draft treaty from Congress. U.S. Congress so hostile that President Truman signs GATT as an executive order; it is not submitted to Congress.

NOTES

1 Economist (3 June 1944), pp. 738-739.

2 Ikenberry (1992) p. 320.

3 We now understand the complex issue of the failure of the Truman government to muster the necessary domestic support to win Congressional approval for the ITO. By 1949, the high water mark of U.S. internationalism had passed and the Truman administration had begun to devote its energies to the more immediate military-political threats on its foreign policy agenda such as getting Congressional support for the Marshall Plan and NATO, see Odell and Eichengreen (1996). Without high level Presidential support for the ITO, most major American business organizations turned against its investment provisions, see Diebold (1952, 1998).

4 Quoted in Helleiner (1993) p. 20; Diebold (1952).

5 United Nations Conference on Trade and Employment, *Final Act and Related Documents*, New York: United Nations, Sales No 1948 II.D.4.1 (1948).

6 Jackson (1989) p. 32.
7 Eichengreen (1996).
8 Viner (1947).
9 Krock (1973) p. 3.
10 Maier (1982) p. 341.
11 Gardner (1956); Ikenberry (1992); Ruggie (1992).
12 Carr (1939).
13 Meade (1953).
14 Art. 7, 1.
15 Art. 7, 2.
16 Art. 94 and 95; Charnovitz (1995).
17 Charnovitz argues convincingly that the ITO did not endorse the "labour standards to aid link" but it did connect the improvement of labour standards to the larger trade agenda with respect to investment and development.
18 Alcock (1971) p. 169.
19 Diebold (1952) p. 12.
20 Picciotto (2001).
21 Art. 20, 22, 27.
22 Art. 12.
23 It would take developing nations more than a decade to address all the missing pieces of the puzzle that dropped off the world trade agenda when the ITO disappeared. The establishment of UNCTAD and the high profile UN Development Decade strategy spoke to this reality.
24 Picciotto in Drache (2001).
25 Drache (2001).
26 Significantly, governments are continuing to spend money on non-market activities. Many countries everywhere seem less intent than ever in adopting the American model of less state-less tax or its equivalent, Drache (2001).
27 Oxfam International (2001).
28 So far the WTO trade disputes panel have handled approximately fifty cases in the first five years that directly impinge on health and labour standards. A new study of the effectiveness of the WTO disputes panels revealed just how uneven WTO trade jurisprudence is in these sensitive areas. Almost all panel and appellate decisions have denied that markets have immediate and far-reaching social effects. One dramatic exception was the recent Asbestos decision to ban the import of asbestos and it is the first time in fifty years that article XX of the GATT was used to protect public safety. However important the Asbestos victory is, it does not create an international standard to ban asbestos; it only allows a country to ban asbestos should it wish to. For the full study and executive summary of Daniel Drache and Nirmala Singh, *The First Seven Years of the WTO: Canada at Centre Stage. Trade and the Social Deficit*, go to Robarts Centre for Canadian Studies Internet web site at York University.

REFERENCES

Acheson, K., and J. F. Chant, et al., eds. 1972. *Bretton Woods Revisited.* Toronto: University of Toronto Press.

Alcock, Antony. 1971. *History of the International Labor Organization.* London: Macmillan.

Armstrong, Philip, and Andrew Glyn, et al. 1991. *Capitalism Since 1945.* London: Basil Blackwell.

Brown, Jr., W. A. 1950. *The United States and the Restoration of World Trade: An Analysis and Appraisal of the ITO Charter and the General Agreement on Tariffs and Trade.* Washington D.C.: The Brookings Institute.

Carr, E. H. 1981. (original edition, 1939). *The Twenty Years' Crisis 1919-1939.* London: Macmillan.

Charnovitz, Steve. 1997. "Trade, Employment and Labour Standards". *Temple International and Comparative Law Journal*, 11, pp. 131-163.

Charnovitz, Steve. 1995. "Promoting Higher Labour Standards." *The Washington Quarterly*, 18, no. 3, pp. 167-190.

Diebold, William. 1994. "Reflections on the International Trade Organization." *Northern Illinois University Law Review*, 14, no. 2 (spring), pp. 335-346.

Diebold, William. 1994. "From the ITO to GATT – And Back?" In Orin Kirshner, ed., *The Bretton Woods-GATT System Retrospect and Prospect After Fifty Years.* New York: M.E. Sharpe, pp. 152-173.

Diebold, W. J. 1952. "The End of the I.T.O." *Essays in International Finance No. 16.* Princeton: Princeton University, (October), pp. 1-37.

Destler, I. M. 1995. *American Trade Politics.* Washington D.C.: Institute for International Economics.

Drache, Daniel. 2001. *The Market or the Public Domain Global Governance and the Asymmetry of Power.* London: Routledge.

Drache, Daniel, and Nirmala Singh. 2001. *The First Seven Years of the WTO: Canada at Centre Stage: Trade and the Social Deficit.* Toronto: Robarts Centre for Canadian Studies, York University.

Economist. 1944. "Trade Argument." 151, 26 October, pp. 652-653.

Economist. 1944. "The Principles of Trade I." 1 January, pp. 4-5.

Economist. 1944. "The Balance of Payments II." 8 January, pp. 32-34.

Economist. 1944. "Trade and Employment III". 15 January, pp.64-65.

Economist. 1944. "The Multilateral Approach IV." 22 January, pp. 94-96.

Economist. 1944. "Planned Expansion V." 25 January, p. 137.

Economist. 1944. "The Regional Solution VI." 5 February, pp. 169-170.

Economist. 1944. "The New Liberalism VIII." 19 February, pp. 232-233.

Economist. 1944. "Prices and Markets VII." 12 February, pp. 204-205.

Economist. 1945. "Trade and Employment." 15 December, pp. 869-871.

Economist. 1944. "Employment Policy." 3 June, pp. 738-739.

Economist. 1946. "Trade Make-Believe." 30 November, pp. 859-860.

Eichengreen, B. 1996. *Globalizing Capital: A History of the International Monetary System.* Princeton: Princeton University Press.

Gardiner, R. 1956. *Sterling Dollar Diplomacy: Anglo-American Collaboration in the Reconstruction of Multilateral Trade.* New York: Oxford University Press.

Haas, P. 1992. "Introduction: Epistemic Communities and International Policy Co-ordination." *International Organization*, 46, no. 1 (winter), pp. 1-35.

Hansen, A. 1945. *America's Role in the World Economy.* New York: W.W. Norton.

Helleiner, E. 1993. "When Finance was the Servant: International Capital Movements in the Bretton Woods Order." In P. Cerny, ed., *Finance and World Politics.* London: Edward Elgar Publishing, pp. 20-48.

Helleiner, E. 1995. "From Bretton Woods to Global Finance." In Richard Stubbs and G. Underhill, eds., *Political Economy and the Changing Global Order.* Toronto: M&S, pp. 163-175.

Henderson, H. D. 1955. *The Inter-War Years and Other Papers: A Selection from the Writings of Hubert Douglas Henderson.* Oxford: Oxford University Press.

Ikenberry, G. J. 1992. "A World Economy Restored: Expert Consensus and the Anglo-American Postwar Settlement." *International Organization*, 46, no. 1 (winter), pp. 289-321.

Irwin, D. 1996. *Against the Tide An Intellectual History of Free Trade*. Princeton, New Jersey: Princeton University Press.

Jackson, J. 1989. *The World Trading System*. Cambridge, Mass: MIT Press.

Kock, K. 1969. *International Trade Policy and the GATT 1947-1967*. Stockholm: Almqvist and Wiksell.

Lipson, C. 1985. *Standing Guard: Protecting Foreign Capital in the Nineteenth and Twentieth Century*. Berkeley: University of California Press.

Maier, Charles. 1981. "The Two Postwar Eras and Conditions for Stability in Twentieth Century Western Europe." *American Historical Review*, 86 (April), pp. 327-352.

Meade, J. E. 1951. *The Balance of Payments*. London ; New York : Oxford University Press.

Meade, J. E. 1953. *Problems of Economic Union*. Chicago : University of Chicago Press.

Miskell, R. 1994. "Antecedents of the ITO Charter and their Relevance for the Uruguay Round." *Northern Illinois Law Review*, 14, no. 2 (spring).

Myrdal, G. 1957. *Economic Theory and Underdeveloped Regions*. London: Methuen.

Odell, John, and Barry Eichengreen. 1998. "The United States, the ITO and the WTO: Exit Options, Agent Slack, and Presidential Leadership." In Ann. O. Krueger, ed., *The WTO as an International Organization*. Chicago: University of Chicago Press.

Ostry, S. 1997. *The Post-Cold War Trading System Who's on First?* Chicago: The University of Chicago Press.

Oxfam International. 2001. *Oxfam Briefing Paper: Eight Broken Promises: Why the WTO isn't Working for the World's Poor*. Oxfam.

Picciotto, S. 2001. *Private Rights vs. Public Standards in the WTO: For a Margin of Appreciation in the Interpretation of WTO Agreements*. Toronto: Robarts Centre for Canadian Studies, York University.

Picciotto, S. 2001. "Democratizing Globalism." In D. Drache, ed., *The Market or the Public Domain Global Governance and the Asymmetry of Power*. London: Routledge.

Polanyi, Karl. 1944. *The Great Transformation: The Political and Economic Origins of Our Time*. Boston: Beacon Press.

Reisman, Simon. 1997. "ITO and GATT." In Orin Kirshner, ed., *The Bretton Woods-GATT System. Retrospect and Prospect After Fifty Years*. New York: Sharpe, pp. 82-86.

Ruggie, J. G. 1982. "International Regimes, Transactions, and Change: Embedded Liberalism in the Postwar Economic Order." *International Organization*, 36 (spring), pp. 79-415.

Ruggie, J. G. 1992. "Multilateralism: An Antonomy of an Institution." *International Organization*, 46, no. 3 (summer), pp. 573-598.

Schumacher, E.F. 1944. *Export Policy and Full Employment*. London: Fabian Publications.

Sidelesky, R. 1994. *John Maynard Keynes The Economist as Saviour 1920-1937*. London: Allen Lane.

Stern, B. 1983. *Un Nouvel Ordre Economique International? Recueil de Textes et Documents*. Paris: Economica.

United Nations Conference on Trade and Employment. 1947-48. *Havana Charter for an International Trade Organization*. Washington: U.S. Government Print Off.

Viner, J. 1947. "Conflicts of Principle in Drafting a Trade Charter." *Foreign Affairs*, 25, no. 4 (July), pp. 612-628.

Viner, J. et. al. 1945. *The United States in a Multi-National Economy*. New York: Council on Foreign Relations.

Wilcox, C. 1949. *A Charter for World Trade*. New York: The MacMillan Co.

Chapter 3

Monetary Instability: Are National Currencies Becoming Obsolete?

Benjamin J. Cohen
University of California, Santa Barbara

Nothing signifies the growth of instability in today's international political economy more than the disruptive financial crises that have swept the world in recent years – the speculative attacks on the pound sterling and other European currencies in 1992-93, which broke up the old European Monetary System; the fall of the Mexican peso in 1994, which sparked a worldwide contagion in financial markets that came to be known as the tequila effect; the East Asian crisis of 1997-98, which began with crash of Thailand's currency, the baht, and then spread outward in another contagion, which some this time labelled a case of "bahtulism"; the Russian default of 1998; Brazil in 1999; and the continuing troubles of Argentina, Turkey, and others. In just one decade the world's monetary system has gone to the brink a half dozen times. No wonder there is so much talk – albeit, to date, rather little action – about reform of what we now call the international financial architecture.

Yet in a very real sense, all of these crises may be considered little more than the tip of the iceberg – the outward manifestations of a much more fundamental transformation of the global monetary environment. That transformation, which I wrote about in my recent book *The Geography of Money* (1998), is being driven by a rapid acceleration of cross-border competition among currencies – what in *The Geography of Money* I called the deterritorialization of money. Circulation of national currencies no longer coincides with the territorial frontiers of nation-states. A few popular monies, most notably the U.S. dollar and Europe's new euro (succeeding Germany's Deutschmark), have come to be widely used outside their country of origin, competing directly with local rivals for both transactions and investment purposes. Many weaker currencies, conversely, have been reduced to a minority share of the money supply in their own country of issue. All of the crises of the last decade can be understood as instances of national monies that, in this increasingly unstable environment, have lost their market appeal.

S. McBride et al. (eds.), Global Instability, 29–41.

This instability, then, raises a truly fascinating question. In all markets, we know, the logic of competition suggests that, ultimately, many weaker rivals will be eliminated. And so, we might think, the same should be true in the market for monies. Does this mean that national currencies are becoming obsolete? Are many of the monies around the globe – the diverse kips (Laos), quetzals (Guatemala), pulas (Botswana), and levs (Bulgaria) – destined to go the way of the Dodo bird? The short answer, for many, is almost certainly Yes. Extinction could be the fate of the currencies of even some of the world's richest economies, such as Canada's beloved loonie.

In this paper, I will make three main points. I start with the transformation of today's global monetary environment. The implications of deterritorialization for the survival of national currencies are only beginning to be understood. My first point is that currency competition compels governments to choose from among a limited number of strategies, only one of which involves preservation of traditional territorial money. Second, a good number of national monies will indeed disappear, leading to an increasing population of regional currencies of one kind or another – a distinctly new geography of money. But, third, there is no sure way to predict what that new geography of money will ultimately look like. We have a fairly good idea of the principal factors that are likely to influence state preferences, but many configurations are possible and even probable.

THE NEW GEOGRAPHY OF MONEY

That the global monetary environment has been greatly transformed in recent decades is undeniable. A half century ago, after the ravages of the Great Depression and World War II, national monetary systems – with the notable exception of the United States – were generally insular and strictly controlled. Starting in the 1950s, however, barriers separating local currencies began gradually to dissolve, first in the industrial world and then increasingly in many emerging-market economies as well. Partly this was the result of an increased volume of trade, which facilitated monetary flows between states. But even more it was the product of intense market competition that, in combination with technological and institutional innovation, offered an increasingly freer choice among currencies. Currency substitution widened access for a growing number of actors at all levels of society.

Most scholarly attention has been paid to the remarkable growth in recent decades of capital mobility, reflected in a scale of international financial flows unequalled since the glory days of the nineteenth-century gold standard. The high level of capital mobility today is commonly cited as one of the most visible artefacts of contemporary globalization. But these flows are just part of the story of money's growing deterritorialization. A focus on capital mobility, emphasizing integration of financial markets, highlights only one of the standard functions of money: its use as a store of value. In fact, the interpenetration of monetary systems today has come to be far more extensive, involving all the functions of currency – not just money's role as a private investment medium but also its use as a medium of exchange and unit of account for transactions of every kind, domestic as well as international. Cross-border currency competition means much more than capital mobility alone.

Deterritorialization is by no means universal, of course – at least, not yet. But it is remarkably widespread. Krueger and Ha (1996) estimate that foreign currency notes in the mid-1990s accounted for twenty percent or more of the local money stock in as many as three dozen nations inhabited by at least one-third of the world's population. In all, as much as one-quarter to one-third of the world's paper money supply is now located outside its country of issue. Most currency substitution is concentrated in Latin America, the Middle East, and republics of the former Soviet Union, where the dollar is favoured; or in East-Central Europe and the Balkans, where the DM traditionally predominated. By a different measure, focusing on foreign-currency deposits rather than paper money, the International Monetary Fund identifies some eighteen nations where by the mid-1990s another state's money accounted for at least thirty percent of broad money supply.[1] The most extreme cases, with ratios above fifty percent, included Azerbaijan, Bolivia, Croatia, Nicaragua, Peru, and Uruguay. Another thirty-nine economies had ratios approaching thirty percent, indicating "moderate" penetration.

What are the implications of this transformation for the survival of national currencies? For specialists in open-economy macroeconomics, who typically focus narrowly on capital mobility, the significance of recent developments is restricted mainly to implications for the choice of exchange-rate regime. Traditionally, the exchange-rate issue was cast in simple binary terms: fixed versus flexible rates. A country could adopt some form of peg for its currency or it could float. Pegs might be anchored on a single currency or a basket of currencies; they might be formally irrevocable (as in a currency board) or based on a more contingent rule; they might crawl or even take the form of a target zone. Floating rates, conversely, might be managed or just left to the interplay of market supply and demand. More recently, the issue has been recast – from fixed versus flexible rates to a choice between, on the one hand, contingent rules of any kind and, on the other, the so-called "corner solutions" of either free floating or some form of monetary union. Today, according to an increasingly fashionable argument known as the bipolar view or two-corner solution, no intermediate regime can be regarded as tenable.[2] Owing to the development of huge masses of mobile wealth capable of switching between currencies at a moment's notice, governments can no longer hope to defend policy rules designed to hit explicit exchange-rate targets. The middle ground of contingent rules has in effect been "hollowed out," as Barry Eichengreen (1994) memorably put it.

But that too is just part of the story. In reality, much more is involved here than simply a choice of exchange-rate regime. At its most fundamental, what is involved is nothing less than a challenge to the long-standing convention of national monetary sovereignty. Governments have long claimed an absolute monopoly over the issue and circulation of money within their own territory. Currencies were to be territorial – exclusive legal tender within the nation's frontiers – with strict lines separating one monetary domain from another. However, once we look beyond capital mobility alone to the broader phenomenon of currency competition, we see that in many areas of the world the traditional dividing lines between national monies are becoming less and less distinct. No longer are most economic actors restricted to a single currency – their own home money – as they go about their business. Cross-border circulation of currencies, which had long been common prior to the emergence of the modern state system, has dramatically re-emerged, resulting in a new configuration of currency spaces – a new geography of money. The functional domains of many monies no longer correspond precisely with the formal jurisdiction of their issuing authority.

Currency deterritorialization poses a critical challenge because governments have long relied upon the advantages derived from formal monetary monopoly to promote their conception of state interest. In fact, five main benefits are derived from a strictly territorial currency: first, a potential reduction of domestic transactions costs to promote economic growth; second, a powerful source of revenue (seigniorage) to underwrite public expenditures; third, a possible instrument to manage the macroeconomic performance of the economy; fourth, a potent political symbol to promote a sense of national identity; and finally, a practical means to insulate the nation from foreign influence or constraint. But all these gains are eroded or lost when a government is no longer able to exert the same degree of control over the use of its money, by either its own citizens or others. Instead, in a growing number of countries, policymakers are driven to compete, inside and across borders, for the allegiance of market agents – in effect, to sustain or cultivate market share for their own brand of currency. The monopoly of monetary sovereignty yields to something more like oligopoly, and monetary governance is reduced to little more than a choice among marketing strategies designed to shape and manage demand.

Broadly speaking, for affected states, four strategies are possible, depending on two key considerations – first, whether policy is defensive or aggressive, aiming either to preserve or promote market share; and second, whether policy is unilateral or collective. These four strategies are:

Market leadership: an aggressive unilateralist policy intended to maximize use of the national money, analogous to predatory price leadership in an oligopoly.

Market preservation: a status-quo policy intended to defend, rather than augment, a previously acquired market position for the home currency.

Market alliance: a collusive policy of sharing monetary sovereignty in a monetary union of some kind, analogous to a tacit or explicit cartel.

Market followership: an acquiescent policy of subordinating monetary sovereignty to a stronger foreign currency via a currency board or full dollarization, analogous to passive price followership in an oligopoly.

Of these four options, a strategy of market leadership is of course generally available only to governments with the most widely circulated currencies, such as the dollar and euro. For the vast majority of states with less competitive monies, decision making is limited to the remaining three – a tricky tripartite choice. For these states, the very survival of national money is at stake.

CURRENCY REGIONALIZATION

The basic question for such states is the familiar one of constrained choice. What limits on national policy are they willing to accept? Should governments seek to sustain their traditional monetary sovereignty (market preservation)? Or, alternatively, should they countenance delegating some or all of that authority upward, either to the joint institutions of a monetary union (market alliance) or to a dominant foreign powers (market followership)? Involved is what one source[3] calls a "sovereignty bargain" – a voluntary agreement to accept certain limitations on national authority in exchange for anticipated benefits. Monetary sovereignty is either pooled in a partnership of some sort, shifting authority to a joint institution like the European Central Bank (ECB), or else surrendered wholly or in part to a dominant foreign power such as the United States.[4] The former president of the Argentine central bank put the point bluntly: "Should a [country] produce its own money, or should it buy it from a more efficient producer?"[5] Buying from a more efficient producer necessarily implies a degree of regionalization in currency relations.

Currency regionalization occurs when two or more states formally share a single money or equivalent. With a strategy of market alliance, governments agree to merge their separate currencies into a wholly new joint money, as members of Europe's Economic and Monetary Union (EMU) have done with the euro. This is currency unification, what the economist George von Furstenberg (2000) calls a "multilateral sharing model of monetary union." Examples already in existence around the world include, in addition to EMU, the CFA Franc Zone in Africa and the Eastern Caribbean Currency Union (ECCU). A looser version, called the Common Monetary Area (CMA), also exists in southern Africa, encompassing South Africa and three of its smaller neighbours, Lesotho, Namibia, and Swaziland.

Alternatively, with a strategy of market followership, any single government can unilaterally or by agreement replace its own currency with an already existing money of another, an approach typically described as full or formal dollarization.[6] This much more hierarchical variant of regionalization, which von Furstenberg labels an "uncooperative unilateral monetary union," has long been official policy in a miscellany of tiny enclaves or microstates around the world, from Monaco and San Marino to the Marshall Islands and Micronesia, as well as in Panama and, for many years, Liberia; and was more recently adopted by Ecuador and El Salvador, each of which now uses America's greenback in place of its own former currency. A near equivalent is a currency board, such as has long existed in Brunei, Djibouti, and Hong Kong. With a currency board the home money continues to account for a large, if not dominant, part of domestic money supply. In principle, though, issue of the local money is firmly tied to the availability of a designated foreign currency – usually referred to as the anchor currency. The exchange rate between the two monies is rigidly fixed, ostensibly irrevocably; both currencies circulate as legal tender in the dependent country; and any increase in the issue of local money must be fully backed by an equivalent increase of reserve holdings of the anchor currency. Effectively, the home money becomes little more than foreign money by another name – a proxy for the anchor currency, as it were. During the 1990s new currency boards were established in a number of economies, including most notably Argentina, Bosnia, Bulgaria, Estonia, and Lithuania.

The emergence of regional currencies can be regarded as a logical corollary of the intense competitive contest among monies – a Darwinian struggle where, ultimately, only the fittest may survive. Among informed observers today it is rapidly becoming conventional wisdom that the number of currencies in the world will soon decline.[7] Typical is the prediction of Michel Camdessus[8], former managing director of the IMF, who suggests, "In the long run, we are moving toward a world of fewer currencies." Economist Rudi Dornbusch[9] is blunter. "Convergence on regional monies," he asserts, "is a no-brainer."

Not all local currencies will disappear, by any means. Even in today's globalizing world, many states remain determined to preserve some semblance of their traditional monetary sovereignty – to keep their national currency alive, no matter how uncompetitive it may be. Monetary sovereignty can be defended by tactics of either persuasion or coercion. Persuasion entails trying to sustain demand for a currency by buttressing its reputation, above all by a public commitment to credible policies of "sound" monetary management. The idea is to preserve market confidence in the value and usability of the nation's brand of money – the "confidence game," as Paul Krugman (1998) has ironically dubbed it. Coercion means applying the formal regulatory powers of the state to avert any significant shift by users to a more popular foreign money. Possible measures range from standard legal-tender laws, which specify what money creditors must accept in payment of a debt, to limitations on foreign-currency deposits in local banks and even to the extremes of capital controls or exchange restrictions. Both floating and contingent exchange-rate rules are consistent with a strategy of market preservation.

A desire to continue producing a national money is understandable, given the historical advantages of a formal monetary monopoly. But at what cost? As currency competition accelerates, tactics of persuasion or coercion become increasingly expensive. Growth and employment may have to be sacrificed, more and more, in order to keep playing the confidence game; widening distortions in the allocation of resources may be introduced by controls or restrictions. The costs of defending currency sovereignty are real, a direct result of the transformation of the global monetary environment. And as they continue to mount, the alternative of buying from a more efficient producer becomes increasingly appealing – or, at least, less unappealing. Not surprisingly, therefore, in a growing number of countries, more attention is being paid today to the corner solution of monetary union, in the form of either formal dollarization or currency unification.[10]

In the Western Hemisphere, for example, the idea of dollarization has become a topic of intense public debate since Argentina's former President Carlos Menem, spoke out in its favour in early 1999. Though dollarization by Argentina itself was rejected by Menem's successor, Fernando de la Rúa, the idea was in fact implemented in Ecuador and El Salvador and continues to attract attention elsewhere, including in Mexico and Canada, America's partners in the North American Free Trade Area. Likewise, in East-Central Europe and the Mediterranean, "euroization" increasingly is touted as a natural path for countries with close ties to the European Union (EU) or hopes of one day joining the EU. Should more governments decide to go the dollarization route, it is not too difficult to imagine the gradual emergence of two giant monetary blocs, one centred on the United States and one on EMU"s "Euroland." (Eventually a third bloc could also coalesce around the Japanese yen, though not any time soon, as one observer has predicted.)

By 2030 the world will have two major currency zones – one European, the other American. The euro will be used from Brest to Bucharest, and the dollar from Alaska to Argentina – perhaps even in Asia. These regional currencies will form the bedrock of the next century's financial stability.[11]

Much will depend, of course, on the policies adopted by the market leaders, which could significantly alter the relative costs and benefits of followership as contrasted with strategies of either market preservation or alliance. Unfortunately, these policies cannot be easily predicted. On the one hand, monetary leadership can yield substantial benefits, both economic and political. Economic gains include reduced transactions costs and additional opportunities for seigniorage as well as an enhanced degree of macroeconomic flexibility. Politically, an international currency may yield dividends in terms of both power and prestige. The prospect of such benefits could attract the U.S. and Europe (and/or Japan) to offer explicit incentives to potential dollarizers, especially if, as I have suggested elsewhere,[12] active competition for market share breaks out among the market leaders. But on the other hand there are also considerable risks in monetary leadership, including in particular policy constraints that could be imposed by pressures to accommodate the needs of followers. Suppose Canada were to adopt America's greenback, for instance. It is not at all difficult to imagine that Canada, a major commodity exporter, might experience an adverse terms-of-trade shock even at a time of boom in the United States. Could the Federal Reserve really ignore declining income north of the border while fighting inflation at home? Such risks might prompt Washington and other market leaders to discourage rather than encourage formal adoption of their currencies.

Absent material incentives to dollarize, some governments might prefer instead to look to the idea of currency unification, a less subordinate form of monetary union on the model of EMU. Prospects for monetary alliances have been discussed in almost every region of the world.[13] EMU is clearly viewed as a test case for a strategy of pooling rather than surrendering monetary sovereignty. If Europe's experiment comes to be seen as successful, it could have a powerful demonstration effect, encouraging similar initiatives elsewhere. This would be especially likely for groups of states engaged in a common integration project such as Mercosur, in the southern cone of South America, or the Association of Southeast Asian Nations (ASEAN). Alongside two (or three) major currency zones, a variety of new joint currencies could also eventually come into existence in addition to the euro.

Scenarios of currency regionalization, therefore, seem not only plausible but also perhaps even likely – indeed, arguably for many states the most reasonable outcome to be expected from today's accelerating deterritorialization of money. At present there are more than 170 central banks in the world, as compared with fewer than twenty a century ago; and more than one hundred currencies that formally float more or less freely. Can anyone really believe that such a polyglot and turbulent universe represents a stable equilibrium? The logic of competition suggests that a good number of governments could eventually yield to the market power of more efficient producers, replacing national monies with regional currencies of some kind. Regionalization of the world's monies has happened before, in medieval Europe and again during the nineteenth century, as Eichengreen and Sussman (2000) remind us. Obviously, it could happen again. For Ricardo Hausmann, formerly chief economist of the Inter-American Development Bank, the process has an almost historical inevitability about it: "National currencies are a phenomenon of the twentieth century; supranational currencies are the solution of the future."[14] That formulation may be a bit too deterministic. Nonetheless, there is little doubt that alongside national monies a new geography of regional currencies is beginning to emerge.

PREDICTING THE FUTURE

Can the shape of that new geography be predicted? How will governments decide among the three broad options of market preservation, alliance, or followership? Clearly, the choice is not an easy one, involving a number of potential benefits and costs, both economic and political. On the economic side, currency regionalization would reduce transactions costs, a distinct advantage, but would also mean a loss of both an autonomous monetary policy and seigniorage revenue. On the political side, regionalization means giving up not only a degree of insulation from foreign influence but also a vital symbol of national identity, a role of money that has been especially emphasized by Eric Helleiner (1998). State choices ultimately will depend on how much importance policymakers attach to particular gains or losses, which in turn will depend on each state's individual circumstances.

Scholars are just beginning to explore this critical issue. The most ambitious effort to date has been by the economists Alberto Alesina and Robert Barro (2001), who use formal modeling techniques based on deductive reasoning to forecast when governments might be prepared to give up producing their own money. In my own research, which is still at a preliminary stage,[15] I take a more inductive approach, concentrating on the empirical record to identify key factors that may be expected to influence state behaviour. Significantly, study of the empirical record does reveal some reasonably consistent patterns. Three conditions seem especially influential: (1) country size; (2) economic linkages; and (3) political linkages. In addition, domestic politics must also be assumed to play a key role. But we are still quite a way from anything that might be regarded as a full-scale, positive theory of currency regionalization.

Among the conditions that appear influential, country size clearly does matter – at least for the world's smallest states. Of all the economies that were dollarized until recently, the largest was Panama, with a population of less than three million. Most are truly tiny enclaves or microstates. Small size also dominates among nations that have adopted currency boards and is an accurate description of the members of both the ECCU and CFA Franc Zone. One safe bet, ceteris paribus, is that the smaller an economy's size – whether measured by population, territory, or GDP – the greater is the probability that it will be prepared to surrender the privilege of producing a money of its own. The logic is simple. Smaller states are least able to sustain a competitive national currency. Conversely, these are the economies that stand to gain most from a reduction of transactions costs. Moreover, when considering the option of dollarization, they are least likely to encounter resistance from market leaders because they will have the least impact on the countries whose currencies they adopt.

Next is the intensity of economic linkages between nations. Many of the countries that make use of a popular foreign currency have long been closely tied to a market leader economically. This is especially true of the numerous dollarized systems in the Caribbean and Central America, as well as the several dollarized enclaves of Europe and the Pacific. Likewise, we know that nearly half a century of deepening integration preceded the start of EMU. Another safe bet, ceteris paribus, is that closer economic bonds will also increase the probability that a government will be prepared to surrender the privilege of producing its own money. Here again, the logic is simple. Economies that are already closely linked would, because of the efficiency gains involved, appear to be natural candidates for a regional money of some kind.

Third is the intensity of political linkages between nations, whether formal or informal. Ties may take the form of a patron-client relationship, often descended from a previous colonial or trusteeship association; or they may be embodied in a network of cooperative diplomatic arrangements, possibly institutionalized in a formal alliance. Whatever the form, the influence of such ties is unmistakable – in currency groupings that have failed in the past as well as those that still survive in the present. A third safe bet, ceteris paribus, is that closer political bonds too will increase the probability that a government will be prepared to surrender the privilege of a national money. The logic is that political linkages reduce two of the key costs associated with regionalization – the loss of a social symbol and the increase of vulnerability to outside influence.

Finally, there is domestic politics. Unfortunately, no studies yet exist that directly probe the role of domestic interest groups in currency regionalization. But we do know that the material interests of specific constituencies are systematically influenced by what a government decides to do with its money. State strategies, therefore, are bound to be sensitive to the interplay among domestic political forces as well as the institutional structures through which interest-group preferences are mediated. Most influential, it can be assumed, would be the constituencies that can be expected to benefit most from the openness and stability that would be provided by a regional currency. These would include big tradable-goods producers, banks and other financial-services firms, and large private asset-holders – those that Jeffrey Frieden (1991) refers to as "integrationist" interests. Much will depend on the degree of political influence exercised by such groups as compared with other domestic constituencies, such as producers of non-tradables and workers, who might oppose abandoning a national currency – "anti-integrationist" forces who feel they would benefit more from preservation of some measure of monetary autonomy.

Taken together, do these factors suggest that national currencies are indeed becoming obsolete? The answer, regrettably, is unclear. While the deterritorialization of currency is clearly imposing growing constraints on traditional forms of monetary governance, it by no means dictates the choices that governments will eventually make. A good number of countries will consider some form of dollarization or currency unification – but by no means all. The essential elements of a positive theory of currency regionalization can be identified. What cannot be foretold is how these elements will work out in specific bargaining contexts. At this stage, there is simply still no sure way to predict what the new geography of money will look like. Standard microeconomic theory teaches that when stable monopoly yields to more strategic oligopoly, outcomes become indeterminate and multiple equilibrium are possible. So too, it would appear, is that true in matters of money.

NOTES

1. Baliño et al. (1999). Broad money supply (M2) is defined to include all coins and notes in circulation, demand deposits (checking accounts), and all other "reservable" deposits (time deposits).
2. Fischer (2001).
3. Litfin (1997). See also Mattli (2000).
4. The distinction between pooling and surrender of sovereignty, which is generic to the question of how to organize political authority, is of course a familiar one in political science and is used in a variety of contexts – in analyzing differences between confederal states and empires, for instance.
5. Pou (1999) p. 244.
6. The adjectives "full" or "formal" are frequently added to distinguish this policy choice from the market-driven process of currency substitution, which in the past was also often popularly labelled dollarization (now unofficial or informal dollarization). Dollarization, of course, does not necessarily require the dollar. Some other currency, such as the euro or yen, might also be chosen to replace a country's currency.
7. See for example, Alesina and Barro (2000); Fischer (2001); Rogoff (2001).
8. Camdessus (2000), p. 35.
9. Dornbusch (2001) p. 9.
10. In a complementary analysis Helleiner (2001) stresses the declining benefits of monetary sovereignty rather than, as here, the rising costs.
11. Beddoes (1999) p. 8. See also Eichengreen (1994); Hausmann (1999a), (1999b); Mundell (2000).
12 Cohen (2000).
13. These include prospects in Asia, Eichengreen and Bayoumi (1999), Africa, Honohan and Lane (2001), Latin America, Levy, Yeyati and Sturzenegger (2000), Australia-New Zealand, Grimes and Holmes (2000); and even between Canada and the United States, Buiter (1999).
14 Hausmann (1999b) p. 96.
15 Cohen (2001).

REFERENCES

Alesina, Alberto, and Robert J. Barro. 2002. "Currency Unions." *Quarterly Journal of Economics*, CXVII, no. 2, pp. 409-436.

Baliño, T.J.T., A. Bennett, and E. Borensztein. 1999. *Monetary Policy in Dollarized Economies.* Washington, DC: International Monetary Fund.

Beddoes, Z.M. 1999 "From EMU to AMU? The Case for Regional Currencies." *Foreign Affairs*, 78, no. 4, pp. 8-13.

Buiter, W.H. 1999 "The EMU and the NAMU: What is the Case for North American Monetary Union?" *Canadian Public Policy/Analyse de Politiques*, 25, no. 3, pp. 285-305.

Camdessus, Michel. 2000. "Council on Foreign Relations Address." IMF Survey, 7 February, pp. 33-36.

Cohen, B. J. 1998. *The Geography of Money*. Ithaca, NY: Cornell University Press.

Cohen, B. J. 2000. *Life at the Top: International Currencies in the Twenty-First Century*. Essay in International Economics, 221. Princeton, NJ: International Economics Section.

Cohen, B. J. 2001. "Monetary Governance in a World of Regional Currencies." University of California at Santa Barbara, unpublished.

Dornbusch, R. 2001. "Fewer Monies, Better Monies." Working Paper W8324. Cambridge, MA: National Bureau of Economic Research.

Eichengreen, B. 1994. *International Monetary Arrangements for the 21st Century Washington*. DC: Brookings Institution.

Eichengreen, B., and T. Bayoumi. 1999. "Is Asia an Optimum Currency Area? Can It Become One? Regional, Global, and Historical Perspectives on Asian Monetary Relations." In S. Collignon, J. Pisani-Ferry, and Y. C. Park, eds., *Exchange Rate Policies in Emerging Asian Countries*. London: Routledge, ch. 21.

Eichengreen, B., and N. Sussman. 2000. "The International Monetary System in the (Very) Long Run." In *World Economic Outlook Supporting Studies*. Washington, DC: International Monetary Fund.

Fischer, S. 2001. "Exchange Rate Regimes: Is the Bipolar View Correct?" *Journal of Economic Perspectives*, 15, pp. 3-24.

Frieden, J. A. 1991. "Invested Interests: The Politics of National Economic Policies in a World of Global Finance." *International Organization*, 45, pp. 425-451.

Grimes, A., and F. Holmes. 2000. *An ANZAC Dollar? Currency Union and Business Development*. Wellington, NZ: Victoria University of Wellington, Institute of Policy Studies.

Hausmann, R. 1999a. "Should There Be Five Currencies or One Hundred and Five?" *Foreign Policy*, 116, pp. 65-79.

Hausmann, R. 1999b. "Why the Interest in Reform?" In J. S. Little and G. P. Olivei, eds., *Rethinking the International Monetary System*, Boston, MA: Federal Reserve Bank of Boston, pp. 94-96.

Helleiner, E. 1998. "National Currencies and National Identities." *American Behavioral Scientist*, 41, pp. 1409-1436.

Helleiner, E. 2001. "Why Are Territorial Currencies Becoming Unpopular?" In D.M. Andrews, C. R. Henning, and L.W. Pauly, eds., *Organizing the World's Economy*, forthcoming.

Honohan, P., and P. Lane. 2001. "Will the Euro Trigger More Monetary Unions in Africa?" In C. Wyplosz, ed., *EMU and Its Impact on Europe and the Developing Countries*. Oxford: Oxford University Press.

Krueger, R., and J. Ha. 1996. "Measurement of Cocirculation of Currencies." In P.D. Mizen and E.J. Pentecost, eds., *The Macroeconomics of International Currencies: Theory, Policy and Evidence*. Brookfield, VT: Edward Elgar, ch. 4.

Krugman, P. R. 1998. "The Confidence Game." *The New Republic*, 5 (October), pp. 23-25.

Levy Yeyati, E. and F. Sturzenegger. 2000 "Is EMU a Blueprint for Mercosur?" *Latin American Journal of Economics*, 110, pp. 63-99.

Litfin, K. 1997. "Sovereignty in World Ecopolitics." *Mershon International Studies Review*, 41, pp. 167-204.

Mattli, W. 2000. "Sovereignty Bargains in Regional Integration." *International Studies Quarterly*, 2, pp. 149-180.

Mundell, R.A. 2000. " Reconsideration of the Twentieth Century." *American Economic Review*, 90, pp. 327-340.

Pou, P. 2000. "Is Globalization Really to Blame?" In J.S. Little and G.P. Olivei, eds., *Rethinking the International Monetary System*, Boston, MA: Federal Reserve Bank of Boston, pp. 243-250.

Rogoff, K. 2001. "Why Not a Global Currency?" *American Economic Review*, 91, pp. 243-247.

Von Furstenberg, G. 2000. "A Case Against U.S. Dollarization." *Challenge*, 43, pp. 108-120.

Chapter 4

REDUCING BARRIERS TO INVESTMENT: IS THE NAFTA INVESTMENT REGIME AN APPROPRIATE MODEL?[1]

Maureen Appel Molot
Carleton University

The North American Free Trade Agreement (NAFTA) investment regime[2] created by Chapter 11 is significant for many reasons: it covers two developed and a less developed economy; it includes existing as well as future legislative provisions; and most notably, it provides for investor-state dispute settlement. This chapter addresses the construction and evolution of the NAFTA investment regime – its philosophical and practical underpinnings, provisions, operations, assessment, and the complexities of revision. Although it is often argued that multilateral institutions are preferable to regional ones, regional regimes may provide an opportunity to test and refine cooperation on issues that have yet to be addressed more broadly. This is the case with investment in the North American context since Chapter 11 of NAFTA contains many of the same clauses that were included in the failed Multilateral Agreement on Investment (MAI). Thus NAFTA may be considered a test case for a larger investment accord. Moreover, since the investment provisions of the draft Free Trade Area of the Americas (FTAA) have been influenced by Chapter 11, an evaluation of the functioning of the NAFTA investment regime is directly relevant to what might unfold in the hemisphere.

Any analysis of state regulation of foreign investment crosses the international-domestic divide and therefore generates questions about current and future state regulatory capacity. Among the obvious issues is whether the regime imposes constraints on state legislative and regulatory authority, the "regulatory chill" argument. The analysis also introduces a different philosophy of remedy, with different implications for state obligations. The resolution of a trade dispute does not involve compensation but rather the expectation that the offending state will bring its regulations into compliance with its WTO obligations; in an investment dispute, should a decision go against a state, that state is obliged to pay damages, an outcome that has its roots in public

S. McBride et al. (eds.), Global Instability, 43–63.

international law.[3] Because the three parties to NAFTA are federations, the chapter also briefly considers the implications of the NAFTA investment regime for sub-national governments. The chapter argues that from a governmental perspective that the experience thus far with the NAFTA investment regime has been reasonably positive, but that tribunal decisions have generated procedural and substantive matters that need to be addressed. One recognition of this was the issuance of a "clarifying note" on 31 July 2001 by the NAFTA Free Trade Commission.[4] Chapter 11's critics are far less sanguine about it.

The experience with Chapter 11 illustrates at a regional level of governance the argument made by Prakash and Hart at the state level, that the speed of change and the limits of information make it highly unlikely that state attempts to devise institutions to meet the pressures of globalization will succeed on the first iteration. In their view, changes in state institutions and policies, what they depict as "the rearticulated state," will of necessity be incremental.[5] If institutional and policy change are difficult to accomplish at the state level, how much more complex are they when inter-state negotiations are required. Nonetheless, the history of the GATT, the WTO, and the European Union, demonstrates that changes in international regimes through stakeholder negotiations are indeed possible. In the NAFTA context the challenge is to contemplate revisions that would avoid a full-scale re-opening of the agreement.

MANAGING GLOBAL TURBULENCE: THE UTILITY OF REGIMES

The analysis of globalization and its impact have become something of an industry in international political economy. Scholars debate the causes and consequences of the phenomenon, looking at globalization as both independent and dependent variables. Employing globalization as an independent variable, authors consider the meaning of globalization for states: is it rendering the state impotent, not seriously altering state policy capacity, or encouraging policy convergence?[6] Globalization as a dependent variable is less a subject of controversy. Analysts largely agree that globalization is the result of a combination of factors: technological change, the investment activities of multinational enterprises (MNEs), and inter-state competition for investment.[7] Globalization is the current way of capturing what Richard Cooper once called interdependence,[8] although arguably more complex for all stakeholders.

The pace of change in the global economy is faster now than it was a couple decades ago. State capacity to manage interdependence/globalization has changed little in kind, though it is clearly far more sophisticated in quality: states use national levers of policy and cooperate in the establishment and maintenance of international regimes. Regimes are seen as critical in managing interdependence, as institutional responses to a wide range of international market failures.[9]

The literature on regimes, multilateral and minilateral, is extremely rich. More of it addresses regime establishment than evolution, perhaps because of the great interest in bargaining and negotiation and the politics of getting to yes. Analyses of regime creation or failure (in the case of the MAI) direct scholarly attention to the domestic, interstate, and international (particularly the recent activities of cross-border non-governmental organizations) aspects of the process. However, it is equally appropriate to be attentive to regime evolution, since state and interest group experience with, and perceptions of, existing regimes shape demands for change and the likelihood of attaining it, as well as attitudes toward future regime creation. In a discussion of global governance in which regimes are a crucial component, Lake notes that many of the definitions of global governance conflate two processes, which are and should remain analytically distinct: "bargaining, which divides the available costs and benefits between actors, and contracting, which enforces the bargains reached."[10] In Lake's view we need to be more attentive to contracting side, to the enforcement of bargains since this is one of the factors that engender pressures for regime review and possibly alteration. This chapter makes a small contribution to this debate.

Prakash and Hart make a statement in the domestic context that resonates at the international level: "the politics of rearticulation [are]... complex and ... further complicated by the incomplete understanding of the nature and architecture of the desired institutions."[11] The global economy moves far more quickly than states' capacity to conceptualize and agree on institutions; at the same time the continuous character of change means that assessment of institutional performance is essential. In the case of NAFTA, the negotiators fashioned an agreement whose institutions were purposively limited to interstate ones created as needed (in the case of tribunals) or which meet from time to time (the various commissions). Are the NAFTA institutions, including tribunals created as needed to adjudicate Chapter 11 disputes, appropriate for the purposes for which they were intended, or are changes needed?

One strand of the regime literature evaluates the relative merits of multilateral versus regional regimes. Although there is a strong preference on the part of some scholars for multilateral regimes and therefore marshalling of state efforts to this end,[12] regional economic arrangements have a number of advantages, among them the ease of negotiation, the momentum for increased liberalization beyond the level attainable multilaterally, the opportunity to tackle issues on which multilateral agreement would be more difficult, and their demonstration effect.[13] Although the attribution of a demonstration effect has a positive connotation – other states will see the benefits of liberalization or deepening integration – it is possible that the impact could be in the other direction. Bobrow and Kudrle suggest that regional agreements should be treated as "hedging instruments" under which participating states and other actors retain policy latitude, rather than as instruments to "commit firmly to accelerating, braking, or ratcheting liberalization."[14] In other words, a regional agreement is an opportunity to experiment with provisions, the assessment of which will shape a state's negotiating positions in subsequent regime discussions.

The creation of regimes is not neutral in interest terms. Winners can be states, i.e., the one whose objectives are most closely reflected in regime rules, or actors who solidify existing or derive new gains from the regime. This is one of the reasons the creation of a global investment regime has been so contested. While some argue that in negotiations over the regulation of investment states seek to advantage their own MNEs and that MNEs support regime creation because it constrains states and thereby "enlarges the private sphere,"[15] others contend that the rules of an investment regime do not reflect the relative power of any one state and by requiring national treatment for all foreign investors create a level playing field.[16] Others note that the NAFTA investment regime privileges foreign MNEs over domestic ones[17] and the corporate agenda over that of environmental and other interests.

The debate on the meaning of globalization for states has focused largely on national governments. However, some of the issues under consideration at the WTO and at regional tables include topics that in federal states fall under subnational or joint jurisdiction. Regulation of some aspects of investment and of the environment is among them. In signing the GATT and NAFTA agreements states accept the responsibility to ensure that their subnational governments comply with these international regimes.[18] Under NAFTA the subnational governments were able to identify reservations to the provisions of Chapter 11 and did so expansively. A number of the challenges under Chapter 11 have been directed at regulations and decisions of subnational governments in all three NAFTA members. While the politics of each of the three federations is different, the encouragement of NAFTA sensitivity in subnational jurisdictions is one of the challenges of managing Chapter 11.[19]

These theoretical perspectives influence the analysis of NAFTA's investment regime that follows. Among the questions generated by the literature and discussed on the basis of the experience thus far with Chapter 11 are: identification of the norms of the regime and their evolution; the NAFTA investment regime as hedge or ratchet; preliminary discussions on regime re-articulation; and an evaluation of the demonstration effect of the regime.

Chapter 11 of the NAFTA

The investment chapter of NAFTA was one of the more contentious to negotiate. It went significantly farther than, the investment provisions of the Canada-U.S. Free Trade Agreement (CUSFTA). The U.S. has used bilateral investment treaties [BITs] with developing capital-importing countries to protect the FDI of its nationals in locations where expropriation or the deficiencies of national legal systems rendered these investments subject to local whims.[20] With Chapter 16 of CUSFTA, Canada and the U.S. established a bilateral BIT.[21] Its most important provisions:

i) covered FDI in enterprises, but not portfolio or real estate investments;
ii) defined "investor" in national terms (i.e., an investment controlled by Canadians or Americans);
iii) imposed national treatment obligations but not most favoured nation (MFN) treatment;
iv) protected or "grandfather" non-conforming measures extant at the implementation of the agreement, and;
v) provided for state-to-state dispute resolution (under Chapter 18).[22]

In the NAFTA negotiations the U.S. sought an investment chapter that would go well beyond the same section in CUSFTA; it wanted provisions that were similar to those in the U.S.-Argentina BIT (seen as a model BIT) – a very broad definition of investment, the inclusion of an investor-state dispute resolution mechanism, and language around compensation for expropriated assets that spoke of "prompt, adequate, effective" payment. Canada recognized the need to improve on CUSFTA's investment chapter but was much more content with it than the U.S.; Canada opposed the U.S. demand for a broad definition of investment and wanted to preserve its capacity to screen FDI coming into the country.[23]

Whatever their differences Canada and the U.S. shared one goal – the termination of Mexico's adherence to the Calvo doctrine (under which a foreign investor was subject to Mexican domestic law had to settle disputes in domestic courts, and could not seek protection or assistance from its home state). Mexico's major objective in NAFTA was to make the country more attractive to FDI and to this end reduced its restrictions on investment before and during the NAFTA talks. At the same time Mexico wanted to retain the Calvo doctrine, opposed an investor-state dispute resolution provision, sought a narrower definition of investment than the U.S., and preferred the language of "fair market value" for expropriated assets.[24] In the end, Chapter 11 most closely approximated what the U.S. sought. The major components of the NAFTA investment regime are:

A wider definition of investment than the CUSFTA, which means that virtually all forms of investment are subject to NAFTA's purview.

A definition of investor that includes citizens and permanent residents of NAFTA signatories, their governments or state enterprises and enterprises organized under the laws of one of the partners but not controlled by a national of that country (Articles 1001 and 1113). This definition goes well beyond what had been included in BITs and means that subsidiaries of firms with head offices in non-NAFTA members are covered by the provision of the agreement.

National and MFN Treatment: Subheads (1) and (2) of Article 1102 require that each member of NAFTA treat investments and investors of other NAFTA signatories in the same way it treats its own investors. Subhead (3) of the same Article extends the national treatment provision to subnational governments. Article 1103, the MFN provision, provides that NAFTA signatories treat investors and investments of their NAFTA partners no less favourably than investors and investments of any other NAFTA party or non-NAFTA member.

The expectation that NAFTA members will accord each other the better of national or MFN treatment (Article 1104).

The expectation that NAFTA signatories will accord to investors from other members treatment in accordance with international law, including fair and equitable treatment (Article 1105).

The prohibition (Article 1106) on the imposition on investors of performance requirements such as level of exports, transfer of technology, domestic content, restrictions on sales.

The prohibition of expropriation of an investment by a NAFTA member except for a public purpose (Article 1110 (1)), and compensation should this occur at fair market value and without delay (1110 (2) and (3)).

A provision that recognizes the right of members to require that investments respect environmental concerns and that should not prohibit the relaxation of regulations to attract investment (Article 1114).

The creation of dispute settlement provisions (Articles 1115-1117) that permit an investor of one NAFTA member to challenge treatment received in another.

A range of Annexes, negative lists, and reservations because of which designated industries in each signatory are protected from the clauses of Chapter 11.[25]

Two questions stem from the identification of the major components of the NAFTA investment regime: what are the most important norms and procedures that define it and what are the potential pitfalls in regime evolution? The former can be deduced from the content of the chapter and analyses of other international regimes and buttressed or altered by panel decisions. The challenges to the regime have a number of sources. The first group is enumerated here, with others to follow from the explication of regime norms and procedures.

The conceptual cornerstone of the NAFTA investment regime is national treatment. The additions with NAFTA are MFN for investors and the expectation of best possible treatment. At the same time the rules governing national and MFN treatment are circumscribed by the list of exceptions stipulated in the Annexes by national governments and the right given to subnational governments to determine a list of reservations to the chapter's application. National reservations include a range of sectors deemed sensitive by the signatories, most of which are not subject to phase out provisions. [26] Subnational governments had two years from the date of NAFTA's implementation to list their reservations. All, but particularly the Canadian provinces, found the exercise an enormous challenge and in the end, the NAFTA signatories agreed that all subnational measures inconsistent with Article 11 would be protected without the requirement of specific listings in Annex 1.[27]

A second critical norm is the proscription on the nationalization or direct or indirect expropriation of an investment or the imposition of a "measure tantamount" to these except in very particular circumstances. Despite considerable effort, the negotiators were unable to define the language and so followed the CUSFTA precedent of simply using the terms.[28] What is not spelled out, indeed perhaps could not be articulated, is the line between state actions that affect the economic interests of investors and therefore require compensation and those which may affect property interests but which are taken in the public interest and, as a result, do not oblige the state to pay damages to those who claim adverse impact. Phrased differently, the distinction is between "taking" and "regulation." What is the meaning of "indirect" expropriation and "tantamount to...expropriation"? Decisions of Canadian and U.S. courts have established jurisprudence domestically on the difference between a taking and regulation. There is also considerable international judicial interpretation of state expropriation. Things are less clear at the international level. A state action taken for identifiable public interest purposes, for example protection of the environment, may be seen as crossing the divide between regulation and taking, in other words, from a non-compensable to an arguably compensable action.[29] This article has prompted concerns about a "regulatory chill," the idea that the possibly wide tribunal interpretation of "tantamount to expropriation" might inhibit state policy choices because they fear challenges under Chapter 11. To underline that the investor-state provisions of NAFTA were not intended to impede the capacity of states to act in the public interest, International Trade Minister Pettigrew stated in September 2001, "it is...important that the ability of governments to regulate in the public interests not be compromised by unintended interpretations of investment rules."[30]

A third construct, which addresses a sovereign right and has become important as a result of challenges and the growing priority attached to "green" component of trade, is Article 1114. The intent was to ensure unfettered state capacity to regulate for environmental purposes. The phrase in the article which is proving problematic is "otherwise consistent with this Chapter"; in other words, litigants can/could claim that government environmental measures are inconsistent with the substantive provisions of NAFTA and therefore can serve as the basis for a challenge to regulation.[31]

On the procedural side the critical innovation of the NAFTA investment regime is the investor-state dispute settlement mechanism. Although not unique to NAFTA – investor-state dispute settlement is a component of many BITs – the provision is noteworthy because of the character of NAFTA (two developed and one less industrialized member), the introduction for the first time of this procedure into the Canada-U.S. relationship (dispute settlement under the CUSFTA was state-to-state only), and Mexico's willingness to forego the Calvo doctrine. NAFTA allows private parties, on their own, and on behalf of their investments, to make claims against host states for breaches of Part A of Chapter 11. There is a three-year statute of limitations on bringing a claim under Chapter 11. To some, the establishment of a procedure that permits individual access to dispute resolution is "perhaps the most significant legal development that has taken place through the NAFTA"[32] and may well set the standard for subsequent investment agreements. Like all NAFTA dispute settlement provisions Chapter 11 contains no provisions for the appeal of tribunal decisions. However, NAFTA implementation legislation in Canada and the U.S. provides for review of NAFTA panel decisions by domestic courts.

In any new regime there are uncertainties. The first emerges from the definition and phrasing difficulties encountered by the negotiators around terms, which in turn led to the use of general language and the expectation that issues would be addressed by panels on a case-by-case basis. A second arises because investors can only sue national governments, even if the legislation or action challenged has been taken by a subnational entity. A third is the definition of investment under NAFTA; because the definition is broad, the potential impact of Article 1110 is considerable.[33] A fourth problem ensues from the use thus far of Chapter 11; while investment agreements are normally seen as "recourses of last resort," in other words employed to protect investors in unusual situations, some suggest that threats to use Chapter 11 have become something of a lobbying tactic, an effort to prevent regulation or to press for or against state decisions or to maintain market position.[34] Finally, although Part B of Chapter 11 contains an elaborate listing of procedures for filing a claim, it does not refer to transparency or openness of either the submissions or the hearing process. While there are reasons for this in the international arbitration processes used in Chapter 11 cases, over the years, and with growing disquiet in some circles about globalization, the closed nature of the process has generated considerable criticism.

In sum, Chapter 11 of NAFTA creates an investment regime with considerable breadth and strength as well as weaknesses. The test of any regime is its operation – what happens when provisions are challenged. A second test is the response of states when, as a result of challenges and decisions, they are faced with outcomes that were unanticipated and potentially limiting to state capacity. The next section of the paper looks at Chapter 11 cases up through January 2002 to demonstrate the evolution of the investment regime.

REGIME EVOLUTION THROUGH PANEL DECISIONS

Twenty-four cases have been brought under Chapter 11 from the implementation of NAFTA in January 1994 to May 2002, all but one since January 1997. Each of the three NAFTA states has been sued. A larger number of cases are pending than have been resolved. The challenges against each of the three NAFTA members will be noted, with only the most important cases summarized briefly.

Canada

There have been nine cases against Canada under Chapter 11, two of which have been decided by tribunals. One, Ethyl, launched against Canada in 1996, was withdrawn before a tribunal could hear the case.[35] All involve challenges by U.S. companies operating in Canada. The first of the two cases decided, Myers, involved charges under NAFTA Articles 1002, 1005, 1006 and 1110. Canada argued that its November 1995 ban on the export of toxic wastes from Canada complied with international conventions. Although the ban was partially lifted in 1997, Myers stated that the 15-month restriction gave a monopoly to a waste disposal plant operated by the government of Alberta and thus, among other things, alleged denial of national treatment and expropriation. The tribunal concluded Canada's ban breached the national treatment and minimum standards of treatment provisions of Chapter 11, but did not contravene the articles on performance requirements and expropriation. In its November 2000 decision the tribunal did not rule on damages; this is now underway. In February 2001, Canada decided to ask the Federal Court to overturn the tribunal finding that Canada is liable for damages since the tribunal exceeded its jurisdiction because the issue related to cross-border trade, not an investment.[36]

Two cases against Canada involve corporate complaints as a result of the implementation of the 1996 Canada-U.S. Softwood Lumber Agreement. Pope and Talbot and Ketchum Investments Inc. and Tysa Investments Inc., all U.S.-based firms, maintained that they lost revenue because of the implementation of provincial and company quotas on lumber exports to the U.S. Pope and Talbot claimed Canada violated Articles 1102, 1105, 1106, and 1110 of NAFTA. The tribunal in the Pope and Talbot challenge found that Canada's implementation of its bilateral lumber agreement was consistent with its NAFTA obligations, with the exception of one administrative procedure. Subsequent to the decision in the Pope and Talbot case, the second softwood lumber case was withdrawn.

A case of some interest is one bought by United Parcel Service (UPS), which claims that its position in Canada is being undermined by Purolator Courier, Priority Courier and Xpresspost, which are owned by Canada Post and which are able, as a result, to use Canada Post's national network. UPS alleges these Canada Post courier services are cross-subsidized by other activities of the Post Office and thus that foreign courier companies do not receive the same treatment as those of Canada Post. UPS maintains Canada is in violation of two articles of Chapter 11 (1102 and 1105) as well as Articles under Chapters 12 (Services) and 15 (Competition Policy, Monopolies and State Enterprises). Although the case has yet to be heard by the panel, a decision has been made as to venue (Washington) and to allow amicus curiae briefs from the Canadian Union of Postal Workers (CUPW) and the Council of Canadians.[37] The inclusion of other NAFTA chapters in the statement of claim raises questions about the applicability of Chapter 11 to other provisions of the agreement, in this instance national treatment to service providers and investments in the service sector.

The fifth Canadian case, Sun Belt Water Inc., involves a suit against Canada for a British Columbia (BC) decision to ban exports of fresh water. The company maintains that when it first formed a venture with a BC company the provincial (Social Credit) government allowed water exports and provided the necessary permits. Subsequently the provincial government changed its policy and imposed a permanent ban on water exports in 1995. Sun Belt claims that the BC government compensated its joint venture partner for loss of business, but that it did not receive similar treatment. The company is claiming a violation under NAFTA Article 1102 as well as Chapter 3 which addresses the movement of goods; in banning water exports the provincial governments is interfering with the international flow of goods. Although the case received publicity because it involved the export of water, the basis of the suit was lack of national treatment. The case is currently in abeyance.

One other case against Canada – Trammell Crow which involved challenging an unsuccessful bid on a tender for services to Canada Post – has been settled. A second, Crompton, a manufacturer of chemicals, that is suing the Canadian government for its decision to ban the use of a pesticide, is in its initial stages. There is lastly a case brought by the Council of Canadians and CUPW and involves a challenge to Chapter 11 itself rather than a complaint about investor treatment. Although long unhappy about NAFTA and particularly Chapter 11, this case was prompted by the UPS Chapter 11 case filed in mid-2000. The Council and CUPW maintain that in implementing NAFTA and therefore Chapter 11 with its investor-state dispute resolution provisions, the Canadian government exceeded its lawful authority.[38]

United States

The United States faces seven NAFTA cases, all brought by Canadian companies doing business in the U.S. A number involve complaints against state or municipal governments, but as noted above under NAFTA the defendant is the national government. A case being closely watched is Methanex, which raises fundamental questions about the relationship between Chapter 11, environmental regulation, and the responsibilities/role of subnational governments. Methanex is a Vancouver-based company manufacturing methanol, a component of a gasoline additive MTBE. In March 1999, through executive order, the governor of California ordered the phase-out of MBTE in gasoline by the end of 2002. A number of other states took similar action. This regulation means Methanex could lose a number of its major U.S. markets. In suing the U.S. government for the action of California, Methanex is claiming violation of Articles 1102, 1105, and 1110, in other words that the governor's order deprived the company of national treatment, fair and equitable treatment, and was tantamount to expropriation. The case is significant as it is the first environment case brought against the U.S. and because it was the first in which a tribunal accepted an 'amicus curiae' brief.[39]

The other significant U.S. case is Loewen, a Canadian-based funeral company that claims the U.S. government is responsible for actions of sub-national governments that contravene the rules of conduct set down under the agreement. In this instance Loewen alleges that it did not receive fair treatment when, in late 1995, a Mississippi jury awarded the owners of a small state funeral home and insurance business a settlement in their dispute with Loewen of $500 million (U.S.). The large award surprised many. In its NAFTA claim, Loewen is not challenging either the procedure or the verdict but contends that state law violated accepted standards of justice by requiring Loewen to post a bond of 125 percent of the judgment if it wanted to appeal. Loewen is claiming it received treatment different from that that an American company would have received under like circumstances. Loewen claims breach of Articles 1102, 1105, and 1110. The panel decision in this case is anxiously awaited because it is the first under Chapter 11 to challenge the conduct of the judiciary and because the size of Loewen's claim may have an impact on U.S. views on Chapter 11.

The remaining cases against the U.S. are Mondev International, ADF Group, Canfor, Tembec, and Kenex. The first relates to a court ruling on a real estate development and the second to the application of the "Buy America" provisions. The Mondev case resembles Loewen in that the complaint focuses on court rulings against the company. ADF is significant because it challenges the breadth of Buy America regulations.[40] Canfor and Tembec are Canadian lumber companies suing the U.S. government for losses they have incurred because of export duties on exports to the U.S. under the Canada-U.S. softwood lumber agreement.[41] The Kenex case involved a claim for damages that resulted from decisions of the U.S. Drug Enforcement Agency that effectively banned the company's shipments of hemp products into the U.S.[42]

Mexico

There have been eight cases against Mexico. Tribunals have ruled in three of them (in one instance to dismiss a complaint), one case was never pursued, and four continue. Four cases relate to challenges to the regulatory authority of municipalities, a fifth to excise taxes (Cemsa), and two to property disputes (Adams and Calmark); the subject of the eighth case (Halchette) is not known.[43] Mexico won the first two challenges against it – Azinian and Acaverde. Both cases were brought by U.S.-owned waste firms alleging breach of promises; both filed claims under Articles 1105 and 1110. The most important aspects of the Azinian case were the tribunal's statements that a termination of a contract was not a basis for a case under Chapter 11 and that a tribunal is not an appeals court against the decisions of domestic courts. A claimant has to demonstrate a breach of Chapter 11.[44] The decision in Acaverde case related to a procedural issue – whether the claimant had waived its right to pursue domestic legal proceedings (Article 1121). Acaverde has filed a second Chapter 11 claim against Mexico on the same grounds as the first; the difference in the second case is that the procedural problems have been rectified. The case has not yet been heard.[45]

By far the most significant case against Mexico thus far is Metalclad. This is the first case that Mexico has lost (the company was awarded $US16.7 million) and it is the first tribunal decision to have been appealed to a national court, in this instance the Supreme Court of British Columbia.[46] The facts in the case, yet another involving a U.S. owned waste disposal company, are rather complex. Metalclad purchased a Mexican company that had authorization from the federal government to build and operate a waste management facility in Guadalcazar. The purchase occurred as the Mexican company was seeking construction and operating permits for a larger waste management facility on the site. Shortly thereafter the state governor became less supportive of the project and the municipality decided not to act on Metalclad's application for a construction permit. However, armed with federal permission, the company began construction. Some time later, without giving Metalclad the chance to appear, the municipality denied the building permit. Subsequently the state governor issued a decree declaring the site an ecological preserve. In its claim Metalclad argued Mexico had violated Articles 1105 and 1110.

There are a number of noteworthy issues in the Metalclad case and its appeal. First was the tribunal reference to the NAFTA preamble as relevant for interpretations of the obligations under Chapter 11. Second was the fact that the BC Supreme Court judge struck down the tribunal's use of preamble language dealing with the responsibility of the Parties to "ensure a predictable commercial framework for business planning and investment" as a basis for finding a breach of Chapter 11. Third the tribunal ruled that Mexico failed to provide minimum standards of treatment in a number of ways, among them federal and state rulings about the capacity of the plant to operate and a lack of clear procedures for investors. On the lack of transparency the BC judge disagreed with the tribunal ruling stating that in Chapter 11 "there are no transparency obligations."[47] Fourth, the tribunal maintained that actions that were considered a breach of Article 1105 were similarly a breach of the expropriation provisions of Chapter 11. The BC Supreme Court upheld this tribunal finding, namely that the actions taken by Mexico to prevent Metalclad's from opening its waste facility amounted to expropriation.[48]

What are the major lessons about the evolution of NAFTA investment regime norms that can be drawn from the cases decided thus far? Since there have been only three substantive tribunal decisions and two rulings with respect to amicus curiae briefs to the end of January 2002, the opportunity for analysis is limited. Still some important directions have been established. Overall, tribunal rulings have been cautious, even if they have not interpreted articles under dispute in the same way. NAFTA tribunal decisions have no precedential impact, in other words, the decision of one tribunal is not binding on another addressing the same provision.

Many of the cases claim lack of national treatment (Article 1102). In evaluating this claim panels have to determine whether the claimant was treated differently from national investors or their investments and, if so, whether the circumstances of the foreign and domestic investors are the same. In both Pope and Talbot and Myers the tribunals found that differential treatment of investors in like circumstances could be justified by a policy choice that did not favour domestic over foreign investors.[49] One outcome of the tribunal decision in Pope and Talbot is that Chapter 11 cannot be used to challenge international agreements made by the NAFTA parties. In other words, NAFTA does not trump managed trade arrangements such as that on softwood lumber.

Article 1105, which addresses minimum national treatment, contains unclear language. Is the last phrase ("fair and equitable treatment and full protection and security") independent of the first ("each party shall accord to investments of investors of another party treatment in accordance with international law) and what is the standard of treatment guaranteed by international law? Panel pronouncements have varied and this likely led to the clarification on Article 1105 issued by the Free Trade Commission in the summer of 2001. In its note, the Commission made clear that NAFTA's standard is the customary international law minimum standard of treatment and that the second phrase does not require treatment beyond that established by customary international law.[50]

The Free Trade Commission's interpretive note also stated that a breach of another NAFTA provision or of a separate international agreement does not mean Article 1105 has been breached. This clarification may have resulted from the effort by Metalclad to link the provisions of the investment regime and the rest of the NAFTA, in this instance the NAFTA preamble as well other Articles of Chapter 11. Under Article 1131 of NAFTA, interpretations of the Commission are binding on panels established under the investment regime.

Arguably the most controversial Article of Chapter 11 is 1110 on expropriation because of the possibility for broad interpretation of the phrase "tantamount to expropriation." Tribunal decisions thus far have been conservative in their interpretation of "tantamount," suggesting that it effectively means "the same as." Only in the Metalclad case has the issue of concern to many – the loss of future revenue which might lead to limitations on state regulation – come up; however, in this instance the tribunal's award to the investor was for the costs of the facility only, and not for loss of future profits. Until there is a decision in the Methanex case concern over the meaning of "tantamount" will remain.

Two other regime norms, both procedural have evolved from tribunal rulings. The first relates to transparency. One of the early complaints about the NAFTA investment regime was its lack of transparency. Under the arbitral rules governing NAFTA tribunals, publication of tribunal decisions requires the consent of the parties. As early as 1998 Canada began to express its concern about lack of transparency under Chapter 11 and submitted a paper to the U.S. and Mexico proposing that the NAFTA parties agree to the publication of information about the existence and subject of each Chapter 11 case.[51] The other NAFTA parties eventually recognized transparency as an issue and the Free Trade Commission's July 2001 interpretive note provides for the release of documents submitted to or issued by Chapter 11 panels subject to concerns of privileged or confidential information.[52] The second procedural norm relates to third party briefs. Tribunals in the Methanex and UPS cases accepted arguments that third parties had concerns in these cases and that their views might facilitate the tribunal's understanding of the issues. At the same time, the tribunals would not agree to intervenor status for the parties, i.e., permit them to present oral arguments. Canada and U.S. supported the addition of amicus curiae briefs to panel procedures, while Mexico opposed it.[53] Both of these innovations reveal recognition of the need that the Chapter 11 process be seen as flexible and transparent.

A related procedural norm is that of appeal of tribunal decisions. Thus far two appeals of decisions have been launched, both in Canada but only one, Metalclad, has been heard. Whether appeal becomes the norm remains to be seen. What also remains unclear are the impact appeals may have on current and future tribunals and whether the process might lead to jurisdiction shopping. The decision of the UPS panel to hold its proceedings in Washington, despite Canada's argument that the tribunal should sit in Canada, was in part a result of the appeals launched in Canada and Canada's attitude toward the tribunal process.[54]

Of the cases decided thus far, only Metalclad touched on the relationship of national to subnational governments and the responsibility of the former to ensure that activities of the latter conform to NAFTA. Two of the cases against the U.S. address the same issue – Loewen and Methanex. Both involve claims of damage far larger than what Mexico was assessed in Metalclad. Tribunal findings in these cases will be important in shaping the attitude of the U.S. to the complexities of Chapter 11 and in providing concrete evidence in the U.S. context of Luz's analysis about which level of government pays for subnational government actions. Under NAFTA the signatories are charged with the responsibility to ensure that the policies and actions of their subnational jurisdictions are compatible with NAFTA's provisions. One of the challenges facing the NAFTA parties is to develop mechanisms to sensitise these governments to their obligations under the NAFTA investment regime.[55]

How have the NAFTA signatories assessed the operations of the investment regime after eight years with what pressures for re-articulation? Of the three NAFTA partners, Mexico has been the most sanguine about Chapter 11. Under President Zedillo, Mexico was content to wait for decisions on future cases before taking a position on possible changes to the regime. Mexico's primary concern has been to be seen as a stable, attractive location for FDI in a competitive global environment. With President Fox Mexico became more receptive to a discussion of some clarification of Chapter 11. Some of this change in attitude can be attributed to Mexico's loss in the Metalclad case.

Under President Clinton, differences within the administration meant that the U.S. was unable to articulate a position on possible changes to the NAFTA investment regime.[56] The U.S. attitude on revisions to Chapter 11 changed with the Bush administration as well as growing volubility of some members of Congress about their concerns around transparency.

Decisions in the Loewen (the need to pay huge damages) and Methanex (capacity of subnational governments to regulate in the public interest) cases may produce further changes in U.S. perspectives.

Canada pushed hardest for the issuance of a note of interpretation under Article 1131, expressing concern about Articles 1105, 1110, and transparency. The country also wanted to include in a clarifying note the point made in the Metalclad appeal that other provisions of NAFTA do not apply to Chapter 11. It took Canada some time to persuade its NAFTA partners that some limited clarification of the NAFTA investment regime was needed, but in the end it did succeed in getting agreement on a note that was issued on 31 July 2001.

CONCLUSIONS

This chapter has examined the rules and operation of, and lessons that can be derived from, the NAFTA investment regime. The analysis demonstrates that the investment regime is evolving as a result of tribunal decisions, though uncertainties remain. For the most part tribunal rulings have been reasonably narrow and have not expanded the meaning of the critical norms of the regime beyond what was intended by the drafters. The one more expansive interpretation of Chapter 11– under Metalclad – was reined in on appeal. Thus far at least, concerns that Chapter 11 would impede state capacity to regulate in the interests of the environment have not been borne out. Nonetheless, until tribunals rule on a number of claims currently in process, the regulatory chill issue, as well as others, including those relating to Articles 1105 and 1114, will not be clarified.

Although Canada was frustrated by the time it took for its NAFTA partners to appreciate Canadian concerns about the need for attention to what Lake terms the contractual side of the regime, its point was eventually recognized. The interpretive note issued at the end of July 2001 suggests that the process established for regime clarification does function. Is there a need for additional clarification of regime norms and procedures? Absolutely. Among the issues that should be addressed are:

(a) whether the regime should develop its own procedural rules to replace the international ones currently used;
(b) whether parties beyond the complainant and respondent should be able to appear before tribunals;
(c) whether a permanent list of regime adjudicators should be established;
(d) whether appeals to national courts should be replaced by a Chapter 11appellate body of the sort that exists at the WTO; and
(e) whether efforts should be made to clarify the meaning of some articles still under debate.[57]

Suggestions for possible regime clarification immediately conjure up political difficulties – the problems of getting agreement on changes and the process by which they might be introduced, since none of the parties wants to re-open the NAFTA agreement.

The NAFTA investment regime is one instance in which the provisions of a regional trading arrangement go well beyond anything that has been implemented multilaterally. The track record of the regime thus far has generated considerable credibility, though many of its critics remain unconvinced of its merits. NAFTA itself and its investment regime are sufficiently rooted in North America that it is hard to imagine them as, in Bobrow and Kudrle's term as a "hedging instrument." The larger question is whether Chapter 11 is a model for other regional arrangements such as the

FTAA or even something broader. Here the Bobrow and Kudrle depiction may be more appropriate, though the U.S. will likely push hard for a FTAA investment chapter that resembles Chapter 11. Investors like the kind of protection that the NAFTA investment regime provides, but few MNEs are demanding anything beyond the current BITs. Other stakeholders – environmental groups, NGOs, and unions oppose the inclusion of a FTAA investment regime like Chapter 11. In any FTAA negotiation, the investment chapter will be hotly contested. The debate around other investment chapters will demonstrate the challenges of creating regimes to promote economic growth and manage global turbulence.

NOTES

1 Anita Symonds and Leigh Wolfrom provided research assistance for this paper. A number of interviews as well as participation in the Centre for Trade Policy and Law NAFTA Chapter 11 Conference on 18 January 2001 enriched my understanding of the complexities of Chapter 11. I am grateful to those who agreed to talk with me off the record as well as for the critical comments of Bill Dymond, Michael Hart and Robert Pastor and the organizers of the Conference on Global Turbulence: Instability in National and International Political Economy at Simon Fraser University, Vancouver, BC, 19-20 July 2001.

2 Eden (1996) first used the term "investment regime."

3 Price (2001) pp. 2-3.

4 The NAFTA Free Trade Commission, which meets annually, is comprised of the three cabinet officials with responsibilities for trade. Canada's Minister of International Trade, Pierre Pettigrew, U.S. Trade Representative, Robert Zoellick, and Mexican Secretary of Economy, Luis Ernesto Derbez signed the statement clarifying Chapter 11. It can be found on the Canada's, Department of Foreign Affairs and International Trade Internet web site.

5 Prakash and Hart (1999) pp. 14-15.

6 Prakash and Hart (1999; 2000); and Drezner (2001) pp. 53-78.

7 See Cerny's (1997) statement that "the transformation of the nation-state into a 'competition state' lies at the heart of political globalization," p. 251.

8 Cooper (1968).

9 Krasner (1983); Keohane (1984); Yarborough and Yarborough (1990), pp. 235-59.

10 Lake (1999) p. 33.

11 Prakash and Hart, p. 15.

12 Bhagwati (1992) pp. 535-555.

13 Laird (1999) pp. 1179-1200.

14 Bobrow and Kudrle (1998).

15 The reality is there is little evidence that MNEs are in the forefront in seeking an investment regime beyond the current network of bilateral investment treaties, Lake, p. 47.

16 There are also NGO critics of globalization who contend that liberalization constrains the policy capacity of states and contributes to immiseration rather than improvement of living standards, Prakash and Hart, pp. 17-18.

17 Domestic investors cannot sue their own governments under Chapter 11.

18 GATT Article XXIV (12) and NAFTA Article 105.

19 One of the interesting issues is whether a national government will/can force a sub-national government to pay the costs of an arbitration award, see Luz (2000-01) pp. 35-84. This could become an issue of some controversy when the Loewen case is decided, since Loewen has made a claim for $US725 million against the U.S. government in its case against the state of Mississippi.

20 For a discussion of BITs and their contents, see Johnson (1994) pp. 277-8.

21 Subsequent to the implementation of CUSFTA Canada negotiated a number of Foreign Investment Protection Agreements (FIPAs), then halted the process once NAFTA was under negotiation. Chapter 11 then became the basis for post-1994 Canadian FIPAs. I am indebted to Bill Dymond for this point. For a list of Canadian FIPAs see the Department of Foreign Affairs and International Trade (DFAIT) Internet website.

22 See Johnson, pp. 278-9 for a discussion of other investment provisions of the CUSFTA.

23 A key Canadian objective was to ensure the exemption of culture and other areas from purview of investment chapter.

24 Cameron and Tomlin (2000) pp. 41-2, 85, 100-01.

25 For details on NAFTA Chapter 11, see Foreign Trade Information System (SICE) Internet website; as well as the discussion in Johnson, Chap.7.

26 Gestrin and Rugman comment that the major advantage of the reservations lists is that they make discrimination in the investment rules of the NAFTA signatories more transparent, see Gestrin and Rugman (1994) pp. 77-95.

27 Subnational reservations to Chapter 12 (Services) were handled in the same way. McIlroy makes two interesting points on this process of determining subnational government exceptions: first, BC was the first to decide to file a general reservation after which other provinces followed – to avoid the possibility that the actions of one province might be used against another in a NAFTA dispute; and second (citing a piece in *Inside U.S. Trade*) that it was Canada that initiated the change in the format of the reservation list, see "NAFTA and the Canadian Provinces: Two Ships Passing in the Night?" (1997) pp. 346-7. The parties used an Exchange of Letters dated 26 March 1996 in which they agreed to grandfather all existing non-conforming state and provincial legislation. De Mestral (2000) comments that as a result "it is easier to determine the precise extent of federal as opposed to state and provincial exceptions," p. 297.

28 Johnson, p. 289.

29 Ibid., p. 290.

30 See Pierre Pettigrew, "Notes for an Address by the Honourable Pierre Pettigrew, Minister for International Trade, to the C.D. Howe Institute/Munk Centre for International Studies, University of Toronto Special Meeting" (2001).

31 Gaines (2000).

32 Appleton (1994) p. 149. Price, who was involved in the negotiation of Chapter 11 as well as a number of U.S. BITs, argues that Chapter 11 was "nothing terribly novel" and grew out of a long U.S. treaty tradition, p. 2.

33 Johnson, p. 292.

34 Mann (2001) p. 16.

35 Ethyl challenged the Canadian government's ban on MMT, an additive to gasoline. The matter was settled when Ottawa was persuaded that Environment Canada's legislation, which banned MMT, contravened the Agreement on Internal Trade. The federal government negotiated an arrangement with Ethyl under which the company would drop its Chapter 11 challenge in return for a financial settlement. Although the case received a good deal of attention, with critics of NAFTA arguing that it demonstrated the inability of the Canadian government to regulate for environmental purposes, in fact the lesson was a different one – that governments have to be attentive to jurisdictional competence.

36 See "Canada Looks to its Courts to Limit NAFTA Investor-State Disputes" (2001) pp. 9-10.

37 Amicus curiae or third party briefs are statements by non-state parties to the case. It took some time for the panel to reach a decision on this issue. This is the first case against Canada in which third party briefs have been allowed, although a similar decision was made in the Methanex case. The significance of this decision will be discussed below.

38 The case alleges the NAFTA investor-state investor procedures: (a) deprive Canadian courts of their authority to adjudicate matters reserved to them by s.96 of the Constitution Act; (b) infringe and deny some of the rights and freedoms guaranteed by the Charter of Rights and Freedoms and the Canadian Bill of Rights; (c) exceed the treaty making powers of government under Canadian and international law; and (d) breach fundamental constitutional principles including the rule of law, democracy, constitutionalism and federalism, see Council of Canadians Internet website.

39 The Winnipeg-based International Institute for Sustainable Development (IISD), supported by the Canadian and U.S. governments, petitioned to be able to submit a brief. Mexico and Methanex opposed the petition, see IISD Press Release online, 19 January 2001; and Mann, pp. 98-9.

40 For more information on the Loewen, Mondev and ADF cases, see Bottari (2000) p. 7 online; or Mann, pp. 103-6, 108-9.

41 Kennedy and McKenna (2001) pp. B1, B7.

42 See "Notice of Intention to Submit a Claim to Arbitration," 14 January 2002, online at NAFTALAW.ORG (a.k.a. NAFTACLAIMS.COM) Internet web site.

43 Space does not permit anything other than a brief mention of the other cases against Mexico, CEMSA/Feldman, Adams, Calmark and Halchette. Feldman claims damages under Articles 1105 and 1110 alleging his firm was wrongly denied excise tax rebates and export rights for its cigarette exporting business. No decision has been reached. The Adams case involves a claim for compensation for land seized by Mexican authorities even through the land and the homes on it were returned. Calmark also turns on a land issue; in this instance, land purchased for tourist development; in this instance the claimant is arguing denial of procedural and substantive justice. In Halchette, the Notice of Intent was not made public and no arbitration was begun. Details on these claims can be found online at NAFTALAW.ORG Internet web site.

44 Bottari, pp. 8-9; and Mann, pp.79-82.

45 Bottari, p. 8; and Mann, pp. 82-4.

46 The appeal to the BC court came because the tribunal sat in that province. The governments of Canada and Quebec intervened.

47 DePalma (2001).

48 Description of Metalclad case based on Gaines, pp. 7-10; and Mann, pp. 74-9.

49 For a detailed analysis, see VanDuzer (2001). In Myers, although the panel accepted that policy objectives could justify differential treatment, it found that the intent of the Canadian government's ban on PCB exports was to advantage a Canadian company and found for the complainant.

50 See source cited in endnote 3 above.

51 The Canadian paper was not made public but appeared in *Inside US Trade*, 12 February 1999, pp. 0-1.

52 Source cited in endnote 3 above.

53 VanDuzer, endnote 59, pp. 22-2.

54 The tribunal location decision can be found online at the Canadian Department of Foreign Affairs and International Trade Internet website.

55 In Canada, the Department of Foreign Affairs and International Trade uses its regular quarterly meeting with the provinces on trade issues to discuss Chapter 11 issues.

[56] "Zoellick Cool to Restrictions on Investor State Disputes" (2001) p. 5.
[57] Some of these suggestions for regime change are discussed by Hart and Dymond (2001).

REFERENCES

2001. "Zoellick Cool to Restrictions on Investor State Disputes." *Inside U.S. Trade*, 19, no. 16, 20 April, p. 5.

Appleton, B. 1994. *Navigating NAFTA: A Concise User's Guide to the North American Free Trade Agreement*. Toronto: Carswell.

Bhagwati, J. 1992. "Regionalism versus Multilateralism." *The World Economy*, 15, no. 5, pp. 535-555.

Bobrow D.B., and R.T. Kudrle. 1998. "Regionalism as Accelerator, Brake, Ratchet and Hedge: FDI and Competition Policies." Prepared for the Third Pan-European International Relations Conference and Joint Meeting of the European Standing Group for International Relations with the International Studies Association Vienna, Austria, 16-18 September.

Bottari, M. 2000. "NAFTA's Investor 'Rights' A corporate Dream, A Citizen Nightmare." *Multinational Monitor*, 22, no. 4, p. 7.

Cameron M. A., and B.W. Tomlin. 2000. *The Making of NAFTA: How the Deal Was Done*. Ithaca: Cornell University Press.

2001. "Canada Looks to its Courts to Limit NAFTA Investor-State Disputes." *Inside U.S. Trade*, 19, no. 8, 23 February.

Cerny, P. G. 1997. "The Dynamics of Political Globalization." *Government and Opposition*, 32, no. 2.

Cooper, R. 1968. *The Economics of Interdependence: Economic Policy in the Atlantic Community*. New York: McGraw Hill.

De Mestral, A. 2000. *The North American Free Trade Agreement: A Comparative Analysis*. Offprint from the Recueil des cours 275 (1998) reprinted, The Hague: Martinus Nijhoff Publishers.

DePalma, A. 2001. "Judge Issues Split Decision in NAFTA Rules Case." *New York Times*, 4 May.

Drezner, D.W. 2001. "Globalization and Policy Convergence." *International Studies Review*, 3, no. 1, pp. 53-78.

Eden, Lorraine. 1996. "The Emerging North American Investment Regime." *Transnational Corporations*, 5, no. 3, pp. 61-98.

Gaines, S. A. 2000. "NAFTA Chapter 11 As a Challenge to Environmental Law Making – One View from the United States." Presented at the First Annual EnviReform Conference, University of Toronto, 16-18 November.

Gestrin M., and A. Rugman. 1994. "The North American Free Trade Agreement and Foreign Direct Investment." *Transnational Corporations*, 3, no. 1, pp. 77-95.

Hart, Michael, and William Dymond. 2001. "NAFTA Chapter 11: Where to Go from Here." Unpublished paper presented to the Centre for Trade Policy and Law NAFTA Chapter 11 Conference on 18 January.

Johnson, J.R. 1994. *The North American Free Trade Agreement: A Comprehensive Guide*. Aurora, ON: Canada Law Book Inc.

Kennedy P., and B. McKenna. 2001. "Canfor suing U.S. over lumber duties." *Globe and Mail*, 6 November, pp. B1, B7.

Keohane, R. 1984. *After Hegemony: Cooperation and Discord in the World Political Economy*. Princeton: Princeton University Press.

Krasner, S., ed. 1983. *International Regimes*. Ithaca: Cornell University Press.

Laird, S. 1999. "Regional Trade Agreements: Dangerous Liaisons?" *The World Economy*, 22, no. 9, pp. 1179-1200.

Lake, D. 1999. "Global Governance: A Relational Contracting Approach." In A. Prakash and J.A. Hart, eds. *Globalization and Governance.* New York: Routledge.

Luz, M.A. 2000-01. "NAFTA, Investment and the Constitution of Canada: Will Watertight Compartments Spring a Leak?" *Ottawa Law Review/Revue de Droit d'Ottawa*, 32, no. 1, pp. 35-84.

Mann, H. 2001. *Private Rights, Public Problems: A guide to NAFTA's Controversial Chapter on Investment Rights.* Winnipeg, International Institute for Sustainable Development.

1997. "NAFTA and the Canadian Provinces: Two Ships Passing in the Night?" *U.S.-Canada Law Journal*, 23, pp. 346-7.

2002. "Notice of Intention to Submit a Claim to Arbitration," 14 January, online at NAFTALAW.ORG (a.k.a. NAFTACLAIMS.COM) Internet web site.

Pettigrew, Pierre. 2001. Notes for an Address by the Honourable Pierre Pettigrew, Minister for International Trade, to the C.D. Howe Institute/Munk Centre for International Studies. University of Toronto Special Meeting. "Investor Protection in the NAFTA and Beyond: Private Interest and Public Purpose." Toronto, Ontario, 28 September.

Prakash A., and Hart, J.A., eds. 1999. *Globalization and Governance.* New York: Routledge

Prakash A., and J.A. Hart, eds. 2000. *Coping with Globalization.* New York: Routledge.

Price, Daniel M. 2001. "NAFTA Chapter 11 – Investor-State Dispute Settlement: Frankenstein or Safety Valve?" *Canada-United States Law Journal*, 26, Supp., pp. 2-3.

Rubin, S. 2001. "Canada Post a target after ruling in Germany." *Financial Post*, 21 March, p. C1.

VanDuzer, Tony. 2001. "NAFTA Chapter 11 to Date: The Progress of a Work in Progress." Unpublished paper presented to the Centre for Trade Policy and Law NAFTA Chapter 11 Conference, 18 January.

Yarborough, B.V., and R.M. Yarborough. 1990. "International Institutions and the New Economics of Organization." *International Organization*, 44, pp. 235-59.

Chapter 5

LIBERALIZING "TRADE IN SERVICES": IDEAS IN INTERNATIONAL POLITICAL ECONOMY

Russell Alan Williams
Simon Fraser University

On 30 March 2001, the WTO agreed to negotiate guidelines for an expansion of the General Agreement on Trade in Services (GATS) that will aim to remove barriers to investment and other domestic regulations that impede the expansion of a handful of global service conglomerates.[1] Inclusion of items like the regulation of the energy sector illustrates that these talks have little to do with "trade in services" per se, but rather are an omnibus vehicle for advancing deregulation and global neo-liberalism. The obvious question is: how did we get here? How was the GATT/WTO trade regime expanded to cover investment and domestic service sector regulation?

In the 1980's business argued that services could be traded internationally like goods, and that barriers like domestic service sector regulation must be eliminated via multilateral negotiations. In the Uruguay Round of the GATT, advocates of services liberalization attempted to use GATT norms to force states to deregulate their service sectors. While the GATS did not immediately produce massive liberalization, it did formally institutionalize services into the GATT framework. This protects existing liberalization from future policy changes. More importantly, promotes a substantial redefinition of individual governments' powers to regulate their service economies. Subsequent negotiations, and dispute resolution interpretations of the GATS have deepened the impact of the agreement.[2]

Conceptualizing international exchanges in services as "trade in services" represented a radical redefinition of these activities. Internationally rendered services had been regulated internationally for decades. But the industries involved: shipping, transportation, communications, banking, financial services, business services, insurance, and an array of consulting industries, were not seen as "trade" or as a single economic sector. Instead, they had been regulated on an industry-specific basis through sectoral international regimes like the International Maritime Organization and the International Telecommunications Union. Decidedly anti-liberal, States were:

S. McBride et al. (eds.), Global Instability, 65–85.

> ... more concerned about maintaining control over entry of foreign services than they [were] with regard to entry of manufactured goods because market access for services generally involves the right of foreign firms to establish subsidiaries and to enter into open competition with national firms. This, of course, [was] anathema to states that want[ed] to assure certain market shares for national firms.[3]

Redefining and then liberalizing trade in services challenged existing material interests. By undermining states' ability to set autonomous regulatory policy goals, the GATS will force domestic service sector companies to compete with international firms. One might have expected that companies with protected national monopolies in the service sector would have opposed the GATS. States, ever jealous of their ability to autonomously manage their economies would likely refuse to surrender control over service industries. Negotiators, justifiably suspicious of a new discourse on "trade in services," might have wanted time to assess national interests. However, none of this transpired. Instead, there was a high level of agreement on the perceived benefits of liberalization.[4]

This "consensus" supporting the liberalization of service trade, and the process by which it emerged, suggests that ideas matter in international political economy. The prevalence of these attitudes cannot be explained without some account of the international dissemination of ideas – understood here through Gramscian insights regarding "hegemony."

THEORETICAL BACKGROUND: STRUCTURALLY DETERMINED INTERESTS AND IDEAS

State preferences in trade negotiations are typically represented as the aggregation of rational, domestic interests. Commercial liberal theories of interdependence assumed state preferences to be the product of domestic interests. Likewise, the more sophisticated endogenous trade theory posits that industrial organization and its configuration of domestic political cleavages determine state trade policy preferences.[5] Robert Keohane and Helen Milner's (1996) "pluralist" analysis of interdependence argues that state's trade preferences are derived from rational assessments of self interest within society, which are then transmitted through the policy process to trade policy makers.

Such "interest based" accounts contend that changes in the preferences of actors can be "read off" changes in their position in the global economy. In the case of free trade versus protectionism, the laissez-faire position is dominant because more firms have internationalized, thereby making them opponents of closed markets. Ideas come from interests: an actor's position in the global economy leads to ideological preferences that support these structurally given interests.

The problem for this type of theory is that radical change in the preferences of actors, such as redefining the international service economy as "trade in services," requires a massive change in their objective interests. With the GATS, approaches that rely on purely interest-based analyses would seem to be non-starters. The existing material structures of the service economy, prior to the GATS, should have made an international consensus in support of liberalization difficult.

Gramscian Theory and the Role of Ideas

There are alternatives to narrowly interest-based approaches to trade policy. Globalization can be seen as a political process in which internationally disseminated ideas and the international connections between state and non-state actors affect domestic political outcomes.

For Gramscians, ideas may influence events through class formation.[6] Ideas, and the institutions that propagate these ideas, are the essential glue of social formations. Of course, material factors such as the current structure of the economy are crucial to class formation. Robert Cox, for example, argues that the dominant group within the dominant mode of production will always have a better opportunity to exercise hegemony over other classes. However, hegemony is not inevitable; it is obtained by political struggle, in part over the dominant interpretation of the economic order.

Stephen Gill argues that since the 1970s a laissez faire, or neoliberal set of global economic norms, championed by leading multinational corporations, has dominated global economic management: "This neoliberal shift involves ... the growing strength and positional power of neoliberal ideas, their application in the practices and organizational forms of key social institutions, and the reconfiguration of material power relations and a redistribution of wealth."[7] Neoliberal ideas have been disseminated by organic intellectuals working within corporate-funded institutions like the Trilateral Commission and inter-governmental organizations like the Organisation for Economic Co-operation and Development (OECD). These organizations have "schooled" multinational business interests to understand their common interest in constructing an international economic system in which they will be structurally dominant.[8]

For this Gramscian perspective to be able to explain the formation of the GATS, we should see a number of important indicators: evidence of organic intellectuals and institutions struggling over normative interpretations of the service economy; congruence between the ideas disseminated by these organic intellectuals and the interests of leading multinational; and evidence of a clear interaction between the ideas regarding trade in services disseminated by these organic intellectuals and the broader neoliberal intellectual hegemony.

The Trade in Services Argument

Services have often been scorned by economists and policymakers as an unproductive "burden on society." Because of this prejudice, services were not even identified as a sector of economic activity until 1939.[9] There was a similar blindness to international transactions in services that received little systematic thought or economic analysis. Indeed, a significant contribution of liberalization proponents was getting trade policy negotiators to think of trade in services as a single sector with similar economic characteristics.

Throughout the post-war period there was little interest in liberalizing services trade. Demands for liberalized rules of establishment and investment in foreign markets were largely ignored.[10] For Geza Feketekuty (often given the title of "the father of trade in services" for his role within the United States Trade Representative's office), this was an increasingly problematic view as a revolution in communications and transportation technology was producing an equally significant revolution in the possible scope for transborder service exchange. In simplest form Feketukuty (1988) and other advocates of service trade liberalization argued that:

i) There had been a revolution in the potential scope for international 'trade in services'.
ii) This revolution had made international exchange in services analytically the same as merchandise trade.
iii) This type of trade was challenging the importance of merchandise trade in many countries.
iv) It should therefore be liberalized under the GATT.

These four points cumulatively embody the basic "trade in services argument," or discourse, and played a crucial role in paving the way for a GATS deal.

However, from the outset, this "trade in services argument" was problematic. In the pre-GATS period, most international exchanges in services were not analytically similar to trade in goods. Significant functional differences exist between types of service transactions that make a sectoral definition extremely difficult. Lastly, while technological change made some types of international exchange in services theoretically more likely, a revolution in its volume had not occurred by the late 1980s.

Notwithstanding traditional prejudice against services in classical economics, the only way to define services is by distinguishing them from goods. Generally the production and consumption of a service occur simultaneously and the producer and consumer must interact with one another.[11] Goods can be produced, stored and transported across borders.

Trading goods does not require that the producer move to the country of the consumer, the only thing that need is the goods themselves. Traditionally, international trade liberalization agreements have focused on removing barriers to this type of transaction, and it is to this type of exchange that trade theory has been applied. Trade in services is more complex.

International exchange in services can theoretically occur in four ways:

i) The producer moves to the consumer (such when a ballet goes on tour, entertaining people in foreign cities).
ii) The consumer moves to the producer (such as tourism).
iii) The producer and the consumer move to each other (for example education services).
iv) Neither the consumer nor the producer moves to each other.

While the first three types of transactions require the physical proximity of producers and consumers (unlike trade in goods), the fourth type does not. These types of services can be produced in one country, often can be stored (which is unusual amongst services) and transported to consumers, without the need for the producer to have an establishment in the foreign country. For example, a firm in one country could perform services – data processing, accounting services, legal services, advertising and marketing, engineering, architectural design, data processing, software design, some types of banking services, publishing, and a host of other scientific and technical services – for clients in another country.

It is this type of services, sometimes referred to in official trade accounts as "separated services," as "other," or as "specialized" business services, which advocates of liberalization drew upon. These services are traded like goods in principle. However, discussions of the scope of trade in services included all four types of service transactions. When international negotiations on services began at the GATT in 1986, they covered international service transactions as a whole rather than just these traded services. This distinction between those specialized business services that might be thought of as "traded" and those that require the physical proximity of the producer and consumer is important because when discussion of "trade in services" fails to make this distinction, trade issues are conflated with investment.

Trade in Services and Investment

Aside from tradable or separated services, advocates of services liberalization wanted removal of barriers to investment and local establishment. This was a logical reflection the actual organization of the service economy. Prior to the GATS, an examination of the activities of U.S. service firms operating in Latin America found that despite the broad definition of "trade in services," most international exchange in services was conducted by foreign direct ownership of service companies: "The data suggest that, because many services are difficult to trade, service industry affiliates are less likely than manufacturing industry affiliates to be part of a worldwide allocation of production by multinationals to take advantage of differences in factor prices."[12] Of all the types of service transactions, it was those that involved investment in foreign service firms which mattered most in the GATT dialogue about trade in services – particularly to American advocates of liberalization because this type of "trade ... accounts for almost all of the service industry sales to foreigners by U.S. firms."[13] The degree to which services trade is more about investment than it is about trade was notable.

Thus, advocates of free trade in services were in fact calling for a radical redefinition of the purposes of trade policy generally and the role of the GATT specifically. Advocates wanted the GATT to become an international investment regime. This was radical because unlike barriers to trade in goods, barriers to investment were rarely created with the primary goal of impeding imports of foreign competitors. Rather they were often intended to serve other goals considered to be in the public interest. Proponents of the GATS faced an uphill battle. They needed to convince people that services should be thought of as trade and should be liberalized. They needed to convince the international trade policy community that liberalizing investment was also necessary. Most importantly, they needed to convince people that such liberalization was necessary because of a near-revolution in the volume of such trade, an assumption that was flawed.

The Trade in Services Statistics

Advocates of liberalization argued that a massive globalization of service sectors was occurring.[14] However, between 1970 and the early 1980s, trade in services shrank in proportion to trade in goods.[15] In the U.S. (which was both the largest importer and exporter of services), trade in services declined substantially in proportion to U.S. trade in merchandise.[16] These statistics were especially disappointing to services advocates because they were based on the official Balance of Payments categorization of "trade in services" – most of which is actually investment. "Services" in balance of payments statistics was a residual for all "invisible" transactions and, as such, only a portion of its total represented real exchange in services.[17] With investment removed, the totals for real trade in services were small and showed little growth.

Examples of trade in services were invariably drawn from those services that analytically have qualities like trade in goods. However, the

U.S. real trade in services equaled less than two per cent of manufacturing trade.[18] The data for the European Union and Canada were similar.[19] Even the WTO secretariat has conceded that "trade in services" remains "modest" compared to trade in goods.[20] To bolster the totals, investment in services must be included. But there is a significant contradiction here. If "trade in services" includes investment, the application of trade theory and the theory of comparative advantage to international exchange in services is problematic.

This underlines the questionable and value-laden claims made by the proponents of liberalization. As well, the statistics on trade in services emphasize a low level of globalization in service industries prior to the GATS. Even if global investment in service industries is "trade in services," the interests generated in favour of liberalization remain puzzling. Few of the world's service firms had a significant interest in liberalization via the GATS. Most service industries and most service firms were still organized on a national rather then transnational basis – the scale of transnational services trade was still dwarfed by domestic service industries. Prior to GATS negotiations only eight per cent of services were being traded across borders even when investment in foreign service subsidiaries was considered "trade."[21]

However, where trade in services occurred it was preponderantly through a handful of multinationals.[22] These "Transnational Service Conglomerates" had grown rapidly prior to the GATS. By the early 1980s, of the top 200 multinational corporations, 82 were primarily service exporters; either through trade in services or investment in foreign affiliates in other countries.[23] Indeed, in the United States, many service companies (American Express, Citibank, Pan American, Sea Land, AIG, AT&T, and EDS) were "among the largest companies in the country. These firms [had] become far more conscious ... of the advantage of influencing government policies that affect their ability to deliver services worldwide, and their rapid growth ... [had] given them the clout to get attention from the government. Both business executives and government officials [were] thus more inclined than in the past to look to barriers in services as key commercial issues."[24]

Concentration of services trade within a few companies was paralleled by a second factor – the concentration of exports of services from even fewer nations. In 1981 the U.S. and U.K. had the two biggest trade surpluses in services.[25] In 1983, the five leading countries in total service exports (including investment), the U.S., France, the U.K., West Germany and Japan combined accounted for 53 per cent of total world service exports. Even more concentrated were the net positive trade balances in services trade. If countries with positive net trade balances in services, those that most benefit from trade in services, were separated out, the percentages of net positive service trade accruing to key countries is staggering. In 1982, the five leading net exporters of services, the U.S., the U.K., France, Italy and Spain, combined, accounted for 68 per cent of net positive exports.[26] This concentration of huge positive service trade balances in only a few states is markedly different from trade in goods.

From an "interest-based" approach, such an uneven pattern of development of trade in services implies that countries which had a large surplus in services and for which services constitute a large part of total exports, were likely to have a substantial interest in liberalization.[27] The big losers in service trade, countries like Japan, Canada and the developing nations would have had just the opposite interest. Yet there has been an overwhelming consensus in favor of liberalization of services.

ORGANIZING NEOLIBERAL HEGEMONY, ORGANIC INTELLECTUALS AND THE HISTORY OF THE GATS

Gramscian approaches, in highlighting the importance of ideas in IPE, argue that the formation of an international hegemony requires a far-sighted political consciousness, or leadership, of dominant groups.[28] The dissemination of the trade in services argument can be understood in these terms. Proponents of liberalization, "organic intellectuals," sought to manufacture global neoliberal class consciousness in aid of privileging and protecting the interests of leading service multinationals.

The Early Days of the Trade in Services Argument

A small number of individuals and organizations played key roles as "organic intellectuals." In 1968, Hugh Corbett established the Trade Policy Research Centre, in London. Believing that services were playing an increasing role in the world economy, he commissioned a study of trade in services and restrictions on that trade. This study, the "starting point for much of the subsequent work in the field of services and the Trade Policy Research Centre ... [has] played a key role in the development of international thinking on trade and investment in services since that time."[29] The Centre established all the basic concepts of the trade in services argument, suggesting that services could be produced in one country, exported like trade, and that this "trade" should be liberalized.

At the same time, the OECD sponsored a task force as a precursor to the GATT Tokyo Round (often referred to as the Rey Group). The Rey report contained a short chapter on "trade in services," thereby coining the term. Influenced by the work of the Trade Policy Research Centre, the report framed the crucial arguments that would guide thinking about the issue for years to come. It suggested that services were being transacted across borders, and that these transactions were the same as trade in goods and should be liberalized in a similar fashion.[30]

While this argument gained little momentum in international circles in the early 1970s it found acceptance in the United States. U.S. firms had the most to gain from liberalization and little to lose given the U.S.'s already more lax regulatory barriers to international investment. The first U.S. company to promote liberalization was Pan American, which had run into problems with host countries placing restrictions on its right to bid for national mail services.[31] Such concerns were crystallized by Ron Shelp, vice president of American International Group, into a major campaign for including services in the GATT's Tokyo Round.

Shelp recognized that policy makers, negotiators and business leaders would more readily support the logic of liberalizing trade in services if the idea were dealt with within trade policy discourse: "Internationally, the predominately Anglo-American analysts who first posed the issues established the terms of discourse to which other members later had to respond. The very act of defining services transactions as 'trade' established normative presumptions that 'free' trade was the yardstick for good policy against which regulations redefined as non-tariff barriers, should be measured and justified only exceptionally."[32]

During the Tokyo Round little was accomplished. Too few people took seriously the argument that services were traded: "Without a shared causal belief that services were indeed tradable, it was impossible to discuss the question coherently, much less negotiate."[33] Despite these modest results, the Tokyo Round set the precedent that services were a GATT issue. Echoing Shelp's realization of the importance of placing services within the bounds of the trade policy community, U.S. negotiator Feketekuty noted that Tokyo was important because, "the motivation for all multilateral trade negotiations has been to liberalize trade and the whole intellectual framework that supports trade negotiations is based on the proposition that the reduction of trade barriers will generate economic gains."[34] However, in light of the Tokyo Round, the first step would be to convince people that services were indeed being traded like goods.

The Intellectual Campaign in Support of the Trade in Services Argument

After Tokyo, advocates of liberalization confronted the lack of understanding about liberalization of services trade. Feketekuty argued that:

> very few businessmen, including those in the services sector, looked at international service activities in trade terms. In fact, most people, including

> most economists, thought that one of the principal distinctions between services and goods was that services were not tradable and that economic activity in the services sector was therefore insulated from global economic pressures.[35]

Most trade policy officials also shared these assumptions. Feketekuty claims that he was the first to perceive the need for an international "intellectual campaign" to spread the trade in services gospel and that the success in getting services on the GATT agenda was directly attributable to this intellectual campaign.

In the late 1970s Hank Greenberg (president of AIG, and a colleague of Ron Shelp's) was appointed to the Presidential Advisory Committee for Trade Negotiations that provided U.S. trade negotiators with private sector advice. Greenberg pushed the U.S. Trade Representative (USTR) to take services more seriously.[36] Feketekuty also promoted the issue both as the USTR's representative on the OECD's Trade Committee and as a special counselor to the USTR. Indeed, he served in the U.S.'s defacto "house intellectual" on services. The USTR gradually threw its weight behind service trade liberalization and began to circulate a newsletter to those interested in the issue.

Prompted by business, the U.S. Department of Commerce conducted a comprehensive study, entitled U.S. Service Industries in World Markets. Most subsequent studies have merely restated its conclusions.[37] It argued that international service companies faced investment barriers that prevented them from owning affiliates abroad. While this only emphasizes the degree to which this was an investment issue rather than a trade issue, these contradictions were not explored at the time. This study was thought to be further proof of the need for liberalization of "trade in services."

Efforts inside the government were supported by advocates in the private sector. Ron Shelp persuaded the U.S. Chamber of Commerce to organize a services committee that could monitor the Government's commitment to liberalization in the sector.[38] His most important contribution, however, may have been his influential book, *Beyond Industrialization* (1981), a thorough synthesis of the trade in services argument, which was the first to call for a new round of GATT negotiations on the issue.

American Express executives, Henry Freeman and Joan Edelman Spero, also became active, participating in conferences, publishing articles and lobbying officials to promote service trade liberalization. Spero, Freeman, and Shelp used their influence in business organizations and public policy research institutes, persuading them to launch research studies on trade in services; including the U.S. Council of Foreign Relations, the National Foreign Trade Council, the Committee for Economic Development, the Conference Board, the Center for Strategic and International Studies, and the American Enterprise Institute.[39]

The Spread of the Trade in Services Argument Outside of the United States

Given the structures of international exchange in services it is unsurprising that U.S. multinationals played the leading role in disseminating the idea. However, they consciously tried to "internationalize" the campaign, encouraging international organizations (most importantly, the OECD) to carry out similar research: "These various activities shared a common characteristic, service issues were invariably presented in a trade context, using terminology and concepts borrowed from GATT and other trade agreements."[40] In London, the Trade Policy Research Centre continued to play a leading role in promoting trade in services: "Studies sponsored by the Trade Policy Research Centre ... provided a growing body of literature on trade in services that could be used as background material by governments when preparing their position on issues discussed in the OECD and the GATT."[41] The International Chamber of Commerce promoted the issue, creating a services trade working group that, "produced a clear and forceful statement in support of negotiations on services in 1981.[42]

By 1980 a range of international organizations joined the liberalization ranks. They included the World Bank, the Center for the Study of International Negotiations in Geneva, the Center for Transnational Corporations in New York, the Atwater Institute in Montreal, Promethée in Paris, and the Services World Forum, a private support group headquartered in Geneva.[43] Emphasis on the role of the U.S. in the history of the GATS ignores the fact that non-American groups helped to broaden support by legitimizing the sectional interests of U.S. multinationals.

The GATT Uruguay Round

In 1979 William Brock, head of USTR, was instrumental in getting trade in services included in the 1982 GATT Multilateral Meeting, the first step towards inclusion in the Uruguay Round. The incoming Reagan Administration, committed to more explicitly neoliberal policies, was eager to pursue the liberalization of trade in services.[44]

Various research programs were conducted along analytical lines and assumptions identical to those used by the early "organic intellectuals" in the private sector:

> These assessments indicated that services liberalization might well invigorate a sluggish world economy, offset declining competitiveness and protectionism in goods markets, and yield gains for countries other than the United States. Governments began to reassess the parameters of their reticent stances, and the

OECD ministers declared in 1981 that GATT negotiations merited further consideration.[45]

As a result, the OECD produced a document that laid out the key principles that could serve as the foundation for a future trade regime for services, *Elements of a Conceptual Framework for Trade in Services.* This was not published for public consumption until 1987, although work had been completed in 1981-1982. The paper's biggest "achievement [had] been developing a conceptual framework for service trade modeled on fundamental GATT principles such as national treatment, which requires that imported merchandise receive regulatory and fiscal treatment equivalent to domestically produced products, and transparency of regulations and rules affecting trade."[46] The fundamental beliefs of the trade in services argument had already crystallized among many international business leaders and were becoming intellectual givens when "services trade" was discussed by many policy makers. It was within this way of conceptualizing services that U.S. pressure to include services in the Uruguay Round would be addressed.

In the autumn of 1982, the GATT convened its first Ministerial Meeting since the Tokyo Round. At this meeting, Brock announced that the U.S. would emphasize the new issues of intellectual property and services. Brock put forward his ideas on how GATT negotiations could include services in an article entitled, "A Simple Plan for Negotiating Trade in Services" in *The World Economy* (1982), which was published by the Trade Policy Research Centre. Despite the support of the OECD, many felt that the U.S. proposal was premature. The European Commission had just launched its own study of the issue and members were uncertain about their competitiveness in a liberalized service market. Led by Brazil and India, the Group of Ten rejected the trade in services argument's "conceptual claims" and argued that the GATT regime had no jurisdiction over services.[47] The Ministers kept the possibility of services negotiations alive by delaying a decision, calling for national studies of the issue to be presented at the 1984 meeting.

Once the GATT called for study "governments not only needed substantive input on the nature and trade properties of services transactions but also needed strategic input on what liberalization might mean for their national policies and capabilities."[48] The U.S. presentation to the GATT suggested overwhelming benefits from liberalization. Fifteen other countries (including Canada, the U.K., the Netherlands, Japan, Sweden, and Finland) and the EC Commission completed studies that reached the same conclusions. Essentially, after countries "did their homework" their positions shifted rapidly. They began to believe that they also might gain from liberalization. Trade negotiators, responding to the trade in services argument, began to redefine their perceptions of national interest in accordance with these new ideas.

The cases of Japan and Canada, two early supporters of the U.S. position, are illustrative of the role of ideas. Japan and Canada consistently had the two largest deficits in international exchange in services. Many argued that the Japanese government would reject U.S. demands for the liberalization of services trade as they challenged "Japanese cultural values and national self sufficiency in strategic sectors."[49] Surprisingly, "Japan was the first country to join the American cause and was soon followed by Britain, Canada, France and Switzerland. Japan's national study had shown a trade deficit in services, but the new thinking in and out of government circles was that a regime could stimulate regulatory innovation and the growth of an export capability."[50]

Despite Canada's poor performance in international exchange in services and the potential vulnerability of many Canadian service industries from more competitive U.S. service companies, the Canadian study supported the idea of GATT negotiations on services. Canada was in perhaps the weakest position in services trade due to its physical proximity to the U.S., its (largely) shared linguistic community with the U.S., and the fact that U.S. service companies already had a strong foothold in Canada. In fact, cultural content laws and investment restrictions were perhaps the only thing preventing a full integration of the Canadian services market into the web of U.S. service multinationals. Nevertheless, the Canadian government strongly supported the U.S. initiative.

In order for countries like Canada and Japan to support the idea of negotiating services liberalization via the GATT they had to accept the tenets of the trade in services argument – that this was a trade issue that could be dealt with by the GATT. As such, they had to believe that there was actually a great deal of this trade occurring rather than just investment. Since this was not the case, the importance of ideas at this stage would seem to be crucial. Although the scope of such trade had been consistently overestimated, most developed countries now saw the inclusion of services in the GATT as an opportunity to expand their own exports.

The Developing Nations

Opposition to including services in the Uruguay Round came from the G10 led by Brazil and India. Most in the GATT community felt that no agreement could be completed without the acquiescence of the G10 – which "spoke" for developing countries.[51] The government of Brazil believed it to be "naïve" and "theoretical" to think that unilateral liberalization in services would benefit the Third World.[52] India argued that negotiations on services were a form of "neo-imperialism," a way of extending the privileged position of northern multinationals and that the GATT's own economists did not fully understand the issue.[53] There was a deep-seated concern in India that GATS should not include banking, insurance and the telecommunications sector as these were thought to be key sectors in development.

Given the emergent fault line over trade in services between developed and developing nations, UNCTAD might have played an important role in this story. Sensitive to the needs of developing nations, UNCTAD's intellectual heritage was the embedded liberalism of an earlier age. In response to the growing consensus amongst OECD countries in support of a GATS, UNCTAD launched its own study that initially provided a clear and forceful opposition to the trade in services argument.

> They questioned the applicability of trade concepts and placed quotes around the phrase 'international trade in services' in their reports. They maintained that even if some services transactions could be viewed as trade, these were exceptions to the more typical phenomenon of services delivery via FDI, which was outside the jurisdiction of GATT.... Perhaps most importantly they worried that a liberal regime might benefit the large TNC's that dominated global markets more than it did development.[54]

These arguments, grounded in the facts, might have provided a basis for opposition; however, UNCTAD's profile on the issue steadily declined. Opinions within UNCTAD subsequently shifted. UNCTAD staff may, by accepting the arguments of pro-liberalization advocates, have helped to undermine the basis for opposition to the GATS as they stopped challenging the central premises of the trade in services argument-

UNCTAD's ambivalence aside, it should be noted that in the lead up to the Uruguay Round the governments of many developing nations, influenced by the visible evidence of rapid development in the NIC's, had begun to voluntarily adopt neoliberal policies. As Keynesian ideas unraveled, the idea that the developed countries bore some sort of responsibility for helping poorer countries to develop had eroded: "Any negotiating position based on these premises essentially became irrelevant for real bargaining."[55] While this highlights the relationship between neoliberal hegemony and the trade in services argument, it also meant that Brazil and India, in attempting to speak for developing nations, were on slippery ground. Indeed, opposition to Brazil and India's belief that they could exclude services in the Round on "behalf" of the developing nations led to the formation of the Jarmillo Group, an alternative, pro-free-trade group of nations.

Despite these challenges, some developing countries continued to fight against including services, in the end managing to have services put into a separate "track" of negotiations, the GATT Negotiations on Services (GNS). However, developing country opposition ended abruptly once negotiations got seriously underway as they too came to accept the assumptions of the trade in services argument.

In the autumn of 1985, the Contracting Parties convened for a pre-round meeting to set the agenda. The GATT leadership encouraged the Jarmillo Group to continue promoting a GATS deal.[56] Over the next few months the Jarmillo Group, in conjunction with intellectuals outside of the GATT, succeeded in convincing many developing countries that negotiations on services were in their interests. Indeed, dozens of international organizations became active in studying and promoting "services trade" liberalization. They included the Services World Forum, the Centre for the Study of International Negotiations (Geneva), the Applied Services Economic Center (Geneva), Prométhée (Paris), Centre d'Etude de l'Economie des Services (Lyon), the International Service Institute (Tempe), the Berkeley Roundtable on International Economics, the Netherlands Economisch Instituut, the Canadian Institute for Research on Public Policy, the Pacific Trade and Development Conferences, the Institute for World Economics of the Hungarian Academy of Science, and the EC Commission among many others. A key member in this renewed intellectual campaign was the American Enterprise Institute (AEI), whose book series was the cornerstone of pro-liberalization thinking in the negotiating stage.[57]

A major theme of this renewed intellectual campaign was that liberalizing services was in the interests of developing nations.[58] Many articles argued that the lower labor costs of the developing nations might allow them to expand their "service exports." Of course this would only be the case if it were in fact possible to truly export or trade services on a large scale. Given that most of what was referred to as trade in services was simply investment in services, it is difficult to see how this could occur. Regardless, it was very persuasive. Without any substantive critical exploration of the assumption that services were being traded on ever increasing scale (critical exploration of the type that might have been provided by UNCTAD), the logic of the low-wage-advantage argument became compelling to developing nations such as India.

The 1986 GATT Ministerial Declaration

When the Contacting Parties convened in Uruguay in September 1986, the Declaration, by consensus, argued that services should be included as liberalization could advance the economic growth of all countries, as well as development in the South. Ten years earlier such normative and causal agreement on services would have been impossible. The loose coalition of intellectuals, trade policy makers, and business leaders, which had steadily propagated the trade and services argument, had succeeded in redefining how services were conceptualized by key policymakers:

> Governments would not have confronted this choice if new ideas had not emerged. True, there were by the mid-1970's powerful U.S. based TNC's that wanted greater freedom to sell services abroad in what were heavily regulated markets. But states could have managed these pressures by adopting regulatory

> rules on an industry-by-industry basis. It was only when analysts showed that diverse cross-border, transaction ... had the common property of constituting 'trade' that comprehensive liberalization on a pan-industry basis became an issue on the global agenda.[59]

When this idea first arose, governments had no idea whether comprehensive liberalization would be good: "If anything their existing intellectual frameworks and material interests pointed in exactly the opposite direction ... state institutions and organized social constituencies opposed to open competition were embedded deeply in domestic politics."[60] However, policymakers came to believe that services were traded, that they were being exported on a previously unheard of scale, and that if liberalized, services specialization would be welfare maximizing. It was this change in basic world view that paved the way for GATT negotiations on services.

Negotiating the "New Constitutionalism"

As foreseen by Feketekuty and Shelp in the 1970s, the choice of the trade policy community for service sector liberalization was crucial. Observers have argued that the trade policy community is a closed fraternity of like-minded individuals committed to the cause of liberalization. The level of internal normative consensus over the benefits of "liberalized trade" helped promote consensus on the services issue. Trade policy officials who questioned the assumptions of the trade in services argument were marginalized as "protectionists."[61]

The trade policy regime may have also been to the particular disadvantage of those developing nations that opposed the GATS. According to Chakravarthi Raghavan, the GATT was chosen as a vehicle for the liberalization of services because it was where developing nations were weakest. Hinting at Stephen Gill's "new constitutionalism," Raghavan argues that during negotiations, teams from OECD nations deliberately tried to "bamboozle" opposing countries by using terms like "trade" in incorrect contexts in place of real discussion on the nature of trade in services. The attitude of the developed nations' negotiating teams towards their more reticent developing nation colleagues was "[s]ign now, define its meaning latter."[62] Such an attempt to precipitously "strike while the iron was hot" is the essence of the new constitutionalism. Given time, support for the trade in services argument (or neoliberalism generally) might decline. By that point however, the "rules" would already have been written and it would be too late for developing nations to rethink their positions.

The Results of the Uruguay Round on Services

After lengthy negotiations the final draft of the GATS included three elements:

i) A set of general rules that should apply to measures affecting trade in services;
ii) Specific commitments that apply to those service sectors and subsectors that are listed in a party's schedule to be liberalized ; and,
iii) A set of annexes that take into account the specifics of some sectors to allow for temporary exemptions from the Most Favoured Nation (MFN) obligation of the GATT.

The GATS structure essentially duplicated the four-part typology of modes of delivery for services laid out by proponents of the trade in services argument twelve years earlier All four possible modes of service delivery are covered in principle. The degree to which different modes could be used by foreign suppliers was determined by a country's schedule of commitments.[63] In terms of the results, it was argued immediately after the final deal that "significantly more was achieved than most observers – including optimists – would have thought feasible in 1986."[64] The World Bank suggested that high-income countries scheduled about 45 per cent of their service sectors while low and middle income countries as a group only about 12 per cent.[65]

The GATS was a landmark agreement. It signified the extension of the jurisdiction of the GATT beyond merchandise trade. Subsequent negotiations have expanded its coverage considerably. This was true of the 1997 WTO Agreement on Telecommunications Services. It is also the entire purpose of the new round of GATS negotiations. More importantly, however, the institutionalization of the laissez-faire norms of neoliberalism into the GATT's coverage of services has meant that policymakers will have to respond to these principles regardless of whether the trade in services argument remains accepted. Institutionalization in the WTO means that liberalization is now the privileged goal. This is clear in the case of the various WTO Dispute Resolution Panel decisions that have aggressively interpreted the scope and meaning of the GATS to give it far wider coverage than negotiators may have intended.[66] While inclusions in the Schedule of Commitments have been interpreted broadly, maximizing the depth of the original GATS, exclusions (such as excluded modes of delivery) have been interpreted as narrowly as possible, thereby privileging liberalization.[67]

This is the essence of the "new constitutionalism." Regardless of whether neoliberal Anglo-American ideas remain dominant, the pervasiveness of these ideas is being used to erect institutional structures that will continue to cement the bonds of the new liberal order. Even if ideas change, multinational corporations' interests will still be protected by international treaties like the GATS. The existing rules serve as a brake on any possible backsliding.

CONCLUSIONS

After the landmark decision to include services in the Uruguay Round, advocates of liberalization feared that at any moment the fragile consensus in support of liberalization might be shattered. It was thought that those who opposed the move, albeit few in number, had a "potential ally in a huge but amorphous and un-mobilized interest group: the large majority of service concerns that are not involved in international commerce."[68] However, no organized opposition emerged. The consensus that services were a trade issue and could appropriately be dealt with by the GATT was never seriously challenged by those whose interests might be adversely affected. An explanation of this outcome requires attention to the importance of ideas.

The privileged position of giant, American-based service multinationals in the international services economy was an important aspect of the trade in services story. It was these transnationally-organized companies that put the trade in services argument on the international agenda. However, the broad acceptance of the trade in services argument and the consensus in support of the GATS cannot be explained by this factor alone. The trade in services argument, its international dissemination, and acceptance must also be considered.

The concept of the "organic intellectual," which is a core aspect of Gramscian analysis, focuses attention on the role of trade in services advocates in promoting the GATS. A host of influential trade in service ideologues, enjoying easy access to circles of power and influence, played a crucial role in reshaping how trade policy makers thought about the issue. However, the real utility of Gramscian analysis to the trade in services story rests on its recognition of the normative, contestable, and constructive nature of ideas themselves and on the theory's emphasis on the need to link the trade in services story to broader ideological and political developments relating to transnational class formation. The propagation of the trade in service argument was part of a partisan, normative attempt to apply neoliberal ideology and liberal trade theory to services. As well, the acceptance of the ideas at a number of junctures was "pre-conditioned" by the rising intellectual hegemony of those same neoliberal ideas. For example, the domination of neoliberal, laissez faire ideas helped condition Third World countries' eventual acquiescence to the GATS. Indeed, the simple fact that the trade in services argument was illusory, but accepted by policymakers anyway, only illustrates the degree to which ideas matter in international political economy.

NOTES

1 Sinclair (2000).
2 Weiss (1998).
3 Zacher and Sutton (1996) p. 214.
4 Greenway and Sapir (1992) p. 514.
5 Cohen (1990) p. 264.
6 Cox (1987); and Gill (1990).
7 Gill (1995) p. 69.
8 Cox, p. 359.
9 Nayyar (1988).
10 Petit (1986) p. 107.
11 Nayyar, p. 280.
12 Bloomstrom and Lipsey (1989) p. 1769.
13 Ibid., p. 1770.
14 For example, see Spero (1983) p. 17.
15 Nayyar, p. 285.
16 Extrapolated from United States Department of Commerce (1992) Table 4.1.
17 Indeed, it is not even limited to foreign direct investment in service companies, but rather includes all foreign direct investment as well as payments on external debt – hardly "trade in services."
18 Aaronson and Cowhey (1984) p. 7.
19 See, respectively, Petit, p.84; Statistics Canada (1991) Table 1, p. 15.
20 WTO (1999) p. 2.
21 Gibbs (1985) p. 204.
22 Nayyar, pp. 289-290.
23 Clairmonte and Cavanagh (1994) pp. 27-28.
24 Feketekuty (1988) p. 40.
25 Gavin (1983) p. 194.
26 Based on stats drawn from OECD (1992) Table A.
27 Nayyer (1988) p. 287.
28 Gill (1990) p. 52.
29 Feketekuty, p. 296.
30 OECD (1973).
31 Feketekuty, p. 300.
32 Drake and Nicolaidis (1992) p. 40.
33 Ibid., p. 47.
34 Feketekuty, p. 200.
35 Ibid., p. 305.
36 Feketekuty, p. 305.
37 Benz (1985) p. 101.
38 Feketekuty, p. 305.
39 Ibid., p. 309.
40 Gibbs, pp. 199-200.
41 Feketekuty, p. 310.
42 Ibid., pp. 310-311.
43 See Feketekuty, p. 311.
44 Gibbs, p. 200.
45 Drake and Nicolaidis, p. 51.
46 Shelp (1987) p. 72.
47 For a discussion of the response to the U.S. proposals see, Drake and Nicolaidis,

pp. 52-53.
48 Ibid., p. 54.
49 Gilpin (1988) p. 145.
50 Drake and Nicolaidis, p. 57.
51 Kumar (1993).
52 Raghavan (1990) p. 111.
53 Bhalla (1990) p. 190.
54 Drake and Nicolaidis, p. 58.
55 Kumar, p. 216.
56 Drake and Nicolaidis, p. 65.
57 Ibid., p. 75.
58 For example, see Bhagwati (1985).
59 Drake and Nicolaidis, p. 38.
60 Ibid., p. 38.
61 Gibbs, p. 213.
62 Raghavan (1990) p. 108.
63 For discussion, see Hoekman (1995).
64 Hoekman (1993) p. 1533.
65 Hoekman (1995) p. 327.
66 Weiss.
67 Sinclair.
68 Shelp, p. 78.

REFERENCES

Aronson, Jonathan D., and Peter F. Cowhey. 1984. *Trade in Services: A Case for Open Markets*. Washington: American Enterprise Institute.

Benz, Steven F. 1985. "Trade Liberalization and the Global Service Economy." *Journal of World Trade Law*, 19 (March-April), pp. 95-120.

Bhagwati, Jagdish N. 1985. "Splintering and Disembodiment of Services and Developing Nations." *The World Economy*. Trade Policy Research Centre.

Bhalla, Surjit S. 1990. "India." In Patrick A. Messerlin and Karl P. Sauvant eds. *The Uruguay Round: Services in the World Economy*. New York: United Nations Centre on Transnational Corporations.

Bloomstrom, Magnus, and Robert E. Lipsey. 1989. "U.S. Multinationals in Latin American Service Industries." *World Development*, 17, no. 11.

Clairmonte Frederick F., and John H. Cavanaugh. 1994. "Transnational Corporations and Services: The Final Frontier." *Trade and Development: An UNCTAD Journal*, no. 5.

Cohen, Benjamin. 1990. "The Political Economy of International Trade." *International Organization*, 44.

Cox, Robert W. 1987. *Production, Power, and World Order*. New York: Columbia University Press.

Drake, William J., and Kalypso Nicolaidis. 1992. "Ideas, Interests, and Institutionalization: 'Trade in Services' and the Uruguay Round." *International Organization*. 46, no. 1 (winter).

Feketekuty, Geza. 1988. *International Trade in Services - An Overview and Blueprint for Negotiations*. Cambridge: Ballinger.

Gavin, Brigid. 1983. "New Horizons in International Trade: Towards Free Trade in Services." *The World Today*, 39, (January-December), pp. 194-202.

Gibbs, Murray. 1985. "Continuing the International Debate on Services." *Journal of World Trade Law* (May-June).

Gill, Stephen. 1995. "Theorizing the Integrum: The Double Movement and Global Politics in the 1990s." In B. Hettne ed. *International Political Economy - Understanding Global Disorder*. Halifax: Fernwood Publishing.

Gill, Stephen. 1990. *American Hegemony and the Trilateral Commission*. Cambridge: Cambridge University Press.

Gilpin, Robert G. 1988. "The Implications of the Changing Trade Regime for U.S. - Japanese Relations." In T. Inoguchi and D. L. Okimato eds. *The Political Economy of Japan - Vol 2 - The Changing International Context*. Stanford: Stanford University Press.

Greenaway, David, and André Sapir. 1992. "New Issues in the Uruguay Round, Services, TRIMs and TRIPs." *European Economic Review*, 36, pp. 508-518.

Grey, Rodney de C. 1990. *The Services Agenda*. Halifax: The Institute for Research on Public Policy.

Hoekman, Bernard. 1993. "New Issues in the Uruguay Round and Beyond." *The Economic Journal*, 103 (November).

Hoekman, Bernard. 1995. "Assessing the General Agreement on Trade in Services." In Will Martin and L. Alan Winters eds. *The Uruguay Round and the Developing Economies*, World Bank Discussion Papers, 307. Washington DC: The World Bank.

Keohane, Robert and Helen Milner. 1996. *Internationalization and Domestic Politics*. New York: Cambridge University Press.

Kumar, Rajiv. 1993. "Developing-Country Coalitions in International Trade Negotiations." In Diana Tussie and David Glover eds. *The Developing Countries in World Trade*. Boulder: Lynne Rienner Publishers.

Nayyar, Deepak. 1988. "The Political Economy of International Trade in Services." *Cambridge Journal of Economics*, 12 (June).

OECD (Organisation for Economic Co-operation and Development). 1973. *Report of the High Level Group on Trade and Related Problems*. Paris: OECD.

OECD (Organisation for Economic Co-operation and Development). 1992. *Services: Statistics on International Transactions*. Paris: OECD.

Petit, Pascal. 1986. *Slow Growth and the Service Economy*. London: Frances Pinter.

Raghavan, Chakravarthi. 1990. *Recolonization, GATT, the Uruguay Round and the Third World*. Penang: Third World Network.

Shelp, Ronald K. 1987. "Trade in Services'. *Foreign Policy*, 65 (winter), pp. 64-84.

Sinclair, Scott. 2000. *GATS*. Ottawa: Canadian Centre for Policy Alternatives.

Spero, Joan Edelman. 1983. "Trade in Services: Removing Barriers." *PS*. (winter).

Statistics Canada. 1991. *Volume Estimates of International Trade in Business Services*. Ottawa: National Accounts and Environment Division.

United States Department of Commerce. 1992. *National Income and Product Accounts of the United States, Vol. 2, 1959-88*. Washington: Economics and Statistics Administration, Bureau of Economic Analysis.

Weiss, Friedl. 1998. "Dispute Settlement Under the General Agreement on Trade in Services." In J. Cameron and K. Campbell, eds. *Dispute Resolution in the World Trade Organization*. London: Cameron May.

World Trade Organization (WTO). 1999. *The Developmental Impact of Trade Liberalization Under GATS*. Job no. 2748/Rev. 1.

Zacher, Mark W., and Brent A. Sutton. 1996. *Governing Global Networks: International Regimes for Transportation and Communications*. Cambridge: Cambridge University Press.

PART II DOMESTIC RESPONSES

Chapter 6

LOCAL INDUSTRIES IN A GLOBAL MARKET: A COMPARATIVE STUDY OF THE CAPE BRETON AND QUEENSLAND COAL INDUSTRIES

Bradley Bowden
Griffith University

Andrew Molloy
University College of Cape Breton

INTRODUCTION

Despite their location in opposite hemispheres, Nova Scotia and Queensland have long shared similar problems in adapting to the vagaries of the world economy, with each relying on staples to maintain economic growth. While, in both these provincial societies, coal mining had become associated with a wider process of industrialization by 1914, in the wake of World War II each experienced a series of fundamental changes. Three distinct forces shaped this process of transition. First, there were the economic and technological forces that undercut the viability of local industries. Second, there were government responses to these forces for change. In Queensland, the state fostered the operation of market forces, privatizing state-owned mines and lifting restrictions on the production and marketing of coal. In Nova Scotia, in contrast, public ownership was imposed through the formation of a crown corporation (DEVCO). Despite these differences, however, government policies in both situations were premised on an acceptance of market forces, and of the need for "rationalizations" in the name of economic competitiveness. In consequence, in both Queensland and Nova Scotia, officially endorsed "transitions" were associated with reduced employment and mine closures. An alternative response to change, however, came from organized labour and the various mining communities. In Queensland, in particular, this response was based around a sustained opposition to the operation of market forces, and a defence of existing jobs and mines.

S. McBride et al. (eds.), Global Instability, 89–105.

During the 1970s the officially endorsed "transitions" in both Queensland and Nova Scotia gave the appearance of success. This was particularly the case with the Queensland coal industry, where the discovery of new low-cost coalfields, and the state's proximity to the burgeoning markets of East Asia, made it a dominant force in the global coal trade. By the 1990s, however, both the Queensland and the Nova Scotia coal industries were once again in crisis, as each felt the impact of falling prices and sustained job losses. In Nova Scotia, this renewed crisis was associated with the ending of mining in the Cape Breton coalfields after centuries of continuous operation.

THE INTERNATIONAL COAL TRADE AND GLOBALIZATION

Coal is one of the world's most common minerals, with countless deposits existing around the world. While the demand for coal for both heating and steel making has steadily risen with the progressive industrialization of the planet, coal remains a low-price commodity (the "spot" price for thermal coal in 2000 was approximately US$20). Historically, the low price received for coal has driven producers in a constant search for lower-cost production methods. This, in turn, has resulted in sustained patterns of industrial conflict that have few parallels in other industries. While coal has long been traded as low-price commodity, however, two factors have restrained the full operation of market forces. First, there is the cost of transporting coal. Given coal's low sale price, distance has acted to fracture the coal trade, rather than produce a single "global market." In consequence, coal production has historically been directed towards domestic, rather than international markets. This remains the case. In 1997, for example, the world's total sea-borne coal trade amounted to approximately 500 million tonnes, effectively divided by distance into two markets – Europe and North-east Asia.[1] By contrast, China, the world's largest producer, mined almost 1,330 million tonnes, almost all of which was destined for local markets.[2]

Despite the fact that most of the world's coal is still consumed in local markets, the industry everywhere remains focused on producing at low-cost. While distance does provide some protection, market forces remain omnipresent. Given these tensions between domestic and global forces, it is the contention of this chapter that developments in the coal industry need to be understood in both a local and global context, with each local industry constantly being torn between regulatory and free market solutions. Whether or not the problems facing nationally-based coal industries can be regulated within a national context is, of course, part of the larger question of whether "globalization is an overwhelming supra-national force that has largely usurped national policy autonomy."[3] While it is not intended to revisit this debate here, the authors consider that nation-states retain considerable policy autonomy. As the noted British economic historian, Eric Hobsbawm has observed: "The international organizations we have only exist by permission of the nation-states. They have no independent power, other than that granted to them."[4]

The Coal Industries of Nova Scotia and Queensland to 1945

Geographically and climatically, Queensland and Nova Scotia stand in marked contrast to each other. Whereas Queensland occupies a vast, tropical landmass of 1,727,200 square kilometers, Nova Scotia is a relative minnow, encompassing a mere 55,000 square kilometers. Despite these geographic differences, however, Queensland and Nova Scotia have both played remarkably similar economic roles in their respective national economies. Historically, both economies have principally acted as suppliers of staples to the world economy. At a national level each province[5] was overshadowed economically and politically by larger, centrally placed provinces with more diversified economies. In this regard, the development of the vast coal reserves of Nova Scotia and Queensland provided the respective provincial governments with similar problems and opportunities. Was the extraction of coal to be simply another staple that was sold on to the national or global market? Or, alternatively, was the expansion of coal mining to provide the basis for a more diversified economy?

Cape Breton: From a Whale to a Minnow

Canadian economic history is replete with problems of regional underdevelopment. Nowhere is this more apparent than in Atlantic Canada, where the Federal government's policy of creating a national market in goods during the late 1800s accelerated the trend towards a crisis in the regional economy of the Maritimes. This regional crisis intensified through the creation of "underdevelopment within underdevelopment" in the case of mainland Nova Scotia and the Cape Breton hinterland. This pattern of underdevelopment has characterized Cape Breton since the British took control of the island in 1763. Initially, Britain banned any land settlement, thus blocking the development of Cape Breton's rich coal resources. When the colony was opened up for development in 1784, mining activities soon revealed a vast coal-field that stretched along a 30-mile corridor of the northeastern shore of Cape Breton.[6] Despite the bountiful supply of coal provided by nature, however, the early history of mining on the field proved a troubled one. Although there were 20 collieries operating on the field by 1870, five years later the colliery owners were complaining that it was impossible to make money due to transportation costs and competition from lower priced American and British coal. The editor of the *Canadian Mining Review* lamented this situation as "an undeviating policy of (operators) cutting one another throats, until one wonders there is anything left of them."[7]

The turning point in the history of the industry came in the early 1890s, when the Nova Scotia parliament opened up the Cape Breton reserves to investors from outside Canada. Following approaches from Henry Melville Whitney, a Virginian railway magnate, the Nova Scotia Premier, W.S. Fielding, amended a new mines and minerals bill in order to grant Whitney's syndicate an "unprecedented" 99-year lease. Speaking in favor of the bill in January 1893, Fielding linked the future of the industry with "progressive globalization," informing the parliament "that what nature intended was that the miners of Cape Breton should sell in the New England market."[8] Following the passage of the bill, the Dominion Coal Company was created on 1 February 1893 with directors drawn from Boston, New York and Montreal. While the newly formed company stabilized the industry through large-scale development, the owners' central strategy of gaining access to the New England market proved unattainable. Fortunately for the prosperity of the Cape Breton industry, this failing was offset by the formation of the Dominion Iron and Steel Company in 1899 – a company with essentially the same ownership structure as Dominion Coal. While an uneasy period of rivalry between these two companies occurred after 1901, when Dominion Coal was sold off to Montreal interests, this ended when a successful merger of the two firms took place in 1910.[9]

As Dominion Iron and Steel expanded, so the fate of the coal industry became tied to that of the steel mills that, by 1914, were consuming most of Cape Breton's annual production of seven million tonnes. Together, the mills and mines produced a vibrant economy in Cape Breton. As Frank has observed: "By the time of the First World War industrial Cape Breton occupied an important place in the national economy. The coal mines supplied more than 44 per cent of Canada's annual coal production, and the iron and steel industry produced more than one-third of the country's pig iron."[10] This rosy picture was clouded, however, by a pattern of increasingly bitter labour relations within the coal industry, as miners sought relief from employment conditions characterized by low wages and long hours.

Prior to 1900, trade unionism was only able to make limited inroads into the Nova Scotia industry. The only union that managed a continuous existence, the Provincial Workman's Association, did so by adopting a passive industrial posture. By 1900, however, Nova Scotia's coal owners found themselves facing a more formidable opponent, as the United Mine Workers of America (UMWA) gained a significant following among the provinces' miners. Although the UMWA saw itself as a "responsible" union that provided industrial peace in return for industrial recognition, Nova Scotia's coal owners refused to bargain with it. In 1909 this intransigence resulted in a bitter 22-month strike that only ended with the use of troops.[11] Despite their success in defeating the UMWA's initial organising campaign, however, the coal owners found themselves forced on the defensive after World War I. With the Nova Scotia coal and steel industries coming under pressure to consolidate during the post-war economic downturn, a new entity was created – the British Empire Steel Corporation (BESCO). BESCO almost immediately began cutting miners' wages, provoking a series of bitter industrial disputes during 1922 and 1923-4. The latter dispute, in which communists figured prominently, caused alarm not only to employers but also for the President of the UMWA, John L. Lewis. Eager to restore peace to the troubled coalfields, in 1925 the provincial government appointed a royal commission that linked its woes to employer intransigence in dealing with the UMWA. Guided by these findings, the provincial government and the Nova Scotia Supreme Court subsequently compelled employers to recognize and bargain with the UMWA.[12]

BESCO's troubled labour relations history was but one component of a general pattern of organizational disarray that involved corporate infighting, lost markets and cries for state support. By 1930, it was apparent that BESCO's financial situation had become untenable and the corporation was dissolved.[13] Despite this failure, however, government support for the ailing industry continued, allowing the Dominion Coal and Steel Company (DOSCO) to rise from BESCO's ashes. In the short term, this policy of continued state intervention showed promise of remedying the industry's problems, as Cape Breton's coal production peaked in 1940. However, this success could not mask the fragile state of the industry. Reflecting on the government's support for the industry at this time, Kent has noted: "For the next forty years a foreign owned coal and steel industry would be maintained thanks only to increasing government subsidies and at the price, nevertheless, of deprivation for miners and their families."[14]

Queensland: Regulating and Sustaining a Minnow

While, by 1914, the Cape Breton coal industry had become part of a large, integrated industrial complex, in Queensland the industry remained the domain of undercapitalized, family-owned operations. Despite a rapid expansion of the industry between 1906 and 1914, Queensland's total production in 1914 still amounted to little more than one million tonnes. This sorry state of affairs was the product of a vicious circle, whereby small-scale mining operations proved incapable of capturing sufficient national market share to allow for further expansion. In consequence, Queensland's producers continued to be overshadowed by larger competitors based in the neighbouring state of New South Wales, despite the existence of huge Queensland reserves. As one Queensland government report observed in 1900: "It has generally been supposed that we cannot compete with New South Wales.... One very effective reason for this is, unquestionably, the small scale on which our operations are necessarily carried on."[15]

To enable the industry to break out of the vicious circle in which it found itself, the Queensland government pursued a number of strategies between 1900 and 1945 that involved a progressive increase in government control. Prior to 1914, state intervention principally involved the imposition of tariffs and rebates to encourage shipping companies to use Queensland coal, rather than coal from NSW. These measures proved highly effective, and by 1909 almost half of Queensland's coal was used for such purposes. Following the election of the Ryan Labor Government in 1915, government intervention took on more direct forms, as the government established a number of large, mechanized state-owned mines in Central and North Queensland. The impact of such measures, however, was constrained by the continued absence of a large-scale manufacturing sector, such as occurred in Cape Breton. In consequence, the state-owned mines remained aberrations in an industry that continued to be characterized by small-scale production. In 1934, for example, the average annual production of Queensland's 85 collieries amounted to a mere 11,000 tonnes.[16]. With the industry having only a limited capacity for expansion, in December 1933 a newly elected Labor government passed a *Coal Production Regulation Act* to control the production and marketing of coal within Queensland.[17] Unfortunately, while this legislation protected existing jobs, it did little to encourage increased investment or mechanization, thus condemning miners to jobs characterized by the most primitive working conditions.

Industrially, the passage of the *Coal Production Regulation Act* cemented a compact between organized labour and owners in the Queensland industry, in which each side focused on the maintenance of local markets. While the key union within the Queensland industry, the Queensland Colliery Employees' Union (QCEU), participated in the formation of a national Miners' Federation in 1915, it followed a much more conservative path than the federal body. By the mid-1930s, however, this employer-union compact was threatened by the growing militancy of miners employed in Queensland's central and northern districts. After 1942, miners drawn from these districts assumed a dominating role in the internal affairs of the Queensland branch, pushing the union well to the left. This state of affairs reflected, in large part, an organized Communist Party (CPA) campaign to expand its influence in the union. By 1937, for example, the miners at both the Collinsville and Scottsville mines in North Queensland were having donations for the CPA deducted from their pay, along with their union dues.[18]

Following the Queensland union's election of a communist leadership during 1942, both the provincial and national leadership of the Miners' Federation were united in urging policies that would further curtail market forces. While the union's demands for nationalization remained unfulfilled, by the mid-1940s a unique regulatory environment was established in the industry. Nationally, industrial relations came under the control of the Coal Industry Tribunal (CIT), which enforced an effective union-closed shop within the industry. In addition, special federal-provincial legislation was enacted to establish coal boards that were given special powers for economic regulation. In passing the *Coal Industry (Control) Act, 1948* the Queensland parliament extended its already considerable powers to regulate the production and sale of coal. Under this Act, the newly created Queensland Coal Board was entrusted with the task of regulating the industry in a manner "calculated to best serve the public interest."[19] Unfortunately for Queensland's coal miners, hopes that this regulatory environment would protect existing mines and jobs were soon dashed.

Crisis and Adaptation: From the 1940s to the 1980s

By 1945, the coal industry was a key component of both the Queensland and Nova Scotia economies. In each instance, however, coal production had become geared towards the needs of the provincial economy, rather than national or international markets. For Cape Breton producers, the continued profitability of their operations had become increasingly tied to the needs of the province's steel industry. In Queensland, a policy of ever increasing state regulation protected jobs, despite the predominance of inefficient, small-scale mining ventures. In both provinces, however, the post-war decades were to be ones of crises, as the previous patterns of ownership and regulation proved unsustainable in the face of new global trade patterns. In Nova Scotia, the once burgeoning steel mills proved to be the coal industry's Achilles heel. As the steel mills declined in importance, only the imposition of public ownership proved capable of sustaining the industry. By contrast, the incorporation of the Queensland coal industry into new global trade patterns proved its salvation.

Cape Breton: The Long Goodbye

By the 1960s it had become clear that the future of industrial Cape Breton did not lie in coal or steel. In 1965, DOSCO estimated that the Sydney mines had just 15 years of life left, and that new mines would not be profitable.[20] For its part, the federal Liberal government also recognized that to avoid "social devastation," the mines of industrial Cape Breton would have to be brought under public ownership. In 1967, therefore, the federal government decided to purchase the mining operations from the British owners, thus guaranteeing the jobs of 6,300 workers. After some consultation, a federal crown corporation – the Cape Breton Development Corporation (DEVCO) – was created with the uneasy mandate of balancing regional development with the management of the region's coal operations.

Unfortunately for the future of mining in Cape Breton, DEVCO was not created with any great hopes of developing the coal industry but rather to "reduce mining employment gradually enough to provide time for effective economic and social adjustments."[21] The coal industry was to be phased-down as part of a long, slow adjustment process. Part of this process involved creating new mines, which would hopefully provide reduced employment opportunities for another 25 years. New pension plans for the miners were coupled with the "25 year" life span of the new mines in order to stabilize family incomes. Wages also rose (from C$28.00 to C$33.00 per day in the 1970s), partly offsetting the community impact of falling employment.

While initially public ownership was associated with improved wages and employment security, the public cost of Cape Breton coal mining now began its long spiral upwards, with an estimated C$1.7 billion of taxpayers' money being expended by January 1999. Although the industry received a boost from the 1974 "oil crisis," any increase in demand for coal was reduced due to the imposition of a federal government oil importation subsidy. Although DEVCO at least brought a level of stability to the mining industry, a much more difficult task lay ahead – the need to diversify the Cape Breton economy. The extent of the problem grew with the continual problems of the Sydney steel plant, which was now under provincial government control. Other than steel, there was little else in the way of industry in Cape Breton. Government support for diversification, however, produced mixed results. Some strategies simply produced "white elephants" – the Glace Bay heavy water plant is often cited as the one best example (its rusty shell still dominates the Glace Bay harbour today). More successful initiatives involved increased funding for education and training. This resulted in the establishment of the University College of Cape Breton (UCCB), an institution that combines traditional university programs with technological training.

The best that can be said about DEVCO, according to its most notable President Tom Kent, was that the crown corporation endeavoured to "work from inside Cape Breton" instead of imposing economic solutions from the outside. In 1984, however, the corporation's developmental role ended when the federal Progressive Conservative government created regional economic development agencies for Western and Atlantic Canada. This move exacerbated DEVCO's problems, for while the federal government cared little for the declining coal industry it did not amend the original statute that created DEVCO. The significance of this anomaly was demonstrated when management attempted to "balance the books" through an abrupt series of lay-offs. Exploiting DEVCO's statutory obligations, the UMWA and the various mining communities pressured the federal government into forcing binding arbitration on DEVCO because of the "original statutory obligation to minimize hardship arising from the downsizing or closure of a mine."[22]

While DEVCO management was forced to reevaluate their position in the wake of the binding arbitration ruling, the Federal government served notice that Cape Breton coal mining would either be privatized or closed down. This came to a head with the federal budget of 1992, which made clear Ottawa's intention to prepare DEVCO for sale. At this point, however, the industry won a reprieve, with the government being defeated in the 1993 federal election. Unfortunately, the reprieve was to prove short-lived.

Queensland: Entering the Global Market

From its inception in the 1840s the Queensland coal industry was dominated by small-scale, underground operations. Sheltered from change, and operating in a highly regulated environment, employment in the Queensland industry reached an historic peak of 3,741 in 1954. The next 13 years, however, were to be terrible ones for Queensland's miners, as mechanization and the closure of the state-owned mines led to massive job losses. By 1967, Queensland's tally of underground miners was reduced to a mere 1,498 souls.[23]

If mechanization and declining government support were grievous blows, an even more significant change came through the growth of a large, export-oriented open-cut sector. While open-cut operations were not new in Queensland (small-scale operations had existed since the 1920s), their expansion had historically been constrained by government controls. These restraints were removed in 1957, when a newly elected conservative government encouraged a number of new entrants into the industry, all of whom saw the vast Queensland reserves as a source of raw materials for the expanding economies of East Asia. Of these new entrants, the most important were the San Francisco-based Utah Development Company and Australia's then largest company, BHP; companies that were to merge into a single entity in 1983 following BHP's purchase of Utah. During the early 1960s, it was Utah who was to act as the principal pioneer for change in the Queensland industry, driven by a strategic vision that saw the Pacific Basin as the centre of world economic growth.

With Utah's discovery in 1962 of the vast reserves of Central Queensland's Bowen Basin, Queensland's place in this new economic order was clearly identified. To exploit these reserves, Utah created a world-class production system that revolutionized coal mining in Queensland and, indeed, the Pacific Basin. The key features of this new model was not so much its use of open-cut techniques, as in the economies of scale produced and the linkage of this new production system into new global trade flows. Whereas Queensland's coal exports were virtually non-existent prior to 1961-2, by 1980 they exported 21.3 million tonnes, of which 17.4 million tonnes came from just five huge Utah-controlled pits.[24] As other producers followed Utah's example, Queensland's coal exports continued to soar. By 1997-8, production exceeded 105 million tonnes annually. Of this, more than 86 million tonnes was exported. As one official report noted, this export volume made "Queensland the world's largest seaborne coal trader."[25]

If Queensland's growing dominance in the Pacific Rim coal trade represented a fundamental transformation of the way in which coal was produced and traded as a global commodity there were, nevertheless, parallels to be found in the pre-1945 experience of Nova Scotia. First, whereas the growth of coal mining in Nova Scotia was tied to locally based steel mills, so the post-1960 expansion of the Queensland coal industry reflected its role as the principal supplier to the Japanese steel mills. In the boom period between the early 1960s and the mid-1980s, the excessive reliance of the industry on these markets could be conveniently overlooked. Nevertheless, the inevitable downturn in demand would reveal this dependent relationship to be the industry's Achilles' heel, just as it had previously been for the Cape Breton coal producers.

From the 1960s onwards, both the private and public sector in Queensland have remained enthusiastic supporters of an expansion of coal production. Of all Queensland's civic institutions, only the Miners' Federation sustained a prolonged opposition to the transformation of the industry, arguing that the policy of unregulated expansion represented a poor usage of finite crown resources. Reflecting this stance, the Miners' Federation enforced its policy of uncompromising opposition to "continuous production" in the open-cut sector, even though this policy necessarily involved a loss of short-term employment. During the 1990s, this policy was to make the Miners' Federation the principal opponent of the industry's increased engagement with the international coal trade.

Communities in Decline: The 1980s and 1990s

During the 1970s and early 1980s Queensland's entry into the international coal trade enabled it to surpass Nova Scotia for the first time as a coal producer. While jobs were lost in the traditional underground sector, these losses were more than compensated for by increased employment in the open-cut mines. For the new mining communities of Central Queensland, however, this engagement with the international market was to be an increasingly unhappy experience after 1986, as job opportunities fell despite massive increases in both production and exports. This fall in employment, which cannot be explained by new technology, clearly indicates that the conquest of new markets does not necessarily translate into employment growth.

Cape Breton, 1990 – 2001: Privatization or Closure?

Stripped of its developmental responsibilities in 1984, DEVCO was left to flounder as a deeply indebted operation. To add to its woes, in March 1990 DEVCO was informed by the federal government that it must become self-sufficient by 1995. Subsequently, a Senate Special Committee was established to examine DEVCO's success in achieving this goal. The recommendations of this Committee, handed down in June 1996, primarily focused on a "competitiveness agenda" for DEVCO that would allow it some financial "breathing space." In recommending such an adjustment process, the Committee noted the importance of DEVCO to industrial Cape Breton:

> As Cape Breton's largest employer, DEVCO's economic importance is undeniable. Its direct contribution to the economy of Cape Breton was more than 170 million in 1995-96: 90 million in wages, salaries and benefits; 46 million in pensions; 2 million in grants in lieu of taxes; and roughly 32 million in expenditures on goods and services.[26]

DEVCO's positive contribution to the provincial economy was, unfortunately, offset by continuing operating losses that amounted to C$34.1 million during 1996-7, largely due to historical social cost expenses (i.e. non-contributory pension and retirement plans).[27] Despite the Special Committee's recommendations, the federal government refused to forgive outstanding loans or to fund historic social expenses such as pension plans. This decision significantly hurt DEVCO's financial attempts to become self-sufficient. Debt problems also hindered DEVCO's attempt to secure capital for future mine development; particularly the 1.3 billion tonnes which were estimated to exist in the "last major block of coal in the Sydney coal fields," the Donkin Reserve.[28] When, during 1997, the DEVCO board signed a letter of intent with Donkin Resources Ltd (DRL) for the private development of these reserves, obvious questions were asked about the future of public ownership. The answer clearly lay in a strategy to create a public-private partnership that could evolve into a private company.

Like other attempts to revive the flagging fortunes of the Cape Breton field, however, the DEVCO-DRL joint venture proved still-borne. Following the proposal's collapse, in January 1999 the federal government announced that it would shed the majority of DEVCO's work force of 1,167, mine out the Phalen Colliery and close the Lingan mine within 20 months. Prince Colliery in Point Aconi, along with all other service operations was offered for sale. A C$111 million package was offered to displaced workers, mostly for pensions and severance. A further C$80 million in adjustment funds was allocated for community economic development. Events soon followed, however, that led to an even earlier end to mining operations, as repeated rock falls led to the premature closing of the Phalen Colliery with the loss of 400 jobs.

With Nova Scotia's coalmines facing permanent closure, miners engaged in a wildcat strike to defend their jobs, blockading generating stations and occupying the Prince mine. This strike only ended in January 2000 when the federal government agreed to participate in a joint union-management committee established to revisit the worker displacement package. With the strike over, negotiations were commenced to sell DEVCO's assets to the Florida-based Oxbow Carbon and Metals. Unfortunately for the miners of Nova Scotia, the UMWA's ability to act as a defender of the local industry was soon curtailed, when in August 2000 the union's District 26 was placed under trusteeship by the international office due to the precipitous loss of dues-paying members. With the UMWA in crisis, the fate of coal mining in Cape Breton hinged on a private operator taking over. Unfortunately, negotiations with Oxbow Carbon and Metals broke down on 16 March 2001.[29] Consequently, on 16 May, the federal government announced that the Prince Mine – Cape Breton's last working operation – would close in September 2001 with the loss of 440 jobs.[30] Any remaining hopes for the industry ended when negotiations between DEVCO and a second, unnamed buyer collapsed due to the buyer's plans to employ a maximum of 235-250 workers without recourse to union seniority clauses.

Cape Breton coal mining has always lived on borrowed time. With the end of preferential national policies and foreign investment regulations, coal is no longer king. There is cheaper and better coal elsewhere. Coal mining may be possible again in Cape Breton, but the labour-intensive industry that has existed for more than two centuries on the island is disappearing.

Queensland, 1987-2001: Profitless Prosperity

During the 1960s and 1970s the massive expansion of the Queensland coal industry was intimately linked to the demands of the Japanese steel mills. In 1986-7, however, this demand suddenly waned. While demand subsequently recovered, prices did not, with coking coal prices dropping from US$57.49 per tonne in 1986-7 to approximately US$42 in the 1990s. In Australia, this price fall, paradoxically, fostered increased production, as producers sought to maintain profits through additional output. In consequence, Australian exports grew from approximately 100 million tonnes per annum in the early 1990s to 171.63 million tonnes in 1999. In large part, this increased Australian output was sourced from the low-cost opencut operations of Central Queensland, with Queensland's production reaching a record 123 million tonnes in 1999. This increased Queensland production had devastating consequences for other coal exporting nations, notably the United States and Canada. Between 1990 and 1999, coal exports from the United States, historically the world's predominant exporter, fell from 96 to 53 million tonnes.[31] In western Canada, where producers were in direct competition with Australian suppliers, five export mines closed during 2000 alone with the loss of over 1,000 jobs. Even in the Atlantic trade, however, the ripple effect of increased Australian production was felt as far away as Alabama, where low international coal prices forced further mine closures.[32]

The increasing dominance of Queensland sourced coal was the central fact in the world coal trade during the closing decade of the twentieth century. This development, however, cannot be explained in terms of improved technology, which remained essentially unchanged. Indeed, the period of increased Australian output during the late 1990s was actually associated with a dramatic fall in capital investment.[33] Instead, the increased Australian output can only be explained in the context of a remorseless assault on labour costs. Initially, during the period 1987 to 1996, this managerial assault on labour costs was focused primarily on increasing output through the removal of union-imposed restrictions on shift-work, weekend work and work demarcation. Despite the opposition of the Miners' Federation, these goals were largely achieved by 1988. With mines now operating 24 hours per day over 363 days per year, output per employee rose by 42 per cent between 1990 and 1996. During the same period exports rose by 32 per cent. As the Miners' Federation had long feared, however, the removal of the constraints on "continuous production" undercut industry employment, which fell by 19 per cent throughout Australia between 1990 and 1996, dropping from 29,618 to 24,088.[34]

Unfortunately for Queensland's coal miners, the job losses and productivity gains that characterized the industry during the early 1990s did little to achieve security of employment for those that remained. As coal prices continued to fall, so the employers engaged in more radical measures. Initially, this second employer assault on established union conditions was led by Australia's second largest coal producer, Rio Tinto. Aided by the passage of new labour relations legislation in the form of the *Workplace Relations Act, 1996*, Rio Tinto offered non-union individual agreements at a number of its mines from March 1997. Despite union opposition, by 2001 Rio Tinto had scored a number of victories. At one Queensland operation, Kestral, a totally non-union workforce was established. Elsewhere, the union was forced to concede the elimination of seniority in redundancies, massive job losses and unlimited use of contractors.[35]

Despite dramatic increases in output and exports, it is nevertheless clear that the period of employer-driven workplace change between 1996 and 2001 was associated with yet another crisis of employment. Between 1996 and January 2000 total employment in the Australian coal industry fell by a further 28 per cent to 18,888.[36] Such developments, however, failed to restore overall industry profitability, as the industry found itself in a classic deflationary spiral. During 1997-98, for example, Australian coal producers lost A$0.09 for every tonne of coal produced.[37] By 1999, even a senior executive of Rio Tinto characterized the state of the industry as one of "profitless prosperity."[38] For the mining communities of Central Queensland things were even bleaker. As jobs were lost, families left the region, leaving a legacy of abandoned homes and empty shops despite record production levels. As one union official noted:

> Without job security, people will not spend money and communities suffer... Small business owners have been forced to close because the reduction in trade has not enabled them to learn a living... Sporting clubs [are] no longer able to offer competition to children of our communities because of lack of members.[39]

Given that it is highly unlikely that the Australian coal industry will witness a return to a regulatory model, it is probable that the industry will witness a continuance of current industrial and economic trends. For the coal miners of Central Queensland, their status as the principal suppliers of coal to the world market is likely to be increasingly associated with further job losses and increased work intensity.

CONCLUSION

A comparison of the experiences of the Queensland and Nova Scotia coal industries is illuminating for a number of reasons, despite their location in opposite hemispheres. First, it demonstrates that, for the coal miners of these two provincial economies, the issues of globalization and transition are hardly new. For over a century and a half, coal mining communities in both provinces have led a precarious existence, given the fluctuating national and international demand for their product. As early as 1893, the coal miners of Nova Scotia were being informed of the benefits of 'progressive globalization', where the removal of trade barriers would open up new opportunities. More than a century on, the language of globalization and international competition is even more pervasive. The benefits of globalization remain, however, as illusive as ever for the mining communities of both provinces. Mine closures and job losses remain the order of the day.

If "globalization" has been a constant feature of life in the coal industries of Queensland and Nova Scotia, a second insight that a comparative study provides is the inability of either government intervention or free market solutions to provide stability or continuity for "staple" industries such as coal. For both provinces, the heyday of the coal industry was to be found during periods when market forces were allowed a relatively free reign. For Nova Scotia, the high point of the industry was to be found in the period prior to, and during, World War I, when local coal fuelled the expanding steel mills of Cape Breton. In Queensland, the industry's emergence as a truly global force in the 1970s and 1980s also corresponded to its embrace of market forces, as Queensland became the principal supplier of coal to the steel mills of Japan. This temporal relationship between industry expansion and growth, however, should not be seen as a causal relationship. Instead, state intervention should be seen as a response to market failure, with the state increasing its regulation of the industry in both provinces during periods of crisis and retreating during periods of growth. While this pattern of state intervention and privatization differed in terms of timing, the overall similarities are nevertheless clear. In Nova Scotia, state controls were progressively relaxed during the late nineteenth century, as private financiers gained control. As the industry began its long decline, however, state intervention increased, leading to federal government control being imposed in 1967. By contrast in Queensland, a long period of government regulation during the first half of the century was gradually relaxed from the late 1950s as new market opportunities opened up.

Perhaps the most valuable insight to be gained from a comparative study of the coal industries of Nova Scotia and Queensland, however, comes from a realization of the ephemeral benefits that the coal mining communities of both provinces secured even during periods of industry "success." Even during the heyday of the Nova Scotia industry, wages and conditions of work were poor. Protests and strikes were met with strikebreakers and machine guns. Similarly, after a brief period of high wages and employment growth in the 1970s, Queensland's coal miners found themselves caught in a vicious cycle of falling prices, increased work intensity and falling employment. It is, unfortunately, too easy to see the process of globalization and transition as one of industry "winners" and "losers." For those living in the local communities that produce for global markets, however, the problems of employment security and decent working conditions remain constant. In the battles to secure these goals, strategies aimed at securing greater state intervention have not provided enduring answers. Instead, in both Nova Scotia and Queensland coal miners and their unions have been left to fight a relatively isolated battle to preserve their local communities.

NOTES

1 International Energy Agency (1998) p I-1.2.
2 Carrington Coal Company (1999) p. 68.
3 International Labour Organization (1996) p. 14.
4 Hobsbawm (2000) p. 78.
5 In Canada, the component parts of the federation are referred to as "provinces" while in Australia they are called "states." This chapter will use "province" as the common descriptor.
6 Frank (1977) pp. 3-24.
7 Cited MacGillivray (1979) p. 52.
8 Ibid., p. 55.
9 Frank, p. 12.
10 Ibid., p. 7.
11 Fudge and Tucker (2001) pp. 70, 72-4.
12 Ibid., pp. 119-20, 125-30, 146.
13 Frank, p. 33.
14 Kent (2001), p. 2.
15 Queensland Department of Mines (1900) p. 248.
16 Queensland Department of Mines (1936) p. 156.
17 *Queensland Parliamentary Debates* (1933) p. 106.
18 Henderson (n.d.) pp. 16-89.
19 Queensland Coal Board, p. 2.
20 Canadian Broadcasting Corporation (2001).
21 Kent, p. 3.
22 Ibid., p. 7.
23 Murphy, 29 July 1967.
24 Galligan (1989) pp. 27-8.

25 Queensland Department of Minerals & Energy (1999) p. 2.
26 *Special Committee of the Senate on the Cape Breton Development Corporation* (1997) p. 28.
27 Ibid., p. 22.
28 Ibid., p. 28.
29 Stewart (2001) p. 1.
30 Hayes (2001) p. 1.
31 Jonker (2001) p. 10.
32 *World Coal* (2000) pp. 19-20.
33 Jonker, p. 10
34 Carrington Coal Company, p. 26.
35 Bowden (2000), pp. 374-82.
36 Jonker, p. 27.
37 Ibid., p. 10.
38 Tronson (1999) p. 3.
39 Pierce (2001) n.p.

REFERENCES

Bowden, B. 2000. "A Collective Catastrophe: Productivity Maximisation and Workplace Bargaining in the Australian Coal Industry." *Journal of Industrial Relations*, 42, no. 3.

Canadian Broadcasting Corporation. 2001. *Indepth Cape Breton*. Toronto: Canadian Broadcasting Corporation.

Carrington Coal Company. (1999). *Coal 1998*. Newcastle, Australia: Carrington Coal Company.

Frank, D. 1977. "The Cape Breton Industry and the Rise of the British Steel Corporation." *Acadiensis*, vii, no. 1.

Fudge J., and E. Tucker. 2001. *Labour Before the Law*. Toronto: Oxford University Press.

Galligan, B. 1989. *Utah and Queensland Coal*. St. Lucia: Queensland University Press.

Hayes, C. 2001. "Prince to Close, Growth fund to get bulk of $28M." Sydney: *The Cape Breton Post*, 17 May.

Henderson, J. n.d. *Memoirs of a Communist*. Brisbane: Manuscript, held J. Henderson.

Hobsbawm, E. [trans. Allan Cameron]. 2000. *The New Century: In Conversation with Antonio Polito*. London: Abacus.

International Energy Agency. 1998. *Coal Information 1997*. Paris: International Energy Agency.

International Labour Organization (ILO). 1996. *World Employment Report 1996-97: National Policies in a Global Context*. Geneva: International Labour Office.

Jonker, Barlow. 2001. *BJ Coal 2000*. Hong Kong: Barlow Jonker.

Kent, T. 2001. *Cape Breton Provides Pointers for the Adjustment Programs Required by the Decline of the Old Economy*. Kingston: Queen's University School of Policy Studies.

MacGillivray, D. 1979. "Henry Melvillve Whitney Comes to Cape Breton: The Saga of a Gilded Age Entrepreneur." *Acadiensis*, ix, no. 1.

Murphy, D. 1967. "Report to the Central Council of the Miners' Federation." *Common Cause*, 29 July.

Pierce, S. 2001. *Mining Towns Are Dying*. Moranbah: Press Clipping (held by CFMEU).

Queensland Coal Board. 1953. *First Report of the Queensland Coal Board, 1949-52*. Brisbane: Government Printer.

Queensland Department of Mines. 1900. "Annual Report of the Southern District Inspector of Mines." In *Queensland Votes & Proceedings*. Brisbane: Government Printer.

Queensland Department of Mines. 1936. "Annual Report for 1935." In *Queensland Parliamentary Papers*. Brisbane: Government Printer.

Queensland Department of Minerals & Energy. 1999. *Queensland Coal Industry Review, 1997-8*. Brisbane: Department of Minerals and Energy.

Queensland Parliamentary Debates. 1933. Brisbane: Government Printer.

Special Committee of the Senate on the Cape Breton Development Corporation. 1997. Tabled in The Senate, 15 December, Sessional Paper No. 1/36-353S.

Stewart, W. 2001. "DEVCO Sale Collapses, Corporation Officials to Begin Discussions with Second US Firm." Sydney: *The Cape Breton Post*, 17 May.

Tronson, K. 1999. *History and Significance of the Hunter Valley Dispute*. Sydney: Rio Tinto.

2000. *World Coal*, 9, no. 3.

Chapter 7

THE FUTURE OF INDUSTRIAL POLICY IN A WTO WORLD

Marc Lee[1]
Canadian Centre for Policy Alternatives

INTRODUCTION: WHAT IS INDUSTRIAL POLICY?

There is little agreement on how to define "industrial policy": government intervention and participation in the economy has changed over the 20th century and across nations and regions. The prevailing orthodoxy is that governments cannot create wealth directly, but can only create the conditions for wealth creation in the private sector. This stresses policy changes to reduce taxes, to privatize state enterprises and public services, to deregulate environmental protections, labour laws, consumer protection, and to stress export-oriented economic development. These measures should be considered to be "passive" industrial policy, at one end of a spectrum of choices around the degree of intervention by the state.

Traditionally, industrial policy had a more interventionist flavour, consistent with the idea of an activist state. Such "active" industrial policy focused on protecting infant industries, developing infrastructure, placing restrictions and conditions on foreign investment, plus other forms of government intervention to subsidize and support wealth creation. A wide range of public sector activities, including state monopolies, state trading enterprises and public services, also fall within this conception of industrial policy, which connotes deliberate or strategic intervention, whether or not successful in terms of actual outcomes.

Industrial policy is important because markets alone are insufficient to achieve high levels of economic and social development. There is debate around the *degree* to which markets work effectively. There are specific markets that work relatively well, some that produce less than ideal results, and others that fail altogether. The market mechanism can be an effective coordinator, but left on its own, "the market" – or capitalist economic

S. McBride et al. (eds.), Global Instability, 107–127.

development – often leads to sub-optimal outcomes within specific industries, and across society more broadly.

The nature and types of market failure are well known in the economics literature. Markets tend to underproduce basic research, where it is difficult to keep the fruits of that research proprietary. Markets fail to produce public goods and vital infrastructure. Markets can lead to externalized costs, in the form of resource depletion and polluting behaviour. Markets lead to an inequitable distribution of income. Markets can fail when all agents do not have adequate information or do not have access to the same information. The presence of market power in many markets differs greatly from the idealized "free market" based on perfect competition.

Research on the role of technology and economic growth also suggest a more active role for the state in facilitating industrial clusters, knowledge and learning factors, increasing returns to scale, and spillovers.[2] These can lead to historical path-dependence: economies or firms that amass a lead (due to cunning strategy, luck or other factors) can perpetuate it into the future. Hence, government intervention can lead to dynamic efficiency gains that raise incomes and living standards, although it is also possible that interventions will make things worse. However, the critical question is not *whether* the state should intervene in the market, but *how* to intervene in a way that improves standards of living.

In the context of globalization, industrial policy highlights the degree of flexibility different nations have to enact laws, regulations and policies aimed at promoting domestic capabilities and economic growth. It speaks to the *terms* on which countries integrate into the global economy, including the pace and timing of reforms and liberalization. Earlier industrial policy instruments aimed to foster the domestic industry by deterring imports (tariff walls, import substitution policies) and/or increasing exports (subsidies, drawbacks[3] and other incentives). Globalization and the advent of multilateral trade rules have dramatically shifted the parameters of this trade context.

The topic of industrial policy, then, is of vital interest to poorer countries seeking to raise the standard of living of their citizens, and is an essential ingredient of a more far-reaching development policy. Industrial policy is also of interest to advanced economies, including middle-powers with small domestic markets, like Canada. Many regions in Canada are still heavily dependent on the export of primary commodities, and Canada faces distinct challenges in terms of its proximity to the U.S.

First we examine the history of industrial policy, from the early industrializers to the much-heralded Asian economies in recent decades. Then we consider the demise of active industrial policy under the rules of the World Trade Organization, the implications of WTO rules and the remaining options available to countries. The case is made that a renewed public sector can serve as an anchor for industrial policy in the future.

A SHORT HISTORY OF INDUSTRIAL POLICY

Northern governments often lecture poor countries about the need to open up their markets and integrate into the global economic system to increase economic growth and improve standards of living. But, while export markets can be very important, no country has gotten rich by pursuing trade liberalization as a "catch up" strategy. Indeed, there has always been a strong role for government protection and intervention in industrial development. Historically, the U.S., the U.K. and other European nations pursued deliberate industrial strategies, as have the most successful Asian economies more recently.

Early Industrializers

Early industrializers protected their domestic "infant industries" through tariffs, and had substantial government involvement in trade flows. The state played a large role in boosting capital accumulation, institutional development, building infrastructure, and undertaking research and development. Military might and colonial structures were very important in meeting political and economic objectives.

Britain was the dominant world power during the late 18th and 19th centuries. High tariff levels prevailed up to about 1850, when Britain began the shift to a free trade policy. However, free trade came only *after* Britain had consolidated its industrial base – it was preceded by many decades of selective industrial protection in the areas of wool and cotton products, iron and other metals, ship building and fisheries. Imports of silk and cotton from India, which had great cost advantages over Britain, were prohibited altogether. Exports of machinery were also prohibited. By the 1860s, when free trade was fully implemented, Britain was in the advantageous position of exporting manufactured goods (well-established and subject to increasing returns to scale) while importing raw materials.[4] Free trade can thus be considered an adjunct to domestic industrial policy, serving to expand export markets, while lowering production costs through economies of scale.

Like Britain, the United States protected its domestic market through tariffs. Protection was selective, and included cotton cloth, wool and iron. Raw materials were allowed in duty-free and drawbacks were provided for commodities re-exported within 12 months. Protective tariffs lasted from the post-independence period up to the end of the Second World War (although there were ebbs and flows of liberalization and protection). When the U.S. shifted to a trade liberalization framework it held a large post-war industrial lead over European countries devastated from the war.[5]

Both the U.S. and Britain, placed less emphasis on direct intervention in the domestic economy than other early industrializers, but government involvement was still a major factor in the expansion of infrastructure, support for R&D, institutional development, and controls on navigation. Both also benefited from having large domestic markets.

Only when countries become powerful do they tend to be enthusiasts for free trade. (Indeed, in the case of Britain, "free trade" was forced on other countries by military force if need be – witness the Opium Wars with China from 1839-42, leading to the establishment of Hong Kong as a British colony.) This pattern is also evident in today's advanced economic sectors, with the leading nations pushing for liberalization in services, e-commerce, telecommunications and biotechnology – all areas where they have the upper hand. This is also true of the push for strong intellectual property rights to maintain technological and commercial advantages.

Industrial policy in Canada emerged in the shadow of the U.S. and U.K.. Canada's National Policy was introduced in 1879, based on the belief that the domestic market, linked by a transportation infrastructure, would be reserved for Canadian companies. High tariffs were put in place to develop a domestic manufacturing base. However, this policy came in conflict with the need for export markets, since the small Canadian market limited the ability of producers to benefit from economies of scale. This meant that Canadian policy efforts sought to secure market access to either the U.S. or Britain – an early version of an export-led growth strategy – while at the same time "developing ever more sophisticated versions of the National Policy. Successive governments gradually sharpened their use of export and production subsidies, valuation procedures, tariff classification, special antidumping duties, and other devices meant to give Canadian producers advantage over their foreign competitors in the domestic market."[6]

Other examples of industrial policy have centred on the needs of the domestic market. Like many other countries, Canada limited the application of patents in the domestic market by issuing "compulsory licenses" that enabled domestic producers to use a patent without the authorization of the patent holder. This led to a significant reduction in prices, and to the development of a Canadian generic drug industry.[7] Cultural policy is another rich area where Canada has enacted numerous policy measures to ensure the development of domestic cultural industries.

Canada is also an illustrative case of a "mixed economy" approach to industrial policy. This includes the expansion of public services and the creation of Crown corporations. These public sector initiatives shaped the development of particular sectors, such as health care, education, rail and electricity, which in turn had spin-off benefits through to other sectors of the economy. While privatization of Crown corporations and erosion public services have occurred in recent years, the public sector still represents a major presence in the Canadian economic scene.

Asian "Miracles"

East Asia (including Japan, Korea, Singapore, Taiwan and Malaysia) was a modern "miracle," according to the World Bank (1992), at least up until the Asian crisis in 1997-98. The "Asian model" is essentially a pragmatic strategy based on addressing a number of market failures: uncertainty problems related to investment in infant industries; externalities of investment and innovation; first-mover "disadvantage" due to spillovers; small, under-capitalized companies, but that require massive investment and fixed costs. The Asian model also encompasses the idea that governments do manage and plan economies, and channel resources into strategic areas. It is rooted in the notion of manipulating markets to their competitive advantage, usually to reduce the amount of risk and uncertainty.[8]

As the World Bank points out, trade played a significant role for the Asian economies through a highly successful export-led growth strategy. But this trade context was very different from the unilateral opening of borders generally advocated by the Bank. Exports were stimulated through subsidies, tax credits and other incentives to producers, but protecting the domestic market was also given high priority through foreign exchange controls, import quotas and tariffs. When the Asian economies did liberalize, it was on a more gradual basis, as domestic industries became more internationally competitive.[9] This step-by-step process is still evident with China and India.

The Asian lessons are interesting as examples of late industrializing countries, pursuing technological catch-up strategies to compete in already established world markets. Countries face formidable barriers to entry in such circumstances due to the advanced states of technology, capital accumulation, market power, and presence in established markets of advanced industrial economies. Market forces alone in such cases are unlikely to be sufficient, while more intervention by government may be necessary the later the timeframe of industrialization.

Development and Industrial Policy

In a recent study, Weisbrot et al (2001) looked at changes in economic growth, plus health and education indicators for 116 countries, comparing the 1960-80 period against the 1980-2000 period. After sorting countries into five groups based on common starting points, they found that economic growth rates for all five groups were much lower in the second period than the first period. Indeed, the poorest group went from average per capita GDP growth of 1.9 per cent per year from 1960-80 to –0.5 per cent per year from 1980-2000. The second lowest group dropped from 3.6 per cent to less than 1 per cent. The study also found that progress in health and education indicators was reduced for most countries.

This empirical result is an indictment of the period of globalization. The authors note that this presents "a very strong prima facie case that some structural and policy changes implemented during the last two decades are at least partly responsible for these declines. And there is certainly no evidence in these data that the policies associated with globalization have improved outcomes for most low and middle income countries."[10]

The latter period was one in which the International Monetary Fund (and to a lesser extent, World Bank) tied access to loans and the international financial system to economic reforms through structural adjustment programs. These programs required that countries: reduce the public sector by cutting back on public services like health care and education, privatizing state enterprises, deregulating the economy, and eliminating government supports and subsidies; reorient the domestic economy towards export production, and remove constraints on trade and capital flows; and, maintain high interest rates in order to control inflation and stimulate the confidence of foreign investors. These policy frameworks have been increasingly locked into place through trade agreements such as the WTO.

In contrast, the 1960-80 period was characterized by more inward-looking development strategies, such as import substitution policies, protections for domestic industry, as well as performance requirements for foreign investors that required purchases of local inputs or the transfer of technology. Like the Asian examples, many countries in the South used these tools to develop their own industrial bases. Import substitution had its problems, such as cases of corruption, and "dead-ends," where the supporting infrastructure was weak or non-existent. But by and large, this strategy was successful, producing good results in terms of industrial development and economic growth, accompanied by improved standards of living. Rodrik (2000) notes that there is little evidence that these policies were plagued by inefficiencies that would justify the knee-jerk pessimism that they invoke from neoliberal commentators.

Import substitution policies were abandoned not so much due to their own failings, but due to a period of immense turbulence in the international economy: two oil price shocks, higher interest rates, commodity boom and bust cycles, and the collapse of the Bretton Woods fixed exchange rate system. The combined impact of these forces precipitated the 1982 "debt crisis," with massive debt problems that continue to this day. Neoliberal structural adjustment programs became IMF and World Bank policy in the wake of the debt crisis, and have been used as leverage to diminish the capabilities of debtor countries to engage in active industrial policy.

INDUSTRIAL POLICY MEETS THE WTO

Trade agreements are a pillar of neoliberal globalization, with an overwhelming emphasis on restricting the state's potential role in economic management. Ostensibly, these prohibitions are intended to promote freer trade and investment flows, although increasingly trade agreements specify rules that go well beyond border measures to include domestic regulation, public services and investment. The launch of the World Trade Organization in 1995 expanded the scope of multilateral trade rules to new areas not previously considered in "trade" negotiations.

Thus, the rules of the WTO dramatically limit the options and strategies available for economic development. Trade agreements and industrial policy intersect in a multitude of ways.[11] Seven broad areas under the WTO framework are of importance with regard to their implications for industrial policy: tariffs and quotas; subsidies; investment; services; intellectual property; safeguards for the public sector; and exemptions for national security.

Tariffs and Quotas (GATT)

Industrial policy has long been associated with protection of the domestic market from foreign competition by tariffs, quotas and bans, typically aimed at enabling "infant industries" to grow through capturing the domestic market prior to the onset of international competition. The WTO system restrains the ability of states to protect the domestic market.

Article XI of the General Agreement on Tariffs and Trade (GATT) generally prohibits the use of quantitative restrictions, such as bans or quotas (with some general exceptions allowed under Article XX). Instead, tariffs are the only legal border measure for controlling inflows and outflows of trade. At the end of the Uruguay Round (1986-94), many Southern countries had to convert existing quotas into tariffs in order to be WTO consistent. The GATT seeks continual reductions in the level of tariffs specified by countries (known as the "bound" level). Tariffs are subject to downward pressure due to "progressive liberalization," the ongoing process for lowering barriers to trade through new negotiations.

Despite such downward pressures, it is worth noting that countries retain the right to impose tariffs to protect the domestic market in areas of importance. However, countries are effectively locked in at existing tariff levels (there is a ceiling but no floor). Only in the event of emergency – such as a balance of payments crisis– can a country *temporarily* introduce higher tariffs. Countries that wish to raise tariffs in specific areas must negotiate compensating concessions to parties with a "substantial interest" at amounts equivalent to the value of the change (or else face trade sanctions).

Subsidies, Antidumping and Countervailing Duties

The WTO system also restricts the ability of states to subsidize domestic producers. Based on the notion of creating a "level playing field," WTO rules specify that countries cannot unfairly subsidize their industries in a way that affects trade, and that if they do, other nations are allowed to impose countervailing duties against imports equivalent to the amount of the subsidy.

The WTO Agreement on Subsidies and Countervailing Measures specifies different rules for different categories of subsidies. Export subsides are prohibited altogether due to their impact on trade (this agreement only applies to non-agricultural trade; export subsidies in agriculture remain a contentious issue). This includes subsidies contingent on export performance or on the use of domestic goods over imported goods. Certain very poor countries are allowed to maintain export subsidies until their per capita GDP reaches a certain level. Most developing countries have negotiated a phase-out period for certain prohibited subsidies.

Subsidies are permitted, and cannot be challenged by other WTO members, in certain areas. This includes subsidies to disadvantaged regions, for research and development, and for environmental purposes. These represent potential loopholes for a limited range of industrial policy activity, although richer nations are more likely to be able to afford them.

A final area of subsidies exists in a grey area, called "actionable," meaning a subsidy is allowed, but if another Member can prove "adverse effect" as a result of the subsidy, the Member can take action through the WTO dispute settlement process or by imposing countervailing duties. This latter area places a "chill" over the use of subsidies, in that countries may not be willing to use them for fear of retaliation.

Subsidy issues in international trade are also notable because countries can use countervailing duties to protect domestic industries. Under the WTO, use of antidumping and countervailing duties has increased. All countries, however, are concerned about the unilateral application of U.S. trade law. In sensitive areas, countries that have been successful in exporting products to the U.S. have often been accused of illegal subsidization or dumping, and have had their products hit with punitive duties. For the affected country this has meant insecure market access, long delays and legal battles, which consume time, money and resources. The use of countervailing and antidumping duties primarily benefits those with large markets, i.e. the already rich countries. Thus, even with the so-called "rules-based system," power politics plays its role, and the strong have significant advantages.

Investment (TRIMs)

Investment rules pose challenges for industrial policy to the extent that they codify the mobility rights of investors. Government interference is minimal. Including investment issues in trade agreements has been controversial. The Trade-related Investment Measures (TRIMs) Agreement emerged from the Uruguay Round negotiations that created the WTO. Proponents intended that a global investment agreement would be a centrepiece of the negotiations, but due to objections from Southern countries, the resulting TRIMs was much watered down, amounting to a restatement of existing GATT provisions with interpretive examples.

The essence of the TRIMs Agreement is to ban any laws, policies or administrative arrangements that favour domestic producers. The TRIMs Agreement specifically prohibits: local content policies; trade balancing measures (that limit the import of inputs relative to the level of exports); and foreign exchange balancing requirements (that limit foreign exchange outflows relative to inflows). For Southern countries, this means that most of the policies used successfully by East Asian countries are forbidden under the TRIMs Agreement.[12]

The launch of the Doha Round of WTO negotiations in November 2001 marks the return of investment to the negotiating table. The Quad countries (Canada, Japan, E.U. and U.S.) have been the major proponents of deeper investment liberalization at the WTO, seeking to consolidate thousands of bilateral investment treaties into a multilateral framework. The "ideal" model for investment agreement can be found in the North American Free Trade Agreement, which contains an expansive definition of investment, and recourse to an investor-to-state dispute settlement process. It remains unclear how new investment negotiations at the WTO will unfold. Southern countries were highly resistant to new talks on investment prior to the WTO Ministerial in Doha.

Services (GATS)

The General Agreement on Trade in Services (GATS) is another new area for multilateral trade rules. Like the GATT in the goods-producing sector, the GATS has implications for the development of domestic capabilities in services sectors, and the ability to retain the fruits of economic activity.

GATS rules are a hybrid of horizontal rules that apply across all sectors and more liberalizing rules that apply in sectors where countries have made full commitments. In the case of the latter, countries must abide by "national treatment" and "market access" commitments that place constraints on the ability of states to retain domestic benefits in the supply of services. Under national treatment commitments, countries cannot require foreign suppliers to involve local people in management, to hire and train local staff, to pay differential taxes on their earnings, or to transfer technology. Market access commitments prohibit countries from putting limits on the number of service suppliers or on the number of people employed in a sector, and from placing restrictions on foreign involvement and on the total value of an activity.

These GATS commitments have implications for local control over, and benefits from, service industries. For many Southern countries, tourism services are important sources of revenue, but many have difficulty keeping the income from tourism ventures in the domestic economy, due to the presence of foreign corporations that gain the lion's share of airline and hotel revenues. Environmental measures may also come under attack. In the example of whale watching tours, a country that had made full commitments under the GATS would not be able to limit the number of boats as a conservation measure.[13]

The GATS contains a "progressive liberalization" clause that mandates new negotiations even in the absence of agreement by Members to launch a new round of negotiations. GATS negotiations have been underway for a couple of years, and are now rolled into the new Doha Round. The commitment to ongoing negotiations means that countries seeking to protect key service sectors will face continuing pressure to liberalize.

Intellectual Property (TRIPs)

Copying, imitation and adaptation greatly enhanced the diffusion of technology for early industrializing countries. Indeed, the theft of others' intellectual property was effectively a legitimate development policy until quite recently. U.S. and German industrialization made great use of British manufacturing innovations without paying, Japan borrowed extensively from U.S. technological innovations, and Koreans copied U.S. and Japanese product and process technologies.[14]

This is no longer the case under global intellectual property rules, backed by strong dispute settlement through the WTO. The Trade-related Intellectual Property Rights Agreement (TRIPs) reflects the interests of those who control technology, rather than those who favour technology diffusion. In the area of patents, TRIPs provides a general level of protection for 20 years. This includes semiconductors, computer chips and other technological innovations that are necessary ingredients to industrial processes, and thus raises the cost of acquiring technology (this runs in the face of oft-repeated language promising "technology transfer" from North to South, and "technology spillovers" through foreign direct investment). The beneficiaries of IP protection are companies with large investments in technology that are patentable, and the countries within which these companies are based (usually the advanced industrial countries). Copyright laws have a similar bent with regard to protecting the works of the software and entertainment industries.

By conferring monopoly rights, patent and copyright laws are essentially a form of protectionism, amounting to the opposite of free trade.[15] The implications for industrial policy are much higher costs of acquiring technology, and limited possibilities for reverse engineering.[16] The scope of the TRIPs agreement and the costs of establishing institutions to protect the rights of foreign corporations, has been a point of contention among Southern countries.

Public Sector Services and Enterprises

The broader public sector can be considered an important component of industrial policy. The use of public sector delivery of core services, such as health care and education, is evident in Canada and many European countries, as is the use of state monopolies (Crown corporations in Canada).

In many countries, WTO entry has been accompanied by "grandparenting" of existing public enterprises that might otherwise be contrary to the spirit of the WTO Agreements. This puts many Southern countries, that have been coerced by IMF or World Bank structural adjustment programs to privatize state enterprises or public services, at a disadvantage.

However, protections for public services are arguably thin.[17] Under the GATS Article I.3, services "provided in the exercise of governmental authority" are excluded from the agreement. But this is defined very narrowly, as "any service which is supplied neither on a commercial basis nor in competition with one or more service suppliers." This exemption poses challenges due to the mix of public and private delivery of public services in many countries, leaving a grey area that has not yet been tested in WTO case law.

State trading enterprises, another mechanism of collective action, are allowed under WTO rules (GATT 1947, Article XVII). However, an important caveat is that they act "in a manner consistent with the general principles of non-discriminatory treatment" and make purchases or sales "in accordance with commercial considerations." This blunts a potentially powerful instrument for shaping outcomes for domestic producers and consumers.

State enterprises and monopolies (Crown corporations) are loosely covered by Article VIII of the GATS. State monopolies are allowed, provided that they do not act in a manner inconsistent with most favoured nation commitments, and that they do not abuse their monopoly position in competition with services outside of the scope of the monopoly. Establishing new state monopolies under WTO rules, while permitted, faces a hurdle in that a country must offer alternative and equivalent concessions. The thrust towards greater liberalization via the Doha Round may affect state enterprises more directly due to the inclusion of negotiations on competition policy.

National Security Exemptions

Interestingly, the dominant mode of U.S. industrial policy – the $300 billion U.S. military budget – is exempted from international trade agreements. A sizeable share of these funds is allocated to science and technology research, plus massive procurements of weapons, vehicles, planes, and other technologically-sophisticated equipment.

Large U.S. government expenditures in this area would violate any number of WTO rules (subsidies and procurement, for example), but are cleanly carved out of the WTO through "national security" exemptions, Article XXI of the GATT and Article XIV of the GATS. Unlike other exemptions in the WTO Agreements, national security exemptions are self-defined, which makes spending through military channels immune from challenge by other countries via WTO dispute panels. Indeed, this model of an exemption demonstrates how other important areas, such as public services, could be removed from the purview of trade agreements, if there was political will to do so.

The national security exemptions allow the U.S. to pour billions into the development of basic and advanced research. They enable the U.S., and U.S. corporations, to maintain a massive technology advantage in areas that are ostensibly about the military but that have massive spillover effects into commercial markets (the Internet, developed by the Pentagon, is possibly the latest and most potent example).

Given U.S. technological and economic hegemony, and the nature of intellectual property protection and the massive barriers to entry in this field, the national security exemptions offer only a veiled hope of being loopholes that countries can use for industrial development. But to the extent that they are (for larger countries), these exemptions skew the allocation of vital resources toward military ends. Staples (1999) notes that South Africa is moving down such a road, using its military spending to leverage new foreign investment.

WHAT'S LEFT OF INDUSTRIAL POLICY

The policy landscape in the wake of trade agreements suggests a creeping return to the pre-Great Depression era faith in laissez faire, free markets, with a corresponding shift in the nature of the state. This is reflected in the dismantling of public services, Crown corporations, public interest regulation and so on. Such moves have ideological roots that are independent of trade agreements like the WTO. But neoliberal initiatives at national or sub-national levels are linked to globalization to the extent that such moves get locked in by trade agreements and also in the sense that such measures are seen as improving the business climate for investment, and in particular, foreign investment.

Arrested Development

The rules of the WTO, supported by a powerful dispute settlement system to ensure compliance, greatly limit the capacity of nations to engage in a variety of industrial policy measures. The Uruguay Round acted as a transformational matrix that reinforced the position of the already developed nations, while weakening the capabilities of less developed nations.

At the top, the United States emerged in a strong position. It gained from new international rules on intellectual property and moves to liberalize trade in services, two areas of strength. Like Britain in the post-1840 era, free trade benefits the U.S. because it can export high technology goods and services, while importing primary commodities and light manufacturing. U.S. industrial policy also came out relatively unscathed from the Uruguay Round, as national security is exempted from both the GATT and GATS Agreements, and the U.S. continues to be able to use countervailing and antidumping duties to protect the domestic market. Indeed, the WTO poses a development framework that resembles the current (but not historical) U.S. model. But ultimately, this model benefits the U.S. most, as the world's industrial, military and technological leader.

Middle-power nations like Canada generally held their ground in the Uruguay Round negotiations, although there may be slippery terrain ahead as new negotiations demand further liberalization. A major loss is the incapacity to attach conditions to foreign investment. However, as a wealthier nation, Canada is able to provide very generous R&D tax credits, as well as interest free loans and export credits through bodies such as Technology Partnerships Canada and the Export Development Corporation. Canada has also maintained core public services, Crown corporations, dairy and milk marketing boards and the Canadian Wheat Board, although these areas continue to be subject to trade challenges and erosion from within. A serious threat for Canada is that internal pressures to outsource and privatize services and Crown corporations, will be locked in by WTO rules.[18]

Weiss (2001) looks at industrial policy transformations in Korea and Taiwan[19] in the context of globalization pressures. In these cases, the state's capacity for industrial transformation has been limited by WTO rules, but not ruled out altogether. Non-actionable subsidies and a shift of the costs of industrial policy to industry itself are cited as areas of focus for Taiwan, although this is rooted in very tight networks of government, business and research institute players. In Korea, the state is leading the drive to restructure the *chaebol* industrial conglomerates in order to create new "national champions" to withstand market entry of foreign companies.

For poorer countries, however, many tools used by advanced and newly industrialized countries have been banned as a condition of WTO membership. This leaves the poorest countries with much less flexibility to choose policy instruments that would serve their development ends, and greatly reduces their bargaining power vis-à-vis transnational capital. Indeed, these rules not only limit the scope of action by Southern countries, but have also strengthened the hand of advanced countries through the inclusion of intellectual property rights and services liberalization. The Doha Round (November 2001) will, in all likelihood, exacerbate this dynamic.

The areas of industrial policy that remain may be unattainable for Southern countries, although much depends on their current position in the international hierarchy, and on delays negotiated for implementation of some of the WTO's disciplines. In countries with large foreign debts, many public services and state enterprises have already been privatized, because of IMF and World Bank conditionality. Other aspects, such as defence spending and R&D tax credits, may not be readily affordable. While there may be some room for creative policy initiatives, the WTO framework generally strips the use of core aspects of early industrial development policy: tools to develop domestic capabilities; and the ability to exert leverage over foreign investment.

In effect, the WTO system serves to lock in place the pre-existing hierarchy of economic development.[20] While this case should not be overstated, the WTO entrenches a form of globalization highly favourable to the large transnational corporations and financial services firms that are based in advanced countries. Given the historic role of state activism in enabling and coordinating economic development through industrial policy, these measures in the WTO that limit such capacities in the future reduce the odds for successful economic development projects along the lines of South Korea or Malaysia.

Neoliberalism vs. Democracy

WTO restrictions on industrial policy lead to integration into the global economy on weak terms. The WTO and leading industrial nations strongly recommend that the poorest countries integrate themselves into the global economy, but at a handicap. Without the tools to step up to the next level of development, many Southern countries risk ongoing marginalization within the world trade system, while limiting the scope for more democratic forms of development.

A passive industrial policy based around integration into the global economy amounts to a leap of faith and a foreclosure on alternative development options. Rodrik (2000) argues that integration into the world economy is not a substitute for a development strategy. There are significant costs to integration, including the financial costs of implementing changes to comply with WTO Agreements and the opportunity costs related to alternatives (such as providing infrastructure, education and health care). At the same time, the benefits of integration are highly uncertain.

Calls to "get the fundamentals right" to attract foreign direct investment (FDI) should be taken with appropriate caution because of their impact on national economies. Balanced government budgets, lower corporate income taxes and lower personal income taxes at the high end (lower top marginal tax rates), more "flexible" labour markets, and looser environmental regulations, among other things, are supply-side "carrots" designed to make locales more appealing to foreign capital. In many countries, promoting FDI also consists of measures that cost the treasury: offering tax holidays, waivers of duties on imports, providing generous subsidies and land.

There is little empirical support to justify such extravagant and costly measures. FDI is supposed to bring large, positive externalities through the channel of workers learning by brushing up against superior technology. In practice, however, these spillovers tend to be insignificant, while the presence of foreign firms may actually diminish the productivity of domestic firms by reducing their markets and pushing them into narrower market niches.[21]

Promoting FDI as a strategy of encouraging economic growth and development explicitly favours expanded foreign control of domestic assets over other options, such as licensing of technology for use by domestic companies. From the investor perspective, motives for FDI are relatively straightforward – it links with the corporate objective of maximizing shareholder value (i.e., short and longer term profits). Attempts by officials of international financial institutions to paint FDI as acts of benevolence and goodwill must be viewed as more spin than substance. To the extent that new investments generate income, the essential issue is distributional: what share flows outside the country to shareholders, and what share stays inside in the form of wages paid to workers. This calculus must also include the environmental consequences of investment, in terms of depletion of resources, pollution from wastes, loss of biodiversity and so on.

Of course, FDI inflows can be beneficial in some cases. The general difficulty with FDI in a WTO world, however, is that countries cannot attach conditions to investment. Trade balancing requirements, local content policies and agreements to transfer technology and train workers and managers would all greatly enhance the domestic spin-offs of foreign investment. FDI may have a place in an industrial development strategy, but it alone is a poor substitute for more active measures involving the state.

While the prospects of a passive industrial policy based on foreign investment and primary commodity exports seem bleak, this should not be taken to mean that active industrial policy is dead. A first step is to recognize what has been lost and not to go further down the path of neoliberal rule-making that seeks to limit the scope of what is possible. Gill (2000) sees the rules of the WTO as part of a "new constitutionalism," but adds that this project is not complete because it is premised on the subordination of democracy, which provokes resistance.

Secondly, within the current paradigm there is some room to manoeuvre in terms of a more active industrial policy, although as noted above this space is larger for wealthier countries. In the short-term, given the more limited prospects of rolling back certain WTO rules, countries should at least make full use of available options so that their industrial policies are tangential to WTO rules.

One clear space is provided in the WTO Subsidies Agreement. Subsidies for R&D, environmental purposes and regional development are legitimate options available under WTO rules. Numerous other subsidies not conditioned on exports are also permitted, although they may be challenged. The dangers of a challenge could be mitigated by provision of subsidies on equal terms to domestic and foreign companies.

In the area of drug policy, for example, Canada eliminated compulsory licensing in 1993, despite its proven success in lowering drug prices for Canadians and stimulating the growth of a domestic generic drug industry. The Canadian government argued that this was necessary due to international trade agreements, but the WTO's TRIPs Agreement (and the NAFTA) permit the use of compulsory licensing in certain circumstances, such as public health emergencies. While these circumstances are limited, they do exist, and governments should at least use available tools to the extent permitted by trade agreements. Not to do, as is currently the case, amounts to foreclosing on a potentially valuable policy option. A bolder Canadian state might use this first step to treat drug policy as a public health matter to move towards a national, public drug (pharmacare) program.

The lack of states' political will to act is as much an issue as the actual rules negotiated in trade agreements. In many aspects of trade agreements, there are grey areas that have not been tested before dispute panels. While being cognizant of the narrow, trade-liberalizing interpretations that panels might take, if history is any guide,[22] this does not nor should not preclude states from being bold for fear of litigation. Self-censoring by governments is exactly the "chill effect" intended, and this serves as yet another form of the discipline of capital over the state.

Reinventing the Activist State

The future of industrial policy is integrated with the role of the state more broadly. The state has been the author of neoliberal globalization as much as its victim (at least in the case of the advanced industrial countries). In countries like Canada, the state has become more accommodating to the needs of capital (foreign and domestic), diminishing its role in areas of interest to the majority of citizens (especially the most poor and vulnerable), while enhancing its role in areas of interest to capital (such as strengthening intellectual property rights)[23].

However, despite the success of the political right in spurring antipathy towards the state among the population, the degree to which the state has been cut back in certain areas is testimony to the potential of the state to play a stronger, more activist role. The challenge is to recreate, as an idea and in practice, the state as a space for democratic decision-making rather than a space for supporting the interests of capital. The alternative is improving the accountability, transparency and democratic input and oversight of the public sector, not shrinking it.

Thus, industrial policy should not be limited to what the public sector does to stimulate the private sector, but must include the activities and roles of the public sector itself. This includes "traditional" public services, such as health care and education, as well as state enterprises and monopolies, but with a reform agenda based around democratic and progressive alternatives. It also includes new areas, such as the development of public child care, and renewed investments in social housing and mass transit, all areas where market mechanisms are insufficient to meet needs.

Expansion of public services and Crown corporations pose challenges in the context of trade agreements, which seek to curtail such moves and lock in privatization when it happens. The bottom line in trade agreements, however, is compensation. The state retains the right to take such actions provided compensation is provided either directly to those with an "interest" or indirectly by accepting sanctions on other export sectors. These cannot be taken lightly, but neither should it prevent governments from taking action in vital areas.

Translating public action into broad-based gains should also include actions that have served to shape markets in the past. These might include the role of fiscal and monetary policy in relation to a full-employment strategy, a tougher competition policy to diminish excessive market power, labour market policies that support workers' rights through collective bargaining and minimum wages, new public infrastructure projects and utilities, and public support for collectivist institutions that enhance the market power of consumers and small producers (marketing boards, trading enterprises, cooperatives).

Exploring innovative alternative approaches to industrial policy is important in the context of resources. Countries like Canada are rich in resources, but these must be developed within a framework of public policy in order to ensure ecological sustainability and employment stability for communities. In a recent study, Marshall (2001) sets out a number of institutional changes to promote value added investment in British Columbia's resource sector, while meeting goals of environmental sustainability and job creation. Stanford (1999) proposes a number of strategic investment areas that a public investment fund might support. In particular, the importance of water and energy whose seems likely to increase in coming decades.

New approaches, like public investment funds, may brush up against existing WTO rules to varying degrees. The potential for challenges, however, should not scare governments away from developing new policy frameworks that meet local needs. Ensuring market access to the U.S. will continue to be an issue for Canada, but trade challenges should be met as they arise and fought to the greatest extent possible.

An alternative approach should reframe the debate in terms of the very nature and types of institutions required to meet social needs, and this means moving beyond dependence on market/capitalist institutions. The alternative to maximizing trade flows is to find their optimum level, while insulating core sectors of the economy to the greatest extent possible from transnational corporations and global finance.

This path would return to the idea of a "mixed economy" by balancing private, public and other institutional activity. It recognizes and reasserts the capacity of the state to alter market outcomes. Social movements may already be moving in this direction through initiatives like the Council of Canadians' *Citizens Agenda*, which aims to move from protest and opposition toward building and creating economic alternatives through grassroots mobilization.

CONCLUSION: TOWARDS A NEW INDUSTRIAL POLICY

This chapter has taken a broad view of industrial policy, including the range of public sector activities that have economic development consequences for citizens. While the history of industrial policy was in the context of an activist state, this has changed over the past few decades of neoliberalism. A focus on industrial policy is a microcosm of the broader discourse on the role of the state in the face of globalization.

Industrial policy is too important to be left to the market. The passive industrial policy advanced by neoliberals has little basis in history and little support from empirical evidence. Ongoing efforts to constrain states with legally binding international rules at best maintains the existing hierarchy of power and development, and suggests further marginalization of the poorest countries.

Instead, the path forward should be to capture the best elements of an activist state for industrial policy, while immersing it in deeper democratic participation and development. Because it involves issues of governance and democracy, industrial policy is about how people together create the institutions and organizations that support a high standard of living. Industrial policy is about democracy thinking about the economy. It is about holding economic and political institutions up to the light and seeing them as capable of being changed by an engaged and effective citizenry.

Historically, the state, as a prominent force of collective action, has played an important role in the development of advanced capitalist economies. Unfortunately, this lesson is frequently absent from policy advice given to (or imposed on) Southern governments, instead posing neoliberal policies and integration into the world economy as holding the largest development payoff. Rather than one-size-fits-all prescriptions, policy should emphasize flexibility for countries to choose among industrial policy options based on local needs and priorities. A diversity of approaches should be promoted, particularly when the experience of successful industrialized countries runs so counter to the neoliberal orthodoxy.

The WTO places restrictions on industrial development that constrain countries' ability to engage in industrial development, and this is most severe for the poorest countries. Although the door is not completely closed, industrial policy in this context will entail trade-offs and difficult choices. Countries must use all existing space available under the WTO agreements, while pushing back further attempts at liberalization and pushing for renegotiation of elements of the WTO. The biggest obstacle may be finding the political will to act.

NOTES

1 Thanks to Marjorie Griffin Cohen, Stephen McBride and Jessie Smith, who provided comments on a draft of this paper. Any errors are the responsibility of the author.

2 See Lipsey (1996) for an overview of this literature.

3 A drawback is a reimbursement for tariffs paid on imported goods that are subsequently exported.

4 See Shafeaddin (1998).

5 Ibid.

6 Hart (1998).

7 Lexchin (2001); and Correa (1999).

8 Kwon (1998).

9 UNCTAD (1994).

10 Weisbrot et al (2001).

12 Ibid., p. 75.
13 Gould (2001).
14 Bello (1999).
15 See Baker (2001).
16 Bora et al (1999).
17 See Sanger (2001); and Sinclair (2000).
18 Canada also faces industrial policy limitations through the North American Free Trade Agreement. The NAFTA's implications are not discussed here.
19 Taiwan became a member of the WTO in December 2001. Weiss looks at the changes taking place in preparation for joining the WTO.
19 McBride (2001).
19 Hanson (2000).
19 See Shrybman (1999).
19 McBride.

REFERENCES

Baker, Dean. 2001. "Drug Prices in Crisis: The Case against Protectionism." In *Dollars and Sense* (May/June).

Bello, Walden. 1999. "Building an Iron Cage: Bretton Woods Institutions, the WTO and the South." In *Views from the South: The Effects of Globalization and the WTO on Third World Countries*. San Francisco: International Forum on Globalization.

Bora, Bijit, Peter Lloyd, and Mari Pangestu. 1999. *Industrial Policy and the WTO*. United Nations Conference on Trade and Development, Policy Issues in International Trade and Commodities Study Series, no. 6.

Correa, Carlos. 1999. *Intellectual Property Rights and the Use of Compulsory Licenses: Options for Developing Countries*. South Centre, Trade-related Agenda, Development and Equity (TRADE) Working Paper, no. 5 (October).

Gill, Stephen. 2000. "The Constitution of Global Capitalism." Paper presented to the International Studies Association Annual Convention.

Gould, Ellen. 2001. *The GATS: Impacts on the South*. London: World Development Movement.

Hanson, Gordon. 2000. "Should Countries Promote Foreign Direct Investment?" G-24 Discussion Paper Series, no. 9, United Nations Conference on Trade and Development.

Hart, Michael. 1998. *Fifty Years of Canadian Tradecraft: Canada at the GATT, 1947-1997*. Ottawa: Centre for Trade Policy and Law.

Kwon, Jene K. 1998. "The East Asian Model: An Exploration of Rapid Economic Growth in the Republic of Korea and Taiwan Province of China." United Nations Conference on Trade and Development Discussion Paper Series, no. 135 (May).

Lal Das, Bhagirath. 1999. *The World Trade Organization: A Guide to the Framework for International Trade*. Penang: Third World Network.

Lexchin, Joel. 2001. *Globalization, Trade Deals and Drugs: Heads the Industry Wins, Tails Canada Loses*. Canadian Centre for Policy Alternatives, Trade and Investment Briefing Paper Series, 2, no. 8 (November).

Lipsey, Richard. 1996. *Economic Growth, Technological Change and Canadian Economic Policy*. CD Howe Benefactors Lecture

Marshall, Dale. 2001. *Re-Capturing the Wealth: Investment Solutions for Jobs and Environmental Sustainability in BC's Resource Sector*. Vancouver: Canadian Centre for Policy Alternatives.

McBride, Stephen. 2001. *Paradigm Shift: Globalization and the Canadian State*. Halifax: Fernwood Publishing.

Rodriguez, Francisco, and Dani Rodrik. 1999. "Trade Policy and Economic Growth: A Skeptic's Guide to the Cross-national Evidence" (April). Available online.

Rodrik, Dani. 2001. "Trading in Illusions." In *Foreign Policy* (March-April)

Sanger, Matthew. 2001. *Reckless Abandon: Canada, the GATS and the Future of Health Care*. Ottawa: Canadian Centre for Policy Alternatives.

Sinclair, Scott. 2000. *GATS: How the WTO's New Services Negotiations Threaten Democracy*. Ottawa: Canadian Centre for Policy Alternatives.

Shafaeddin, Mehdi. 1998. How did Developed Countries Industrialize? The History of Trade and Industrial Policy: The Cases of Great Britain and the USA." United Nations Conference on Trade and Development Discussion Paper Series, no. 139 (December).

Shrybman, Steven. 1999. *A Citizen's Guide to the WTO*. Ottawa: Canadian Centre for Policy Alternatives.

Stanford, Jim. 1999. *Paper Boom*. Ottawa: Canadian Centre for Policy Alternatives and Lorimer.

Staples, Steven. 1999. "The WTO and War: Making the Connection." In proceedings of *The WTO and the Global War System*, published by the International Network on Disarmament and Globalization.

Stiglitz, Joseph. 1998. "Towards a New Paradigm for Development: Strategies, Policies and Processes." UNCTAD Prebisch Lecture 1998.

United Nations Conference on Trade and Development. 1994. *Trade and Development Report*.

Weisbrot, Mark, Dean Baker, Egor Kraev, and Judy Chen. 2001. *The Scorecard on Globalization 1980-2000: Twenty Years of Diminished Progress*. Washington: Center for Economic and Policy Research.

Weiss, Linda. 2001. "Guiding Globalization in East Asia before and after the Crisis." Paper presented at *Global Turbulence: Instability in National and International Political Economy* conference, 19-20 July 2001.

World Bank. 1992. *The East Asian Miracle: Economic Growth and Public Policy*. Washington, DC.

World Trade Organization. 1999. *The Legal Texts: The Results of the Uruguay Round of Multilateral Trade Negotiations*. Cambridge: Cambridge University Press.

Chapter 8

TURNING THE TITANIC? POLICY MAKING AFTER NEOLIBERALISM

John Wiseman[1]
RMIT University

"It takes a lot of things to change the world:
Anger and tenacity, Science and indignation,
The quick initiative, the long reflection,
The cold patience and the infinite perseverance,
The understanding of the particular case and
the understanding of the ensemble;
Only the lessons of reality can teach us to transform reality."
Bertolt Brecht, Einverstandnis[2]

The aim of this chapter is to contribute to discussions about public policy directions and processes after neoliberalism, informed by reflection on the initial development of the *Growing Victoria Together* policy framework in the Australian State of Victoria.

The chapter begins by noting the key features of the rapidly expanding international debate about alternatives to public policy paradigms based on a narrow focus on economic rationality, free market decision making and organizational managerialism. It is argued that successful implementation of alternative paradigms will require revaluing and reinventing:

i) more balanced and integrated relationships between economic, social and environmental logics;
ii) the role and capacity of the public sector including developing more effective and accountable relationships with communities and stakeholders;
iii) better ways of engaging citizens, communities and stakeholders in informed and democratic decision making processes.

The second section of the chapter outlines the steps and actions involved in the initial development of the Victorian Labor Government's *Growing Victoria Together* policy framework. This framework has been developed to articulate a more integrated approach to economic, social and

S. McBride et al. (eds.), Global Instability, 129–146.

environmental directions, to engage communities and stakeholders in future priority setting and implementation and to guide medium term public sector policy and resource allocation priorities.

The chapter concludes by reflecting on some of the lessons that can be learned from this experience for exploring the path towards policy making directions and processes.

AFTER ECONOMIC RATIONALITY, MARKET FUNDAMENTALISM AND MANAGERIAL CERTAINTY

Three important international trends are leading to new debates about public policy and the roles of government after a period of over twenty years in which market ideas and instruments have dominated the thinking of many policy makers.

First there is increasing recognition of the interdependence of policies and in particular the need for policy settings that are sustainable – economically, socially and environmentally. The economic policy settings implemented in most industrialised societies over the last twenty years have been associated with increased economic growth (as measured by GDP). They have also been linked to significant increases in inequality, with a growing gap between rich and poor; included and excluded; secure and insecure.[3] At the same time there has been increasing recognition of the need to recognise and address the full range of environmental externalities – and the full environmental, economic and social costs – arising from the assumption that energy and waste disposal resources are infinite.[4]

A more balanced understanding of economic, social and environmental logics leads to the realization that, in the medium term it is neither desirable nor possible to continue down a policy path based on maximising economic growth at all costs and then hoping to fix up the social and environmental costs later. The detailed, practical implications of sustainable, 'triple bottom line' development remain a work in progress but the core argument is compelling.[5] It makes sound economic, social and environmental sense to develop ways of working, ways of doing business and ways of making policy that start by valuing and understanding the complex relationships between environmental, social and economic logics, values and forces.

Second the increasing volatility and uncertainty of a globalizing, fragmenting world has led to renewed expectations that government will play a significant role in meeting the complex challenges of achieving more inclusive, democratic and sustainable prosperity.[6] These expectations have been reinforced by increasing transparency and rapid circulation of information that has provided individuals and organizations with more detailed understandings of the consequences of policy choices and increased expectations that governments can and should be held accountable for their actions.

The third public policy legacy of the last twenty years to have come under significant criticism is the managerialist faith in hierarchical, rational planning mechanisms linking mission statements, goals, objectives, programs and performance in straightforward chains of cause and effect.[7] Numerous critiques of managerialist public sector direction setting and changing management strategies have demonstrated their limitations in a world where the knowledge and capacity needed to predict and address increasingly complex policy problems comes from many sources. A world of complex relationships requires learning a great deal more about new ways of involving and engaging citizens, communities, community organizations, businesses, trade unions – and government – in policy making and implementation.[8]

The alternative to public policy making driven by economic rationality, market forces and managerialism does not lie in nostalgia for a vanished world of administrative rationality and bureaucratic processes. In an increasingly interconnected, volatile and globalized policy environment, governments and policy makers face three linked challenges:

i) developing and articulating a sense of direction which integrates economic, social and environmental goals <u>and</u> is simple and focussed enough to form the basis for seeking shared understandings and agreements with citizens and stakeholders;
ii) improving the capacity of governments, in partnership with citizens, communities and stakeholders, to set clear directions, manage complex policy challenges and be appropriately accountable for their actions in an increasingly volatile, complicated and fragmented world;
iii) drawing upon a broader base of knowledge, experience and expertise by involving and engaging citizens, communities and stakeholders in policy making and implementation.

These were the three challenges that led down a winding – and at times contested path – to the development of the Victorian Government's policy direction statement, *Growing Victoria Together.* The next section of this chapter outlines the initial steps in the development of this framework in order to illuminate some of the challenges facing communities, governments and policy makers endeavouring to achieve more sustainable, engaged and accountable policy making in a complex and uncertain world.

INITIAL WORK ON GROWING VICTORIA TOGETHER

The State of Victoria, with a population of about 4.7 million, is the second most populous of the six states (and two territories) which make up the Commonwealth of Australia. While initial economic development was founded on gold mining and agriculture, manufacturing industry became the cornerstone of economic growth during the twentieth century. Competition from cheap imports from low wage manufacturers led to a deteriorating outlook for many Victorian industries and workers during the 1980s and 1990s – creating the familiar picture of a once prosperous manufacturing economy being transformed into a crumbling, "rust belt."

While Victorian politics has been dominated by conservative Liberal and National Party governments for most of its history, a Labor Government led by Premiers John Cain and Joan Kirner governed the State between 1982 and 1993. While these Governments achieved a range of significant social and economic policy "goals," most commentators agree that the final election defeat of the Victorian Labor Government in 1993 was based on a media portrayal and a public perception of poor financial management.[9]

The incoming Liberal National Party Government of Premier Jeff Kennett was at the forefront of international experiments in neoliberal public policy, combining deep cuts to public expenditure (particularly in health and education) with an extensive program of privatization, competition and outsourcing.[10] The Government's underlying philosophy is well captured in Premier Kennett's assertion that "life is not about equality of opportunity and you don't have equality of outcomes ... There is no such thing as equality. We live in a competitive world. If you try and make the thin man fat the thin man ultimately dies. We have got to encourage the fat man to become fatter so that the thin man becomes fatter."[11]

The Government was also fiercely committed to the restoration and maintenance of the Victorian government's Triple A credit rating with international credit rating agencies and frequently identified this outcome as the single most important test of its policy success.

Despite vocal opposition from a diverse range of community groups concerned about issues of public sector cuts and democratic processes, high levels of economic growth and a sense that Victoria was "on the move" appeared to be continuing to shore up strong electoral support for the Kennett Government. It was therefore a profound shock to all commentators and most voters when the September 1999 election led to the defeat of the Kennett Government and the election of a Labor Government led by Premier Steve Bracks.

Firmly burned into the minds of incoming government Ministers was the memory of the way in which the media had characterized the previous Cain and Kirner Labor Governments (1982-1993) as financially irresponsible. The impact of this legacy was to create a culture of cautious reform in which "balancing the books" remained a paramount objective.

The new government faced four other significant constraints. First, it was a minority government dependent on the ongoing support of at least two of the three independent members of parliament. Second, the Victorian Upper House (the Legislative Council) remained under the control of the Liberal and National parties. Third, the members of the newly appointed Ministry were inexperienced, some without previous experience of being in Parliament, much less running a Department. Fourth, the skills and capacity of the

Victorian public service had become increasingly focussed on outsourcing and contract management with a diminished capacity to explore and develop broader options and processes

The initial directions of the Bracks Government focused on the implementation of the independently costed election policy document known as the Labour Financial Statement (LFS). The focus of the LFS was as a framework for initial, "first term" directions rather than a comprehensive long term policy agenda. In order to provide a focus for communicating the Government's broader directions, the following "four pillars" were identified by the Premier as overarching themes:

i) financial responsibility
ii) revitalizing democracy
iii) restoring services
iv) growing the whole State, not just part of it.

The initial legislative program focussed on democratic accountability issues through restoring the powers of the Auditor General and the independence of the Director of Public Prosecutions. The Government's first budget (2000-2001) included new expenditure commitments of $426 million, primarily aimed at improving education, health, police and community services. The Budget also included a $1 billion "Growing Victoria Fund" to support new infrastructure investment.

A major focus of the first twelve months was the initiation of an extensive range of policy reviews on issues such as public education, preschool services, primary health and community services. A range of broadly based consultation processes were also trialled including Community Cabinets, Policy Summits and "Roundtable" discussions between the Premier, Ministers and social, environmental, business and trade union stakeholders.

In March 2000 the "Growing Victoria Together" Summit, held at Parliament House, and chaired by former Australian Prime Minister Bob Hawke, brought together 100 participants from business, unions, community organizations, State and local government.

Despite an understandably high level of initial scepticism from both the media and participants, there was a broadly held view that the event provided a useful basis for key stakeholders to review common aspirations and ways of working. The opening paragraph of the Summit Recommendations noted: "the Summit agrees on certain fundamental principles and processes for achieving our shared objectives of Growing Victoria Together. We have been able to do this because of: first, a mutual recognition of the legitimate aspirations of the various interest groups represented at the Summit and second, a shared realization that these aspirations are most likely to be achieved by a cooperative approach to maximising economic growth within a just and inclusive society."

Importantly the Summit Recommendations also included a commitment to develop a "triple bottom line approach to policy making" and "to establish a Victorian Economic, Environment and Social Advisory Council" to provide ongoing advice and input from key stakeholder organizations.

By mid 2000 a number of forces were converging to create pressure for work to commence on the next steps in setting future directions. The emphasis on consultation had pleased some stakeholder groups, tired of the more directive processes of the previous government. Other groups, including much of the media, were raising expectations about the need for the Government to "get on with it" and articulate a clearer sense of purpose and direction. This was not a simple challenge given the lack of a clear groundswell of public opinion pushing the Government towards a particular vision. Nor was there any specific direction emerging from the ALP policy processes.

Nonetheless Ministers and senior public servants were increasingly aware that much of the substantive content of the Labour Financial Statement would soon be implemented, leaving the "four pillars" as a limited foundation for setting and communicating future priorities.

A second force for change was the growing recognition across the Government of the limitations of the output structure used for budgeting and performance measurement. It was becoming apparent to Ministers that the output structure was neither designed for, nor capable of being used as a strategic planning framework. Like all output structures the architecture is both complex and dense, with over 90 outputs across Departments and over 800 measures of performance. Whilst useful for tracking the ways money has been spent and measuring technical efficiency such architectures are not useful for long term planning. Nor do they provide a sufficient basis for transparent communication about the ways in which government action is actually making a positive difference to the lives of individuals and communities.

The logic of developing a longer term planning framework was becoming clear. Such a framework could provide a sense of vision and direction from the government to guide the public sector. It could also provide an umbrella for the output structure and guide choices by Ministers. Finally, it could form the basis of a communications strategy for the Government to express its aspirations to Victorians.

This combination of factors provided the stimulus for the Premier to request work to begin within the Department of the Premier and Cabinet on three economic, social and environmental policy frameworks. The choice of these three dimensions was consistent with the logic of a triple bottom line approach and most Government activities could be aligned with one or more of these policy areas. Responsibility for each of the three frameworks could readily be allocated across Ministerial portfolios and Departments. Other options, involving the development of cultural, fiscal and governance were considered. However this would have added additional complexity and for some additional frameworks (cultural and governance) there was no clear alignment with Ministerial or Departmental responsibilities.

Rather than risk losing mandate and momentum at an early stage the decision was taken to leave the issue of integration until the basic frameworks were constructed. Whilst in many ways this seems contrary to integrated planning there was no point seeking an integrated approach if the process was to fall over at the starting line because of perceived complexity. By commencing with separate economic, social and environmental frameworks Ministers had the opportunity within their specific structures (such as Cabinet Sub-Committees) to focus on their particular issues but do so in the context of Cabinet oversighting the process.

To ensure the opportunity for an integrated approach the same basic template was constructed for each of the frameworks and a set of broad outcomes agreed. By commencing with agreed, whole of government outcomes (via Cabinet) and using the same template, the logic of integration was embedded in the process. Integration was achieved by the end of 2000 pre-empting a potentially destructive competition for dominance between the economic, social and environmental frameworks. It was precisely this kind of bitter competition for pre-eminence that had bedevilled the relationship between the Economic and Social Justice Strategies of the previous Cain and Kirner Governments.[12]

Importantly there was strong and continuing support for the integrated policy framework approach from the Premier and senior Ministers as well as from the Secretary of the Department of Premier and Cabinet. This support, expressed through relevant Cabinet and Cabinet Sub Committee decisions endorsing key stages in the development of the framework, provided the essential mandate and momentum for work to proceed. Much of the early work on *Growing Victoria Together* involved establishing the mandate and ownership of a process from the key stakeholders and building *Growing Victoria Together* into the key processes of Government. Other key organizational structures and relationships included:

i) the Policy Development and Research Branch of the Department of Premier and Cabinet, established in mid 2000 which coordinated policy input, liaison and communication tasks;
ii) the Frameworks Interdepartmental Committee convened by a Deputy Secretary of the Department of Premier and Cabinet and involving a senior representative from each Department which provided a mechanism for ensuring that all Departments were kept informed and involved;
iii) Chiefs of Staff meetings, convened by staff from the Premier's Private Office, which provided a mechanism for ensuring that Ministers' private offices were kept informed and involved;
iv) the Victorian Economic, Environment and Social Advisory Committee which provided an ongoing forum for checking views of key stakeholders.

The importance given to creating a short, sharp document and to winning real ownership from Ministers and Departments led to a long, arduous writing and editing process with dozens of substantial iterations. In total over 90 drafts were generated. Content was informed by a number of sources including Government election policies, the views of Ministers after 12 months in Government, the recommendations of the Growing Victoria Together Summit, policy review and consultation outcomes, policy research checking whether proposed content and language resonated with Victorians from different backgrounds and comments from members of the Victorian Economic, Environmental and Social Advisory Council.

During the period from October 2000 to October 2001 when the *Growing Victoria Together* process and content was being refined, the process was already having a significant impact on the corporate and business planning of Departments. The significance of *Growing Victoria Together* was also reinforced by including references to maintaining the momentum in performance agreements for senior executives. This had the effect of gaining the attention of many senior staff who otherwise may have maintained a "wait and see" attitude.

The Growing Victoria Together Booklet[13]

The *Growing Victoria Together* booklet, launched by the Premier in November 2001 had three key purposes:

i) to communicate the Government's integrated economic, social and environmental directions to Victorians;
ii) to provide a medium term (5-10 year) policy framework for the Victorian public sector;
iii) to provide a basis for engaging stakeholders in implementing future directions and actions.

The booklet begins with an introduction from the Premier noting that *Growing Victoria Together* "expresses the government's broad vision for the future. It links the issues important to Victorians, the priority actions we need to take next and the measures will use to show progress. *Growing Victoria Together* balances economic, social and environmental goals and actions. It is clear that we need a broader measure of progress and common prosperity than economic growth alone. That is the heart of our balanced approach – a way of thinking, a way of working and a way of governing which starts by valuing equally our economic, social and environmental goals."

This is followed by a summary of the Victorian community's strengths and challenges leading to the following broad vision statement: "By 2010 Victoria will be a State where:

i) innovation leads to thriving industries generating high quality jobs;
ii) protecting the environment for future generations is built into everything we do;
iii) we have caring, safe communities in which opportunities are fairly shared;
iv) all Victorians have access to the highest quality health and education services all through their lives."

The bulk of the document consists of outlining the progress measures and initial priority actions in relation to eleven "Important Issues for Victorians." The issues and related progress measures are summarised in Table 1 below. The Priority Actions are summarised in Table 2.

The progress measures are the "sharp end" of *Growing Victoria Together*. A good deal of the work involved in finalizing the content of the document consisted of reaching agreement on reducing hundreds of suggested measures to a smaller number of 32. The inevitable trade offs involved in achieving agreement mean that the specificity of the measures is extremely mixed, ranging from precise benchmarks to broad "improvement targets." However keeping the list short was essential to ensure that the overall package of measures provided a reasonably sharp focus for setting future priorities.

The criteria used for choosing the progress measures was that they:

i) provide a sensible and integrated basis for reporting on progress in addressing the social, economic and environmental issues important to Victorians;
ii) be linked to the capability of the state Government and be achievable over time;
iii) be able to be measured using readily available, valid and reliable data;
iv) be able to be expressed in plain language;
v) be able to be used to show progress for particular places and groups.

Table 1: Important Issues and Demonstrating Progress Measures Included in Growing Victoria Together

Important Issues:	**Demonstrating Progress Measures:**
Valuing and investing in lifelong education	Victorian primary school children will be at or above national benchmark levels for reading, writing and numeracy by 2005. Ninety per cent of young people in Victoria will successfully complete Year 12 or its equivalent by 2010. The percentage of young people 15-19 in rural and regional Victoria engaged in education and training will rise by six per cent by 2005. The proportion of Victorians learning new skills will increase.
High quality, accessible health and community services	Waiting times and levels of confidence in health and community services will improve. Health and education outcomes for young children will improve. Waiting times for drug treatment will decrease, as will deaths from drugs, including tobacco and alcohol.
	An annual budget surplus.

Sound financial management	Victoria's taxes will remain competitive with the Australian average Maintain a Triple A rating.
Safe streets, homes and workplaces	Violent crime and fear of violent crime will be reduced. Road accidents and deaths will be reduced by 20 per cent over the next five years.
Growing and linking all of Victoria	The proportion of freight transported to ports by rail will increase from ten per cent to 30 per cent. Rail travel times will be reduced to Ballarat, Geelong, Bendigo and the Latrobe Valley. Travel in Melbourne taken on public transport will increase from nine per cent to 20 per cent by the year 2020.
Promoting sustainable development	Renewable energy efforts will increase. Energy consumption in Government buildings will be reduced by 15 per cent and the use of electricity from Green Power by Government will be increased to five per cent by 2005. Waste recycling efforts will increase and the use of landfill as a waste disposal method will be reduced. Waste water reuse in Melbourne will increase from one per cent to 20 per cent by 2010.
More jobs and thriving, innovative industries across Victoria	Victoria's productivity and competitiveness will increase. We will see this through increasing GDP per worker. There will be more and better jobs across Victoria. The proportion of Victorians learning new skills will increase. A greater share of innovative R&D activity will be in Victoria.
Building cohesive communities and reducing inequalities	The extent and diversity of participation in community, cultural and recreational organizations will increase. In a crisis there will be more people Victorians can turn to for support. Inequalities in health, education and well being among communities will be reduced.
Protecting the environment for future generations	The Snowy River will be returned to 21 per cent of its original flow within 10 years and over time to 28 per cent.[14] The quality of air and drinking water will improve. The health of Victoria's catchments, rivers and bays will improve. The area covered by native vegetation will increase. There will be a real reduction in the environmental and economic impact of salinity by 2015.
Promoting rights and respecting diversity	The proportion of Victorians aware of their legal and civil rights will increase. More Victorians from all backgrounds will have the opportunity to have a say on issues that matter to them.
Government that listens and leads	More Victorians will be consulted on issues, which matter to them. There will be regular reports on progress in improving the quality of life for all Victorians and their communities.

Table 2: Important Issues and Priority Actions Included in Growing Victoria Together

Important Issues:	Priority Actions:
Valuing and investing in lifelong education	Improve participation and achievement in education and training. Provide better links between schools, business and communities. Expand opportunities for training and learning all through life.
High quality, accessible health and community services	Build, improve and integrate hospitals and community health services. Link and invest in services for mothers and children through pregnancy to age eight. Support older people to live active lives in the community. Reduce drug abuse and harm. Tackle health issues linked to inequality including mental and dental health.
Sound financial management	Maintain responsible financial management. Invest in long term social and physical infrastructure such as schools, hospitals, roads, public transport and waste management. Provide an annual report showing the link between budget outcomes and progress on issues important to Victorians.
Safe streets, homes and workplaces	Continue to increase police numbers until we have 800 extra police in the front line against crime. Develop new and expanded crime prevention programs. Reduce family violence. Improve road and workplace safety.
Growing and linking all of Victoria	Build faster, better, more accessible transport and communication links. Better link Melbourne and regional ports to industry and agricultural centres across Victoria. Connect more Victorians to the Internet and other new technologies.
Promoting sustainable development	Increase recycling and effective waste management and increase the development and use of renewable energy sources. Improve the productivity and sustainability of natural resource industries such as fisheries, farming, forestry and mining. Facilitate the planting of more trees.
More jobs and thriving, innovative industries across Victoria	Promote the creation and use of new ideas and technologies to attract investment and employment in new and existing industries. Promote growth in information and communications, biotechnology, professional services, design, advanced manufacturing and environmental management. Improve the business environment through competitive business costs, certainty and security of energy supply, high performing, cooperative workplaces and a highly skilled workforce.
Building cohesive communities and reducing inequalities	Support new community building initiatives and develop partnerships with local government around local communities' needs. Enhance community participation and engagement in cultural activities. Encourage employers, workers and families to better balance their work and family responsibilities and their ability to participate in community life. Reduce unemployment and rejuvenate those areas worst affected by social and economic disadvantage.

	Expand the supply of secure, affordable and appropriate public housing.
Protecting the environment for future generations	Improve the health of our rivers and waterways and take effective action to reduce salinity. Increase and provide greater protection for areas of high conservation value including the establishment of a comprehensive system of marine national parks. Ensure water authorities continue to supply affordable good quality drinking water. Encourage increased use of public transport.
Promoting rights and respecting diversity	Improve awareness of rights and promote equal opportunity. Improve access to courts, legal aid, victim support and alternative dispute resolution procedures. Increase racial and religious tolerance. Promote reconciliation between indigenous and non-indigenous. Victorians and move to redress the dispossession of Aboriginal land and culture. Improve access to services for culturally and linguistically diverse Victorians. Increase the diversity of representation on decision making boards and in local government.
Government that listens and leads	Provide strong, clear vision and direction with regular reports on progress. Make Government more democratic, open and inclusive through better access to decision making processes including holding numerous Community Cabinets each year. Strengthen the capacity of the public sector to deliver high quality, responsive, accessible and efficient services.

Communicating, Implementing and Engaging

The external communications objective of *Growing Victoria Together* was initially addressed through the public launch of the booklet that was mailed out to a wide range of community, business, trade union and local government organizations as well as being available through local libraries and local government offices. Advertisements were placed in major daily newspapers informing readers of the availability of the booklet and a web site was established providing downloadable versions as well as translations. Initial reactions from key stakeholders could best be summarised as a mixture of cautious support for the broad directions and intent combined with appropriate scepticism about the prospects for statements of direction being converted into substantive outcomes.

For the public sector, the significance of *Growing Victoria Together* lay in its capacity to inform and guide policy and resource allocation choices. The task of selecting and agreeing on progress measures had already had the valuable effect of focussing Departmental attention on discussion about future priorities. Following the public launch of *Growing Victoria Together,* Departmental Secretaries were asked to ensure that their staff and stakeholders were fully briefed on its content and purpose as well as beginning to address the following implementation questions:

How should progress measures be sharpened into benchmarks and/or continuous improvement goals?
Do you have the data to measure progress? If not, what action is needed?
What does available data show about trends?
Will existing policy settings and proposed priority actions achieve progress? By when? What else needs to be done?
What are the implications for regions and population groups?
How will connections to resource choices, corporate and business planning be shown?
How will you engage and work with other Departments and stakeholders to address cross cutting issues?

At the launch of *Growing Victoria Together* the Premier also made a commitment to working with communities and stakeholders to keep improving the progress measures and to identify ways of working together on important issue. Community Cabinets and the Victorian Economic, Environment and Social Advisory Council were identified as important forums for these discussions but all Ministers were also asked to identify ways of working with local communities and advisory bodies to take *Growing Victoria Together* forward.

By the beginning of 2002 the *Growing Victoria Together* development process had led to the production of a short, simple, integrated policy direction statement which had sufficient Ministerial ownership and support to be publicly launched and distributed. The Important Issues, Priority actions and Progress measures had begun to be used by Departments as the key basis for guiding resource allocation, corporate and business plans and Ministers had begun to consider ways of engaging communities and stakeholders in discussions about next steps. The most significant steps underway include the following:

The alignment of the resource allocation, output and performance reporting systems of government with the *Growing Victoria Together* outcomes. The 2002-2003 Victorian Government Budget papers are, for example, framed and organized to show how outputs and actions will lead to progress in addressing *Growing Victoria Together* issues and progress measures.

The incorporation of *Growing Victoria Together* outcomes and actions and measures into the corporate and business planning of all Government agencies. This involves, for example the development of cross cutting measures and measures of sustainability that are reflected in the corporate and business plans of all agencies and which specifically demonstrates the contribution of those agencies to sustainability outcomes.

The development of enhanced skills capacity in the Victorian public service to support *Growing Victoria Together*. This includes learning about different approaches to policy development (e.g. moving from risk management to managed risk taking); policy development techniques (e.g. community consultation and scenario planning strategies) and new understandings of the relation between policy issues (the implications new thinking about sustainability and triple bottom line approaches). In addition to a range of cross government policy forums and skill development initiatives work has also begun on the development of a Graduate School of Government to provide a focus for significantly upgrading public service skills and capacities.

Work on clarifying and improving measures of progress to enable reporting on *Growing Victoria Together* outcomes to commence. This involves the standardization of data sets (scope, definitions, counting rules) to enable consistent reporting within and across Departments. In some instances (e.g. social capital) this has required the commissioning of new research and data collection work.

The engagement of population groups and places on the "drop down" implications of *Growing Victoria Together.* Agencies with a specific responsibility for population groups are working on ways to make *Growing Victoria Together* relevant to the specific issues and aspirations of, for example, indigenous and aged people in Victoria. This includes discussions between the population groups on key common measures of progress such as health status and education outcomes. A number of pilot projects have also been commissioned to support learning about the best ways of developing progress measures and direction statements at regional and local community levels.

First Steps on a Longer Path: The Potential Significance of *Growing Victoria Together*

The track record of government strategic plans and "vision statements" is littered with stories of failure. Many never make it into the light of day. Many that do become "shelf documents" or public relations glossies with little impact on thinking and action. While it would be wrong to overstate the significance of the *Growing Victoria Together* experiment, and it is clearly too early to make long term judgements about its effectiveness in setting and driving alternative policy directions, there are a number of features of the document and the process behind it which are worth noting.

It Has Medium Term Time Frame

The five to ten year medium term time frame deliberately opens up discussion about policy goals and actions extending beyond the next budget – or the next election to provide the basis for a discussion about the actions needed to address underlying causes and longer term challenges.

It Integrates Economic, Social, Environmental and Governance Issues and Outcomes

As the Premier has noted (in his speech launching the document) this is the Victorian Government's approach to implementing a triple bottom line policy making which balances a range of issues and outcomes – not just GDP growth and triple A rating. "Getting the balance right between economic, social and environmental goals is our greatest challenge. The *Growing Victoria Together* framework lays down an agenda for meeting that challenge."

It Includes a Small Number of Measures of Progress for Which Government Can Be Held Accountable

As noted above, agreement on a small number of progress measures provides an important basis for demonstrating government is serious about public accountability for progress in achieving outcomes on the issues important to citizens, stakeholders and communities.

It Has Significant Ministerial and Public Sector Ownership

The time consuming process of winning Ministerial ownership has been crucial in order to convince Departments to take directions seriously. It is a short simple communications document that can provide a starting point for talking with stakeholders and communities about future directions and priorities. Detail, length and technical policy jargon have been deliberately avoided in favour of a short document written in straightforward accessible language to encourage broad readership and genuine dialogue with community and stakeholder organizations.

Public Policy Directions in a Time of Flux: After Economic Rationalism and Managerialism

Growing Victoria Together is no more – and no less than – a short, simple overview of the work needed to address the most important issues facing Victorians along with ways of demonstrating progress. In this sense it is an initial step on a longer path towards a more integrated and accountable approach to policy making. It is very much a sign post rather than a road map and only time will tell whether it has been effective as a mechanism for turning rhetoric into reality in a way in which has ongoing positive outcomes for citizens and communities.

However the experience of developing and beginning to implement *Growing Victoria Together* does provide an opportunity to open up and reflect on some of the larger questions about future public sector goals and processes. While the debate remains hotly contested, there is increasing evidence that the answers provided by the dominant neoliberal policy triumvirate of narrow economic rationality, market fundamentalism and organizational managerialism have begun to ring hollow.

The final Table 3 is, however, informed by the view that, while the old world shows some signs of passing away, the new world is still some way from being fully formed, named or implemented. In this time of flux it aims to provide a framework for some of the key questions about public policy directions, the role of the public sector and the range of voices needed to address the central policy challenge of our time: *how to deliver sustainable, fair and democratic prosperity in the context of accelerating global flows of information, resources and people.*

Table 3: Public Policy Directions in a Time of Flux

Key Questions	**...from (apparent) simplicity and rationality of markets and managerialism ...**	**...towards balance, accountability and engagement in complex policy environments**
What should be the relationship between economic, social and environmental goals?	Economic growth first – then trickle down and fix up the environment	Fair, sustainable prosperity – through balancing economic, social, environmental outcomes
What can and should governments do about distributional issues?	Inequality and exclusion irrelevant and/or inevitable	Inequality and exclusion important and changeable
What should be the dominant logic in decision making and resource allocation?	Market and price signals	Reconsideration of relationship between market and new ways of engaging citizens, communities and stakeholders in decision making
What should be the relationship between market, state and civil society?	Market dominant	Reconsideration of market, public sector and community sector roles and relationships
What should be the dominant public sector organizational principles?	Rational planning and top down goal setting plus outsourced implementation and delivery	Coordinating and connecting multiple sources of knowledge, experience and expertise
What should be the main roles of the public sector?	Planner/purchaser/contractor	Planner/catalyst/developer/ provider/enabler/broker/purc haser/contractor
What should be the relationship between policy and resource allocation?	Budget focus on outputs - no clear connection to outcomes	Clear and integrated connections between budget strategy, outputs and

		outcomes
What are the most important public sector skills and knowledge sets?	Strategic planning, contract management, risk management	Identifying, sharing and using knowledge; Creativity, innovation and managed risk taking; Managing complex issues and relationships; Engaging stakeholders
What range of voices should be involved in policy decision making?	Narrow- professional bureaucrats and their immediate networks	Broad range of public sector, community and stakeholder networks

NOTES

1 The author is on leave from an ongoing position as Associate Professor in the School of Social Science and Planning at RMIT University in Melbourne. While he currently holds the position of Assistant Director, Policy Development and Research Branch, Victorian Department of Premier and Cabinet, the content of the chapter does not necessarily represent the views of the Victorian Government. An earlier version of some of the arguments contained in this chapter was developed as an article with Dr. David Adams

2 Brecht (1997) p. 84.

3 Stilwell (2000); Tanner (1999); Hamilton (1998); Nieuwenhuysen, Lloyd and Mead (2001).

4 Coombs (1990); Diesendorf and Hamilton (1997); Eckersley (1998).

5 Beder (1993); Elkington (1999); OECD (2001); Yencken and Wilkinson (2000).

6 IFG (2001); OECD (2001); Bauman (1999); Dror (2001).

7 Davis and Rhodes (2000); Saul (1997); Bogason (2000); Considine (1995).

8 OECD (2001); Edgar (2001).

9 Considine and Costar (1993).

10 Alford and O'Neil (1994).

11 J. Kennett cited in interview with M. Gill and G. Kitney, *Australian Financial Review*, 23 October 1992.

12 See Wiseman (1992).

13 Copies of the *Growing Victoria Together* booklet along with related documents and links can be found at Victorian Government Internet website.

14 The Snowy River that flows into the sea near the border of New South Wales and Victoria has an iconic status as a symbol of Australia's environmental heritage. In recent years, the water flow has been reduced to a trickle, largely because of irrigation. Returning water flow to the Snowy was also an important policy objective of one of the independents holding the balance of power in the Victorian Parliament.

REFERENCES

Alford J. and O'Neil, D. 1994. *The Contract State: Public Management Under the Kennett Government.* Deakin University Press: Geelong, Victoria.

Argy, F. 1998. *Australia at the Crossroads.* Allen and Unwin: Sydney.

Kennett J. Kennett intent on fundamental reform." *Australian Financial Review*, 23 October 1992, pp. 8-9.

Bauman, Z. 1999. In Search of Politics. Policy Press: Cambridge.

Beder, S. 1993. *The Nature of Sustainable Development.* Scribe: Newham.

Bogason, P. 2000. *Public Policy and Local Governance: Institutions in Postmodern Society*, Edward Elgar: Cheltenham.

Brecht, Bertolt. 1997. *Das Badener Lehstiick vom Einverstandnis. The Didactic Play of Baden: On Consent.* Brecht, B. Collected Works, 3. Methuen: London.

Considine, M. 1995. *Public Policy: A Critical Approach.* Macmillan: Melbourne.

Considine, M. and B. Costar, eds. 1993. *Trials in Power: Cain, Kirner and Victoria 1982-1992.* Melbourne University Press: Melbourne.

Coombs, H.C. 1990. *The Return of Scarcity.* Cambridge University Press: Sydney.

Davis, G. and R.A.W. Rhodes. 2000. "From Hierarchy to Contracts and Back Again: Reforming the Australian Public Service." In M. Keating, J. Wanna, and P. Weller, eds. *Institutions on the Edge.* Allen and Unwin: St. Leonards, NSW

Diesendorf, M. and C. Hamilton. 1997. *Human Ecology, Human Economy.* Allen and Unwin: Sydney.

Dror, Y. 2001. *The Capacity to Govern.* Frank Cass Publishers: London.

Eckersley, R. 1998 'Perspectives on Progress: Economic Growth, Quality of Life and Ecological Sustainability'. In R. Eckersley, ed., *Measuring Progress: Is Life Getting Better?* CSIRO: Melbourne.

Edgar, D. 2001. *The Patchwork Nation: Re-thinking Government – Re-building Community.* Harper Collins: Melbourne.

Elkington, J. 1997. "Cannibals with Forks: The Triple Bottom Line of 21st Century Business." Capstone: Oxford.

Hamilton, C. 1998. *'Economic Growth and Social Decline'. Australian Quarterly*, May June.

International Forum on Globalization (IFG). 2001. *A Better World Is Possible! Alternatives to Economic Globalization.* Summary Report. Alternatives Committee, International Forum on Globalization, San Francisco.

Nieuwenhuysen, J., P. Lloyd, and M. Mead, eds. 2001. *Reshaping Australia's Economy: Growth, Equity and Sustainability.* Cambridge University Press: Melbourne.

OECD. 2001. *Governance in the 21st Century.* OECD: Paris.

Rees, S. 1995 *The Human Costs of Managerialism,* Pluto Press, Sydney

Self, P. 2000. *Rolling Back the Market.* Macmillan: London.

Saul, John Ralston. 1997. *The Unconscious Civilisation.* Penguin: Harmondsworth.

Stillwell, F. 2000. *Changing Track: A New Political Economic Direction for Australia.* Pluto Press: Sydney.

Stretton, H., and L. Orchard. 1994. *Public Goods, Public Enterprise Public Choice.* Macmillan: Melbourne.

Tanner, L. 1999. *Open Australia.* Pluto Press: Sydney.

Wiseman, J. 1992. "The Development and Outcomes of the Victorian Social Justice Policy." In M. Considine and B. Costar, eds. *Trials in Power: Cain, Kirner and Victoria 1982-1992.* Melbourne University Press: Melbourne.

Yencken, D. and D. Wilkinson. 2000. *Resetting the Compass: Australia's Journey Towards Sustainability.* CSIRO Publishing: Collingwood, Vic.

Chapter 9

RE-INVENTION AND TRANSITION OF THE MEXICAN STATE

José G. Vargas Hernández.
Universidad de Guadalajara

INTRODUCTION

Recently, the role of the state in formulating and implementing economic policies for the achievement of societal growth and development has undergone many changes and transformations. In Mexico, the protectionist, statist and populist regime has been replaced by the so-called neoliberal state model, which has achieved some impressive results in terms of economic growth and development. It should be noted, however, that this growth rate "falls well below the 3.4 per cent GDP growth" that the World Bank considers necessary for the reduction of poverty. Unfortunately, an increase in poverty has been among the most poignant results of the implementation of neoliberal policies. Further disappointing results include growth in the unemployment rate, a decline in incomes, and a widening gap between the rich and poor, which have produced fissures in society and fuelled guerrilla warfare and crime waves.

In fact, at the turn of a new millennium, the debate over the appropriateness of particular state models is taking on greater importance, not only for the more globalized and highly developed societies but also for the less developed ones as well. The main issues of this discussion focus on the fundamental concepts of representation, economic functions and organization.

According to Moctezuma (1997), the debate has gone through three different stages. The first stage involved the need for state reform and enhanced efficiency. The second stage concerned itself with modification of relations within the state and issues of an economic nature. Today, the debate is centred upon the transformation of the state in the presence of a more participatory society.

S. McBride et al. (eds.), Global Instability, 147–159.

MEXICAN STATE IN TRANSITION

Many of the economic policies implemented by states after the Second World War, in accordance with the welfare state model, came to be viewed as failures by the 1980s. However, the same is becoming true of the successor policies. Even the great conservative revolution initiated by Margaret Thatcher in 1979, that replaced the welfare state model by advancing capitalist principles, has been challenged through the acquisition of office on 1 May 1997 by the Labour Party in Britain.

Neoliberal economic reforms, also known as the "Washington consensus," entail public policies that are directed toward tight fiscal discipline, privatization of public sector organizations in order to downsize and achieve balanced budgets, deregulation and lowering of trade barriers. Several economic analysts have expressed concern about the destabilizing impacts of these reforms. Sáenz (1997) believes that the contemporary emergence of ideological unconformities and violent manifestations in many parts of the world indicates that the economic policies of the immediate past and their potential projection into the future will not generate consensus. As Harvard's Mangabeira recently put it in an interview: "the opposition in Latin America is in danger of being represented as a populist backlash of the poor against the rich.[1] Furthermore, other critics' comments "are focusing their attention and energy on the allegation that these same reforms have also spawned high unemployment and a sharp decline in the standard of living of the majority of Latin Americans."[2]

The state model that succeeded the conservative revolution in Britain would be defined by new economic policies that promised to "unmask the myths of prosperity that the Tories divulged and which do not coincide with reality."[3] According to Semo (1997), Blair talks frequently of transcending differences between right and left and of maintaining old loyalties abroad – changes necessitated by our epoch. Thus, the great challenge for Labour will be how to manage the process of economic reform initiated and propounded by the Conservatives and simultaneously satisfy the populist promises made to an electorate weary of two decades of adjustments. Some analysts see the birth of a new politics that may dominate the 21st century.

Until now, the neoliberal state model seemed to be the only course, with privatization, deregulation, tight fiscal discipline and slashing of social benefits and taxes, a formula which "promised a dollop of austerity and little else for the time being."[4] However, the election of centre-left governments in a number of European countries, has demonstrated that "Thatcherism isn't the only path to structural reform" and that a new strategy and model of the state can emerge where "growth and job creation becomes possible" and "a less austere policy would certainly ease the task of structural reform."[5] The return of social policy in Britain weakens the alliance between the successors of the Thatcher legacy and Washington. Almeyra notes (1997b) that several considerations are necessary for the maintenance of an aggressive military policy, these include: social discipline, high military expenditures and political insensitivity, policies that a social democratic government cannot afford without meeting serious problems.

The process is, of course, complex. Much of the Maastricht politics elucidated in Brussels at the margin of national parliaments has expropriated part of the sovereign and democratic decision making powers of governments and imposed restrictions that may spell the end of the remaining social policies.

Even so, a leftward shift can be very contagious in Europe where the south winds blowing over Portugal, Spain, Greece, Belgium, etc., have started to partially unfreeze the sociopolitical European panorama formed during the Thatcher-Reagan Glacial Era. Left-of-centre governments, have demonstrated that "... social institutions need not be cast aside entirely but rather made more competitive."[6] Therefore it is possible that the backlash could reverberate around those countries in Europe where the Social Democrats are in power and could militate against further economic reform.

As an external force, it is evident that the globalization process reveals a profound ideological split. Those who insist that international capital is the only possible frame of reference cannot reconcile their position with those who refuse to accept that the rule of international capital is inevitable.[7] The main challenge for the former then, is how to convince voters of the need to face up to the necessities of economic globalization.

The transformation of the state from one state model to another does not always occur in an orderly and smooth fashion. States that began the process earlier apparently reached and accomplished certain goals. A look at developments in Latin America reveals the presence of great difficulties. Fifteen years after the Mexican government initiated economic reforms oriented toward strengthening the market economy, it is facing tremendous challenges. The trend of revising the mission of the state in Mexico is occurring as it has been elsewhere. The pattern of recent political changes shows that the state is going through a process of transition. Within the political bureaucratic machinery and partisan team many conflicts have not been resolved. Recent elections show an unprecedented democratic process of political transformation that in turn will have important effects on the formulation and implementation of social and economic policies.

Although economic reforms in Mexico have surpassed expectations, the scope of political reform has been limited and has resulted in the acceptance of free market forces on the one hand, and an authoritarian regime which maintains the three fundamental pillars of the Mexican state: presidentialism, centralism and corporatism, on the other. The legitimacy of the Mexican state has decreased considerably over the last few years, giving way to the weak and erratic growth of social organizations, and an increasing role of political parties and civil society. This can be attributed to the economic restructuring process that the Mexican Government has undertaken which has both weakened the state and undermined the fundamental mechanisms of legitimization. Thus, there is a sense of urgency to re-establish equilibrium between economic policy and the political reform of the Mexican State.

There are two political and economic conceptions of the Mexican state, according to Labastida (1997): the revolutionary conception and the presidential authoritarian conception. The Mexican state's revolutionary conception, designed after the Mexican revolution of 1910-17, proclaimed in the Federal Constitution of 1917 as popular republican, sovereign, representative, with a presidential government limited by legislative and judicial powers. Its functions included the following: to respect human liberties; to establish and maintain international relations; to foster conditions which make possible economic and cultural social justice; and to guarantee human and family protection by way of material development founded on the greatest ideals of society. It was a conception of the state based upon the realities of urban workers, peasants, the middle classes, and nationalist entrepreneurs.

To critics, this conceptualization of the Mexican state bears the greatest responsibility for the problems inundating society. Poverty, underdevelopment, lack of economic growth, and unemployment, etc., are all remnants of the welfare state. As with any modern state, it was the best instrument of capitalist expansion. This is no longer the case. Today, the Mexican state is the largest and strongest obstacle for the free movement of capital, goods and services, the necessities of a strategy of economic globalization. The state will thus be expansionist capital's main challenge.

The other conception of the Mexican state forged during the past 30 years, according to Labastida, supposed a violation of the constitutional state to edify authoritarian presidentialism. The main characteristic of this conception was a separation of government from the people. In other words, a transformation of government into the political operator of the dominant higher classes occurred, remaining relatively local during the administrations of López Portillo and De la Madrid and developing an outward orientation starting in 1988 with the rise of Salinas. Through its illegality and illegitimacy presidential authoritarianism led to the demise of any ethical foundation for the state. As a consequence, public and private corruption became rampant, corporatist structures replaced democratic life in civil associations, and a bureaucratic hierarchy dependent almost totally on the executive power's titular became the norm.

Under the first phase of presidential authoritarianism, the so-called period of "stabilizing development," the Mexican economy achieved impressive rates of growth. However, this growth was inequitable and broadened the gap between the rich and the poor, both on an individual and regional level. Governability was effected through an authoritarian and repressive political system as the case of the student's movement in 1968 demonstrated.

Macías (1997) contends that the economy's subordination to foreign capital commenced during this period of "stabilizing development" (1940-1970). This entailed the unequal development and marginalization of the larger southern regions of Mexico where a rise in poverty and migration took place. The nation's land and resources were transferred from agriculture, fisheries, forestry and mining, activities of the Southern communities, to subsidize industrialization projects in the centre, north, northeast and northwest regions of the country. The so-called "Mexican miracle" was characterized by regions that exhibited extreme poverty along side the better developed areas.

During the 1970s an interventionist type of state continued its protectionist policies within a closed-economy context, distinct from free market principles and generating serious distortions. In the 1980s, the forces of globalization led to an alteration in the strategies of Mexico's economic development. The International Monetary Fund (IMF) and the World Bank imposed development and monetary policies based largely on the free market. State intervention was considered the main cause of economic, social and political dysfunction in Mexico.

During this first phase the Mexican state was identified as authoritarian and corporatist as opposed to socialist and distributive, the Keynesian type. The bankruptcy of this corporatist economic model, however, precipitated the need for new political rules not only to guide the activities of the state but also those of the political parties. Lewis (1997) states that the traditional adherence to nationalism, economic protectionism, and one-party rule gave way to policies that more closely resemble those seen in liberal democracies.

The Mexican economic crisis of 1982 demonstrated that the economic structure had serious problems. These problems led to the exhaustion of the developmental model based on import substitution and the orientation of monetary and fiscal policies toward public spending. Such policies resulted in a high foreign debt incurred to support large-scale public intervention, a low rate of productivity growth, a high negative income distribution, a concentration of inequality, an aggravation of extreme poverty, and structural lags in the economy. Poor distribution of economic development remains one of the major sources of social problems and political instability. The prolonged economic crisis of the past 15 years has resulted not only in economic changes, but underscored the need for a political and democratic transition. To what extent the economic crisis has precipitated the need for state-wide political reform has yet to be answered.

Under the second phase of presidential authoritarianism, a new model of the Mexican state, identified as neoliberal, emerged after the economic crisis of 1982: "Based on integration to the global economy and a downscaling of the government,"[8] the model promised to rescue Mexico from the brink of economic and political ruin. The assumption was that the market was the best regulator of economic, political, social and cultural relationships.

Within this new model of the Mexican state, neoliberal elites appear to dominate the upper echelons of the political apparatus. The neoliberal model not only weakens the political autonomy of the state; it also diminishes the capacity of the state to formulate social policies. The adoption of economic neoliberalism has led to an anti-statist ideology. As such, the state's structure and functions have been transformed, allowing for greater assumption of responsibility by the private sector.

The most important structural changes experienced by the Mexican state were linked to economic policies congruent with the new global environment. Some of these changes include the restructuring of productive plants, privatization of the *ejido* (communal property), improvement of public finances, modernization of education, privatization of state enterprises, negotiation of external debt, deregulation of the economy, commercial and financial liberalization, and greater foreign investment. The goals of such changes are economic modernization, creation of wealth, and increased welfare. According to Conger (1997), the model has achieved impressive results. He notes that state-controlled industries have been privatized, foreign investment has increased dramatically, the bureaucracy has been reduced in size, and democratic reforms have been initiated.

The dismantling of the welfare state in Mexico has been accompanied by a weakening of social and political structures. This has been especially problematic since the internal dynamics of the state are not yet compatible with neoliberal orthodoxy, that is, the neoliberal model is dependent upon a form of individualization within social and productive organizations. Mexico, however, has not yet abandoned neocorporatist structures. Thus the neoliberal state model poses a complex paradox within the Mexican State. This has resulted in a mixture of neoliberal and neoconservative ideology with a heavy pragmatic orientation.

Thus, monetarist economic policies have laid down the foundation for the creation of a model of political and social domination based upon capital accumulation and the rule of financial capital. As Banamex-Accival (1997) notes: "The globalization process currently sweeping the world only aggravates dependency and vulnerability, by dividing the world between producer and consumer countries." But also, the same process is disturbing Mexican society. Conger contends that economic development is thus characterized by "the breakdown of economies into vibrant financial and industrial centres and impoverished rural backwaters." Former Mexican President Zedillo conceded that there was a troublesome dualism between the dollar-based, export-oriented sector and the peso-based economy.

As this new financial environment is established and the free movement of financial capital increases, the interdependence of states within the global system will increase accordingly. Mexico has been enmeshed in this process for the past few years. Foreign capital inflows required to fuel development have not been accompanied by investor confidence and general prosperity due to "poor economic management and government corruption."[9]

The "fundamentalist" economic model imposed upon Mexico is based upon the promise or expectation that national and international free markets will solve problems of slow growth and structural unemployment. Sáenz notes, however, the model is ill equipped to secure integral developmental goals.

The economic policies implemented since 1982, although sacrificing the goal of sustainable economic growth, have nonetheless achieved substantial reductions in the rate of inflation. In 1994, when Mexico ratified the North American Free Trade Agreement (NAFTA), the policy of national self-sufficiency was completely abandoned. It is important to note that economic distortions were already present at this time. For example, no more than 800 Mexican enterprises were exporting and the market concentration of the top five exporting firms accounted for 20 per cent of the export value. Meanwhile unskilled Mexicans in dire poverty numbered approximately 40 million, according to an analysis performed by Kerber (1997). Therefore, Conger argues, although Mexican exports have grown at an average annual rate of 20 per cent, 80 per cent of the population "labours in the stagnant, domestic economy and takes home a smaller per capita income, in constant dollars, than it did in 1980."

Market liberalization entailed the indiscriminate entrance of products and ruthless foreign competition leading to the demise of parts of the manufacturing sector and a loss of jobs evident in an increasing rate of unemployment. However, the discrepancy between the rate of inflation in Mexico and that of its major trading partner, the U.S.A., as reflected in the balance of trade, foreshadowed the coming of a profound economic crisis that indeed took hold in 1994 and continued thereafter.

The moral, political and economic crises of the Mexican state that can be traced back to the sixties had climaxed in both 1982 and 1994, demonstrating that the economic structure and the role of the state needed urgent redefinition. As Macías[10] recognizes, Mexico is experiencing a crisis of values in its economic policy and in the daily exercise of public functions. Alliances of cooperation between citizens and special interest groups are hampered by conflicting values and asymmetric power vis-à-vis the state. This crisis is not only a result of over 50 years of presidential centralism and unipolar decision making which had led to a monopoly over power, it is also a product of fraudulent electoral practices. Corruption, that runs throughout the governmental hierarchy and penetrates the core, has also played a determinant role in the crisis.

The structural weaknesses and vulnerabilities of the Mexican economy became quite evident by 1995. Many of the policy measures that had been adopted to remedy the crisis caused the loss of "millions of jobs and sources of revenue." They further resulted in heavy social and political costs causing major distortions and ruining hopes for well-balanced development and growth. These problems seem to have occurred because of the higher priority given to dramatic economic reforms as opposed to significant political and social change.

Overall, the Mexican state's economic policy of the last few decades, as noted by Cordera and Orive (1995), has been characterized by an artificial system of production giving way to capitalistic forces and submitting to the vagaries of the owners of financial capital. In fact, foreign and national financial groups have been known to manipulate the mass media to maintain social control over the market economy.

Due to these changes, the post-revolutionary economic, political and social equilibrium has broken down and a new order needs to be established. Until now, the economic development model implemented in Mexico has resulted in a fiscal surplus and a social deficit. The neoliberal policies adopted in Mexico on the advice of the IMF and World Bank has not met with much success. As critics, like Banamex-Accival acknowledge: "the last three regimes have dismantled the promotional role of the state, sold out national resources, handed out a major share of sovereignty, and destroyed our mixed economy, including the social sector."

Submission to the exigencies of foreign capital meant a lack of attention to the increasing internal social deficit. Without an appropriate and comprehensive political maneuver to alter Mexico's future course, economic performance seems destined to decline. By the late 1990s even the Institutional Revolutionary Party recognized in its economic platform that no matter how essential economic consolidation may be, it cannot by itself cope with the social costs of development.[11]

However, not everyone has come out from the Mexican crisis a loser. An old Mexican saying states "a turbulent river means gains for fishermen." De la Torre (1996) argues that during the eighties, the economic, social and political changes in Mexico, gave rise to a new political elite who used neoliberal policies and pragmatic responses to opportunities offered during the crisis phase to enrich themselves. During the mid-eighties, argue Meyer (1996) and Centeno (1994), a new group of technocrats steadily established power at the pinnacle of the authoritarian pyramid up to the presidency. Their ultimate goal in doing so was the implementation of an elaborate project to reconstruct the economic system in record time. A recuperation of GNP would in turn reinforce the feasibility of the authoritarian system leading to maintenance of power by a small circle of technocrats huddled around the office of the president.

The unchecked presidential system, however, violated its own mandate.[12] Mexico has a strong presidential system due to its historical domination by all-powerful leaders since the pre-Colombian Aztec Tlatoani *emperors*. The elite that took over power following the Mexican Revolution utilized the Institutional Revolutionary Party to consolidate its economic powers and influence. And although the technocrats have reformulated several of the articles of the Constitution to incorporate a philosophy of social liberalism in order to maintain legality and legitimacy, the system is still not accepted by broad sectors of the Mexican population and as such is based on a very weak foundational support. Many Mexicans are pressing the technocrats to depart from the neoliberal economic program. This seems a difficult task while the main macroeconomic objectives include an anti-inflation program, currency stabilization, and a balanced budget for public spending.

Thus, there is a major discrepancy between governmental practice and neoliberal propositions, and more specifically between the authoritarian Mexican political system and the fundamental right espoused by neoliberals to a democratically elected government. According to Meyer changes in the role of the state in the economy dissolved the old capacity of political leadership and at the same time weakened the power of the electorate before an unopposed Institutional Revolutionary Party (PRI). The 1997 election, however, marked an end to PRI rule after 68 years. The presidential system has also been restricted through the democratic election of governors and legislators from the opposition. Meanwhile the plurality of interests has multiplied exponentially and there has been some government response.

The Mexican state is currently undergoing a transition. Some analysts contend that the contradictory effects of recent economic, political and social changes in Mexico are due to the North American Free Trade Agreement and that there should be re-negotiations in order to deal with problems of poverty, social polarization, and potential conflicts in the future. The road to economic development in Mexico, however, cannot be divorced from substantial power and wealth disparities, nor can it occur in isolation of addressing issues of governance and human rights.

There is a shared political perception that the Mexican state transition, as it has been characterized by Huntington as the "third wave," had started with the political reform at the middle of the 1970s and reinforced with the economic reform implemented after the crisis of 1982 and the presidential election of 1988. This Mexican state transition involves an economic and political process that has purposes to abandon an authoritarian regime by dismantling the basic pillars of its sustainability, presidentialism, a hegemonic political party, and society controlled by corporatism. So far, what can be concluded is that in Mexico such a state transition has been only a partial and pragmatic vision of what would have been the project of the nation and the role of the state in the economy during the last two administrations.

An analysis of recent events in state transitions can lead us to understand the trend toward rejection of the neoliberal design of public policies as with the Labour Party in England. Under such transitions, social justice is stressed in the design of public policies. As Blair argues "Social justice, the possibility to make all participate in a just society, is a complement of economic efficiency, not its enemy. We do not have to choose between a less divided society and a more productive society. We can and we must look for both ... no society can prosper economically and socially unless all its members prosper, unless we use the talents and energies of all the people instead of few, unless we live to the height of ambition to create a society in which the community lives for the well being of each individual and each individual works for the goodness of all." Semo concludes (1997), that in England the extreme neoliberal Malthusianism that conquered minds and votes is reaching the end. Not an abrupt end, but slowly and doubtfully, but in spite of all, an end.

Still there are some consequences of these events that in turn will affect future changes in democratic transitions not only in Latin America but also in Mexico. Until now, failure of the so-called neoliberal state and the technocrat class in Mexico has further weakened an already weak country. From another economic perspective, using the welfare state model to solve actual problems in the present situation is very similar to what it was during the depression in the US, in which obviously the government has to spend in order to generate wealth. The urgency of changes in formulation and implementation of economic and social policies is pressing the transitional process and creating confusion and conflict among the different actors and their interests involved, and therefore, generating transitional dilemmas.

Thus, one conclusion is that a transition of the scheme of economic, political and social relations between the Mexican state and the civil society is an imperative that demands immediate attention of the main actors involved. However, the transition must be managed and controlled by the state, which still has an important leadership role in conducting change, creating the necessary economic, social and political institutions, formulating and implementing public policies and strategies to achieve development, and closing the gap between efficiency on one hand and equality, human rights and social justice on the other. In this sense, the transition can trace the characteristics of a new model of state signaled by Nicos Poulantzas (1968): as the cohesive factor of divergent social classes, regulator of equilibrium among productive factors and as the condensation centre between the social and economic resources of the system and the increasing demands for employment, income and social welfare. [13]

The Mexican state has been designed at different periods of time and different circumstances under two different economic models, the so-called welfare state and the neoliberal state. The economic policies derived from the implementation of these two structural designs of the Mexican state have shown dysfunctionalities. Both models have generated social and economic inequalities, although the last one implemented, the neoliberal has deepened the differences and its failure is inherent to its own nature. It must be recognized that the principal limitation of today's social policy neither reside on the covering or efficiency of programs nor on the magnitude of expenses; its fundamental failure is associated with leaving the economy to generate inequalities until they crystallize and become difficult to remove.

A feasible transition to a new step of development and growth implies not only economic reform it also requires effective political reform directed towards construction of new patterns of public behaviour to sustain a frontal combat to traditional characteristics of the system: corruption, presidential arrogance (presidentialism), authoritarian heritage, centralization of decision making process, lack of social participation in public decisions and policies, intolerance, old schemes of social, political and economic relations based on corporatism, patronage, political bosses (caciques and caudillos), etc.

Therefore, any agreement on economic and political transition has its own risks. While the economic transition needs a long-range process of economic re-structuring, political transition is needed urgently. It seems that the actual transition of the Mexican state persists only on a transition agreed, as López (1996) maintains, "among traditional anti-state forces who not only look for the surviving of the actual political regime, but also, its reconstruction, that is, a transition without institutional rupture which guarantees the authoritarian heritage. In this sense, the neoliberal, anti-state ideology is the best instrument of domination by international economic interests.

The most relevant of the reforms must be directed at a deeper and profound level, to change moral, social, political and economic values and attitudes, in such a way that every citizen can be a dynamic and creative agent in the generation of a new scheme of social, political and economic set of relations, capable of making decisions and taking full responsibility and accountability for his/her own decisions. Only when the state is designed under this theory of pure and impure forms of government and the importance of human happiness will the transition be more legitimate. To paraphrase Aristotle: The perfect state is that in which each citizen, can look to the law to be virtuous and to secure citizens' happiness. This is the cornerstone of further political and economic transition toward the development and democratization of social organizations, with independent criteria and performance from the ideological and administrative apparatus of the Mexican state.

In the final analysis, a transition to a more feasible model of the Mexican state must establish a break-even point between its regulatory action and efficiency in the formulation and implementation of policies that respond to the challenges of market dynamics, social participation and political stability. That is, the role of the emerging Mexican state must be to balance market dysfuntionalities by implementing social policies through its social function. The Mexican state must give priority to formulation and implementation of social policy to attend its social demands if it wants to recover democratic legitimacy.

In fact, recent developments have considered the relevance of social policy to the state. Rodrik (1997) for example, argues that any state that makes substantial advancements in external market liberalization, such as the case of Mexico, has more possibilities of social instability. Rodrik is alluding to the main obstacles that any state has and will have in the future to achieve a proper socialization of risks and costs, in such a way that helps the less privileged social groups confront the increasing integration of the economic environment.

The economic, political and social crises of the Mexican state can only be overcome through the democratic legitimization of its public policies, and achieved by social participation in its institutions of government and public management. This proposition coincides with what Mangabeira and others have advocated as a "democratized market economy." Thus, the re-dimension of the Mexican state must take into consideration the demands of a society that has undergone rapid transformations, where changing values and identity need to be adapted to recent developments in global economic restructuring. The strategies for re-defining the Mexican state must be directed toward optimization of economic development's impact and to strengthening of social character, in such a way that preserves national historical character and values.

However, at this point, the state must exercise more efficient capabilities to carry on economic policies with wide faculties of regulation escorted by social policies directed toward reducing inequalities, and the costs of development externalities. Sustainable and equitable development is two main challenges of the Mexican state. The challenges still remain, and any reforms that avoid these facts are condemned to deafening failure.

NOTES

1 Conger (1997) p. 27.
2 Ibid.
3 Tello (1997) p. 12.
4 Kuttner (1997) p. 21.
5 Almeyra (1997b).
6 Kuttner.
7 Almeyra (1997 a, b).
8 Banamex-Accival (1997) p. 8.
9 Ibid.
10 Macías (1997) p. 79.
11 Banamex-Accival.
12 Meyer (1996) p. 213.
13 Poluntzas (1968) p. 114.

REFERENCES

Almeyra, Guillermo. 1997a. "Francia: Cohabitación entre quienes?" *La Jornada*, viernes 30 de abril, p. 16.

Almeyra, Guillermo. 1997b. "Un mundo con hipo." *La Jornada*, domingo 8 de junio, p. 14.

Banamex-Accival. 1997. "Elections and the Platforms of Major Political Parties." *Review of the Economic Situation of Mexico*, LXXIII, no. 858 (May), p. 8.

Centeno, M. A. 1994. *Democracy Within Reason: Technocratic Revolution in México*. University Park, Penn: Pennsylvania State University Press.

Conger, L. 1997. "Tilting at Neoliberalism." *Institutional Investor* (May), p. 27.

Cordera, R., and A. Orive. 1995. "Artículos." *Revista Nexos* (Septiembre), p. 22.

De la Torre, R. 1996. "Más allá de la crítica al neoliberalismo." *Economía Informa*, 248 (junio), p. 14.

Easton, D. 1965. *A System Analysis of Political Life*. New York: J. Willey and Sons.

Forrester, V. 1997. *L'horreur économique*. Paris: Fayard.

Kerber, V. 1997. "Dulce TLC, no nos desampares." *La Jornada* (19 de julio), p. 23.

Labastida, H. 1997. "La lección del debate." *La Jornada* (viernes 30 de mayo.)

Lewis, S. 1997. "Mexico: Emerging from Crisis." *Market: Latin America*, 5, no. 7 (July), p. 34.

López, L. 1996. "Qué trasición política para México." *Memoria*, no. 94 (diciembre), p. 25.

Macías Cardone, L. 1977. "Democracia.legitimidad constitucional y gobernabilidad." *Quorum 2a época*, VI, no. 52, p. 79.

Meyer, L. 1996. "Estado, soberanía y nacionalismo." In *Los compromisos con la Nación*. México: Plaza & Janés.

Moctezuma Barragán, E. 1997. "El Estado democrático frente al próximo siglo." *Examen*, 92, no. 8 (Junio), p. 52.

Poulantzas, Nicos. 1968. Pouvoir Politique et Classes Sociales de L'état Capitaliste. París: F. Maspereo.

Rodrik, D. 1997. *Has Globalization Gone too Far?* Washington: Institute for International Economics.

Sáenz, J. 1997. "El subdesempeño económico de México." *Este País*, no. 74 (Mayo), p. 31.

Semo, E. 1997. "Tony Blair y la reinvención de la izquierda europea." *Proceso*, no. 1073, 25 de mayo, p. 25.

Tello, N. 1997. "El modelo prueba modelo." *Visión*, 16 al 30 de abril, p. 12.

PART III ALTERNATIVES (AND THE NEED FOR THEM)

Chapter 10

DEMOCRACY, COMPLEXITY AND NON-TERRITORIAL PUBLICS: THE CASE FOR FOREST TRUSTS

Gus diZerega
Whitman College, Walla Walla, WA

NEW CHALLENGES TO PUBLIC SPACE

Globalization has increased the force of market pressures on governments. Greater economic integration and expanded definitions of restraint of trade both threaten protection of public values. Money speaks especially loudly today, as politicians explicitly sell "access" to their time and attention. Growing market impersonality squeezes all values but the bottom line from economic decisions.

Traditional political institutions seem ill adapted to this new environment, with public values the loser. Democratic theory arose when polities were far simpler and public tasks few and fairly straightforward. It sheds little light on the many layered interpenetrating publics of the contemporary world. This chapter explores alternative democratic possibilities through examining governance of publicly owned forests.

Contemporary liberal democracies are unimaginably complex. No participant knows more than the smallest part of relevant knowledge in public policy. The classical ideal of the well informed citizen is simply beyond human power to achieve. It is even beyond the power of political professionals who have devoted their lives to public affairs.

In complex liberal polities, relationships between political actors resemble networks more than hierarchies. Boundaries between public and private spheres are exceptionally porous and ill defined. Hugh Heclo observed, "As more and more puzzling, unfamiliar policy issues have been thrust on government, more and more fluid groups have unexpectedly mobilized ... [diffusing] the focus of political and administrative leadership." He adds, "any neat distinction between the governmental structure and its environment tends to break down...."[1]

S. McBride et al. (eds.), Global Instability, 163–180.

Liberal democracies are not coterminous with formal government institutions, for they include as essential elements parties, the media, and interest groups. Their boundaries encompass society as a whole, although only some issues at any time will be public. Like an old growth forest, a modern liberal democracy can only be thoroughly understood by grasping the extraordinarily dense networks of relationships that both constrain and invigourate it.

In complex democracies, citizens do not belong to just a single public. They belong to many. By "publics" I mean groups of citizens concerned with deciding the governing values and decisions that should prevail over their common life and concerns. Some publics are geographically based, such as provincial, state, and city governments. Federalism, as in relations between state or provincial and general governments, offers a way to enable these publics to co-exist.

However, not all publics are geographically based. Some are defined by issues that are truly public but not important to many citizens intermingled with those for whom they are quite important. The polity as a whole is so complex that these public concerns can lack adequate expression because, among citizens as a whole they receive little attention. Nor can these publics be adequately represented by geographically elected representatives; who will be concerned mostly with district interests.

The United States' 147 National Forests are such a public value, as are Canada's crown lands. They are sites of serious contention among citizens concerned with their well-being, but motivated by conflicting priorities and values. Yet these concerned citizens are immersed within a larger sea of citizens for whom these values are of relatively little moment. As a consequence, most elected representatives also find the well-being of forests of relatively little importance. These publics have often been unable to protect public values against the assault of organized private and bureaucratic interests.

WEAKNESSES IN TRADITIONAL POLITICAL MANAGEMENT

American forest policy was originally considered a technical rather than political issue. The U.S. Forest Service was to manage resources in accordance with the best scientific knowledge possessed by professional foresters. Gifford Pinchot sought to institutionalize this ideal while serving as the first Chief of the Forest Service. He even helped develop academic forestry programs to supply reliably trained foresters.

Pinchot's ideal had three problems. First, it ignored the political context for creating a centralized professional organization within an open and complex democratic system. Second, it assumed a large professional organization would remain true to its founding ideal. Third, it assumed that basic decisions over forest policy were appropriately determined by scientific expertise. All three assumptions proved mistaken.

The Congressional Connection

The Forest Service exists under the ultimate authority and oversight of Congress. The Founders' initial ideal for Congress resembled a relatively enlightened town meeting, where representatives chosen by the people, or (for the Senate) their legislatures, would meet to discuss and decide the affairs of the new nation. Hopefully, Madison wrote in Federalist 10, Congress would "refine and enlarge the public views." Congress was designed to deliberate, and widen the perspectives to which legislative proposals would be subjected.

Like all institutions, practice often fell short of the ideal. Nonetheless, for a long time there was at least the opportunity for Congressional deliberation, and a careful consideration of the details of proposed legislation. Today it would appear that Congress's deliberative function has to a significant degree broken down, partly due to the overwhelming quantity of information requiring a Congressperson's attention. The combination of legislative responsibilities, oversight, fund raising, and constituency service has reached such proportions that, even in 1978, average members of Congress had about 11 minutes a day to read about public issues and 12 minutes for writing speeches and proposed legislation.[2] Conditions have not improved.

Congressional staffs have expanded to lighten legislative loads. But reliance upon large staffs breeds its own problems, as elected representatives become increasingly dependent on others for decision-making, and even for crafting legislation. Today no member of Congress reads most of the legislation on which he or she votes. They rely on the advice of other members, staff and trusted lobbyists. They have no choice. In the process they do not deliberate much.

Omnibus legislation increasingly combines a hodge-podge of measures into a single "bill." "Riders" which could rarely be passed into law on their own merits, are often attached to unrelated measures of great public importance. Poor legislation takes good bills and programs hostage. This practice is scarcely new, but apparently its scale is increasing. No likely reform in committee structure or staffing is likely to change this situation. The responsibilities confronting representatives are too vast for much deliberation, even if they did not spend as much as 40 per cent of their time raising funds.

Nor is oversight much better. With respect to the National Forests, committee oversight has proven neither consistent nor particularly in harmony with the legislation's original purposes. While Congress has repeatedly proven capable of legislating to enhance public values, it has proven far less adept at implementing the legislation it passed. Frequently such laws are hijacked to serve very different purposes.[3]

In the case of the Forest Service, oversight committees frequently intervened in Service decisions, strengthening the hand of extractive interests while undermining the Service's ability to make its own decisions. Congress may have known little about forests and cared less, but members knew a great deal about winning elections. Congress frequently over-ruled Service decisions, mandating harvest levels based on what their political allies wanted, not what foresters considered desirable for the forests. Congress responded to demands by the National Lumber Manufacturers Association to limit Forest Service road building only to roads that could be used by loggers to take out trees.[4] Congress also successfully pressured the Service for ever-higher rates of logging, even while cutting funds for reforestation in the name of "economy."[5]

The reasons for these problems lie far deeper than inadequate time. Pressures for Congress to enhance public values tends to be episodic, with popular attention dissipating when the sought-for legislation is passed. However, efforts by private interests seeking to turn these policies towards their own advantage are unrelenting. Nor is oversight by many elected representatives generally in keeping with the laws they pass. Congressional action often undercuts efforts by the Service to rely on its understanding of silviculture alone to manage forests.

More Problems

The rise of highly organized environmental groups has broken the older alliances of the Forest Service with extractive industries and local economic elites. The "Lords of Yesterday" have been decisively weakened.[6] However, the rise of national environmental organizations appealing only to a portion of the community of citizens concerned with the well-being of a forest creates its own problems.

First, national organizations analyze policies through the filter of maintaining a national membership and focusing on power at the national level. Organizational health is maintained by promoting a sense of crisis and threat, whether soundly based or not. These tactics are used by environmental organizations and their opponents alike.

Second, emphasizing crises makes it more difficult to find common ground among citizens concerned with the fate of the forest. The kinds of agreements that environmentalists, loggers, and other local forest users found through the Quincy Library Group are threatening to the hard won influence of the Sierra Club and similar organizations. National environmental groups complained that the Quincy policy was made by local groups with the larger community of concerned citizens mostly excluded. They had a point. But their own national forum is, if anything, even less able to address forest well-being and competing public values.

The Forest Service and Institutional Sclerosis

The U.S. Forest Service was hardly a passive victim of Congressional meddling. It actively manipulated Congressional committees, seeking to strengthen its own budgetary security and political well-being. In the process, the Service elevated logging from being one of many "multiple uses" into the primary use of the national forests, even at a time when recreational pressures were steadily increasing.[7]

The Forest Service has served a relatively narrow definition of its responsibilities for so long that internal reforms have been powerfully impeded by its own often intractable institutional culture. This culture was deliberately designed to insulate the Service from its environment. Herbert Kaufman's admiring 1978 study, *The Forest Ranger,* describes an institution that deliberately reduced diversity and creativity within its ranks, ensuring homogeneous and predictable actions by all employees. Professional foresters made up about 90 per cent of the professional men administering the national forests. Other professions, such as biologists, had few opportunities to advance in the Service.

Frequent lateral transfers further strengthened homogeneity in professional outlook. Service people formed few close contacts with people outside the organization, creating "company men" whose loyalty was to the institution, not its mandated responsibilities. Extensive in-service "indoctrination" and the elaboration of the *Forest Service Manual* further contributed to an insular Forest Service approach to forest policy.

In 1978 Kaufman found these agency personnel practices to be evidence of good management. Nevertheless, he noted, "A new generation of foresters is appearing some of whom admit that Gifford Pinchot would probably not get very far if he entered the Service today; he would be too upsetting to the established order."[8]

The Service's has consistently treated forests as resources where timber extraction was the primary value. The Knutson-Vandenberg Act of

1930 further institutionalized an agency bias towards timber cutting because the Service got to keep funds from such uses, but all other income returned to the Treasury. When the Service did balk at approving harvests from politically connected industries, Congress intervened. Professional hesitation within the Service itself, such as it was, was overridden by political pressures.[9] In such an environment the Service gravitated to a myopic vision of "getting out the cut" as its mission and criterion of success.

Science and Politics

Pinchot's initial motivating ideal was a vision of scientific forestry. He had learned this approach studying forestry in Europe, being particularly impressed with Prussian practices.[10] Adopting German science would, he argued, make the efficient use of our resources possible.

There were serious problems with this ideal. The first was conceptual: efficiency as often defined in science is in energy use, which is different from economic efficiency (serving more desired ends before less desired while leaving a maximum of resources left over for serving less strongly felt needs). Scientific knowledge has little to say as to what is or is not economically efficient, and vice versa. But the problem goes deeper.

In living systems the goal of efficiency is misleading. Steven Jay Gould observed:

> the watchwords for creativity are sloppiness, poor fit, quirky design, and above all else, redundancy.... Bacteria are marvels of efficiency, simple cells of consummate workmanship, with internal programs, purged of junk and slop, containing single copies of essential genes. But bacteria have been bacteria since life first left a fossil record 3.5 billion years ago – and so shall they probably be until the sun explodes.

If evolution operated primarily on the basis of efficiency, Gould concluded it "would generate no structural complexity, and bacteria would rule the world."[11]

When the standard economic or scientific efficiency is applied to managing natural processes, error is inevitable. The scientific community can discover error because multiple centres of innovation exist to challenge reigning orthodoxies.[12] But hierarchical organizations such as the Forest Service, no matter how strong their commitment to science, are resistant to challenges to their way of acting.

External standards of evaluation run the risk of ignoring the needs of complex and incompletely understood ecosystems. By institutionalizing a vision of scientific management that, in retrospect, was bad for German forests as well as ours, Pinchot actually disconnected the Service from real science.[13] As a consequence, the Forest Service had great difficulty integrating scientific advances in practicing sustainable forestry.

Nancy Langston describes the Forest Service's *The Blue Mountains Forest Health Report* (1991), which acknowledged the necessity of insects, disease, and fire as integral to a forest ecosystem. But she notes that its next chapter reads as if the first did not exist, recommending extermination of insect pests and even age stands of intensively managed trees.[14] Regardless of what science may say, the simple agency goal of timber production also served its vision of "economic efficiency."

Economic efficiency is best measured when we have a clear end and competing means for achieving it. Efficient use employs the means leaving the most resources left over for attaining other, less valued, ends. But many citizens have quite conflicting desires regarding forests. No clear hierarchy exists to order decisions. The gospel of efficiency cannot help choose between competing often mutually exclusive ends held by different people. It only provides guidance within a single hierarchy of goals.

Canadian Forests

Canada's political system features a Westminster style parliament that would seem at first glance to be superior to the American system with respect to managing public forestlands. Stronger parties, relatively weaker interest groups, and easier accountability at election time would seem to offer better protection of complex values than does the American example. The evidence does not support this optimistic judgment.

Most public land in Canada is controlled by the provinces. Historically the provinces have used this land to attract investment from extractive industries. The Canadian public has broadened its interests in the kinds of values to be served by forestlands but the provinces have been unresponsive. By 1991 79 per cent of the Canadian public opposed clear-cutting as ecologically unsound and 86 per cent supported preserving old growth forests.[15] Nevertheless, forest policy has not come close to reflecting public values. Nor does it appear that it reflects scientific values either. In a 1990 survey of 4,500 Canadian foresters conducted by the federal government, more than 60 per cent believed that the allowable annual cut in their province was too high. Over 75 per cent believed that "there is a growing scarcity of timber in Canada today."[16]

Leases of forestland to logging companies are even more permissive than is the case in the U.S. In British Columbia, for example, only as late as 1992-3 did Ministry of Forest revenues actually exceed its costs.[17] The supposedly less responsible American system has actually been more protective of forestland than the Canadian.

Neither parliamentary nor presidential systems have proven responsive to public values or able to adequately oversee the protection of public forests. Scientific bureaucracies have not proven capable of effectively serving as protectors of public forests, and have been unable to address the complexity of values such forests serve. Clearly, traditional public institutions have failed to accomplish their responsibilities. This dismal result has led some to recommend abandoning public institutions and values, in favour of using the market as a guide to action.

WEAKNESSES OF MARKETIZATION

Some argue that market incentives can outperform government management. This argument denies that a major difference separates public from private values. For example, Randal O'Toole suggests requiring the Service to raise most of its funds through the sale of forest assets, such as timber and recreation. Congress would cease appropriating funds, a major cause of distorted decision making on the Service's part. Only a very few functions would need to receive political appropriations: threatened and endangered species protection, watershed protection, and research. These, O'Toole suggests, would be best handed over to Fish and Wildlife Service, Soils Conservation Service, and the National Science Foundation, respectively.[18]

Decentralizing forest management, creating Wilderness Trusts, receiving authority over subsurface resources, mitigating the immediate economic disruptions stemming from the end of logging subsidies, and changes in state water laws are other elements of O'Toole's proposal. Many of these proposals are in harmony with the forest trust model described below. However, two problems are inherent in O'Toole's proposal.

First, marketization is not a reliable means for evaluating public values. In *The Economy of the Earth,* Mark Sagoff describes Disney Corporation's proposal for developing the Mineral King Valley in California's Sierra Nevada into a destination resort. In his classes Sagoff had asked how many students had ever visited the valley. Almost no one had. He then asked how many would visit if it were developed into a destination resort. A great many indicated they would like to go. Finally, he asked how many favoured the Disney proposal over leaving the valley in its current undeveloped condition.

The response was nearly unanimous. The students believed that the Disney plan was loathsome and despicable, that the Forest Service had violated a public trust by approving it, and that the values for which we stand as a nation compel us to preserve the little wilderness we have for its own sake and as a heritage for future generations. In spite of their consumer preferences, the students opposed the Disney plan to develop Mineral King.[19]

Economists argue that words are cheap, students lie, and demonstrated preferences are the preferences that count. This is an attempt to deny what each of us can tell from daily experience, that choices are always shaped by contexts.[20] When we choose in the context of consuming we do not always reflect the values we most value as ideals or in other contexts. Students would have voted to bar the resort; once built, they would have used it.

O'Toole's proposal has a second important weakness. While removing Congress from the appropriations process eliminates one source of poor management, both forests and the Forest Service would still remain vulnerable to frequent short sighted political intervention. A major task of elected representatives is servicing the private interests of numerous or politically well placed constituents. It is difficult to imagine that Congress would demonstrate the self-control needed to leave the forests alone.

On occasion Congress can enact genuine reforms, for example, by reducing the distorting impact of tax rules devised to help myriads of special interests. But once those reforms have been put in place, Congress begins undermining them. Impetus for reform is episodic. Temptations to manipulate earlier reforms to favour well connected interests discomfited by them, or simply desiring "small changes" to benefit themselves, is perpetual.

Over time, and probably not very much time, new means of servicing the politically privileged would enter through riders attached to other bills and obscure legislative amendments. O'Toole's marketized forest and the Service responsible for their maintenance lack an organized constituency with a strong incentive to minimize Congressional meddling. Public values without a powerful public are helpless in the face of political and corporate attack.

REQUIREMENTS FOR SUSTAINABLE DEMOCRATIC FORESTS

National forestlands are genuine public values. Privatization and marketization cannot adequately serve such values. But contemporary democratic practices tend to promote divisiveness. What is needed are public institutions open to all, but able to select citizens genuinely concerned with that particular public good, therefore combining the strengths of local collaborative approaches with recognition that forests are properly national.

Our analysis gives us some general guidelines for an appropriate institutional framework for creating sustainable forest practices. There are three:

First, such an institution must have long time horizons. Compared to the needs of maintaining viable forest practices, the electoral cycle, the market's rate of interest, and the politics of the budget are very short term in their outlook. These factors are central to our social and political environment. But if they are also the major institutional influences on environmental decision making, we can be sure many short-sighted decisions will be made, with bad consequences for the forests themselves.

Second, such an institution must be able to learn and adapt. It must be constrained by its environment, its internal composition, or ideally by both, to be open to new information and knowledge, and able to make use of such knowledge. It must be free from the institutional petrification that makes many large organizations increasingly rigid and non-adaptive as time goes on, particularly when their environment is perceived as stable.

Third, it must be public. The public sphere is uniquely suited for recognizing and protecting non-market values. It is the public sphere that must determine how far market values should prevail in society, and when they should be limited by other considerations.

The institutional embodiment of these requirements is the democratic national forest trust. Trusts are a time honoured means by which a person or institution is charged with protecting and managing the property of another. They are widely used in many areas of private life, and are becomingly increasingly important in private conservation efforts. Trusts have also been used by many Western American states to manage their forests primarily for the benefit of schools. In this latter capacity, over 135 million acres are under trust management. These trusts, however, serve financial rather than broader public values. While certain features I describe later insulate them from the worst abuses afflicting National Forests, their financial orientation makes them inadequate models for preserving our National Forests.[21]

Land stewardship trusts, the form closest to that proposed here, remove land from the real estate market, enabling it to be "stewarded" on behalf of future generations.[22] Land trusts are traditionally non-governmental, non-profit, and often charitable organizations created to preserve the ecological, historical, agricultural, or wilderness value of the land. Land stewardship trusts focus on preserving and fostering sustainable forestry and agricultural practices, wildlife habitat, and recreation.

Because the land is removed from the market "in perpetuity" or for an extended period, it cannot be used as collateral for obtaining loans. Operating funds must come from sources such as fees, membership dues, and the like. A firewall is erected between the land and the market. This constraint has not prevented land trusts from becoming very important actors in the field of land preservation.[23]

The world's oldest land trust is the National Trust of England, Wales, and Northern Ireland, which celebrated its centenary in 1995. As of 1996 the National Trust's properties extended to over 1000 square miles in the U.K., including 550 miles of coastline, nearly 18 per cent of the total coastline of England, Wales, and Northern Ireland. Most other trusts in the U.K. and elsewhere are under 25 years old, raising the question of their own sustainability. However, the record of the National Trust, including its consistent acquisition of new land, is evidence not only of the concept's popularity, it also attests to its long term viability. After the Crown, the National Trust is now the largest landowner in the U.K. Its membership is over 2.2 million, and it is quite popular.

Some private land trusts are philanthropically controlled. In their case democracy is not a possibility. Others are democratically run; members simply join and thereby obtaining voting rights. In the U.K. about one-third of independent conservation amenity and recreation trusts elect their trustees or council of management through democratic means.

The National Trust has a Council consisting of 52 members, 26 elected by its membership, another 26 appointed by outside bodies. Direct management of the National Trust is through an Executive Committee, under which are a number of decentralized Regional Committees. Far from being devoid of political debate, the National Trust is frequently the site of vigourous campaigns by members seeking changes in policies regarding hunting issues, recreational use, and the like.[24]

Land stewardship trusts are increasingly relied upon in the U.S. and Canada as well. Trusts represent a time-tested and effective means by which conflicting demands and values can be managed within the context of a strong legal commitment to perpetual sustainability. Even the largest and oldest has apparently been free from the serious problems of mismanagement that afflict the Forest Service.

The Case for National Forest Trusts

National Forest Trusts could be established with primary responsibility for governing American and Canadian national forestland. In the U.S. case one trust could be established for each forest. Boundaries would have to be established for provincial lands. Membership in each Forest Trust would be open to anyone, requiring only that members pay a fee covering membership expenses in order to join. Judging from the dues of modern mass membership organizations, such expenses would not be high. The hurdle of having to pay a small dues for each Trust would, however, ensure that only people genuinely interested in the forest and its fate would usually take the time to join.[25] Perhaps, as Karl Hess has suggested to me, work trade arrangements could be made for people lacking means to pay even these modest fees.

Much experience in resource management suggests that self-governing bodies cannot be successfully imposed from above. Attempts to copy a formula that worked in one situation often fail when applied to different physical and social circumstances in another. Apparently the very act of organizing a self-governing body helps to create the social capital and infusion of local knowledge that enables an organization to survive.[26]

Enabling legislation should make it possible for Forest Trusts to be formed if there is significant interest in doing so, and to guarantee their democratic character. Open procedures and membership, and a means for ensuring a diversity of member perspectives would be required, but little more. Details of organization would be up to the Forest Trust and its governing Board of Directors.

Such a Trust could be established once a sufficient number of prospective members have created an organization meeting these requirements. To prevent one interest grabbing control of a board from the beginning, membership opportunities would need to be widely publicized, after which election to the first Forest Trust Board of Directors or similar body would take place. The Board would take over policy management after some period providing sufficient time for extensive consultation with the Forest Service during the transition.

The number of citizens required to create a Forest Trust should vary because of the widely different circumstances in which the various National Forests exist. Probably some formula reflecting both the number of annual visitors and the immediate population in the region would be best. Clearly different numbers should apply to Humboldt National Forest in eastern Nevada and Umatilla National Forest in SE Washington and NE Oregon, compared to Roosevelt National Forest close to Denver and Wenatchee National Forest near Seattle. In all cases numbers should be high enough to require real organizing effort but low enough that such efforts will have a reasonable chance of success.

Given that there are 2.2 million members in the National Trust of England, Wales and Northern Ireland, the potential for a large American or Canadian membership is high. Each forest trust would probably have thousands of members, some many times that. Some would be residents living close to the forest, some would be involved in extractive industries using forest resources, some would be people making recreational use of the forest, and some would be people concerned with its well-being, even if they had never been there.

To ensure a significant level of citizen knowledge and commitment, and make more difficult a hypothetical "packing" of voter roles by organized interests of any sort, there should be a limitation on the number of forest trusts a citizen could join. Whatever the number, it needs to strike a balance between two values: promoting a reasonably large and diverse constituency for each forest *and* promoting significant citizens knowledge about the issues facing each forest over which he or she shall help determine policy.

Proportional representation would give the wide variety of legitimate interests representation ensuring informed oversight. Elected directors would be under intense pressure to serve all or most interests that have legitimate claims upon the forests. Little opportunity would exist to hide important information from the membership, both because so many different perspectives would serve on the Board, and because of the legal requirement for openness applied to trust governance.

Several possibilities for Board structure exist, and the one selected should be the choice of those joining the Trust. One might be entirely democratically elected, another might have a mix of elected and appointed members, such as from local university Departments of Forestry. However, less than fully elected Boards should ultimately be subject to periodic membership approval.

The Board would decide basic policy and subcontract with service agencies for their implementation. Initially, in the U.S., the Forest Service would be the subcontractor to the Board, charged with implementing its policies. In Canada, provincial agencies could perform the same function. However, to ensure agency responsiveness, the Board must have the option of contracting with other agencies, such as state departments of forestry, if they are dissatisfied with performance.

There is ample precedent for this alternative. Many small U.S. cities contract out police and fire protection to other cities' departments. The arrangement saves them money while the availability of alternatives helps ensure attentive service. The option of such a choice would keep the Forest Service responsive to the Board's priorities, perhaps freeing the Board from ever needing to subcontract with another agency. Absent such an option the Forest Service or equivalent organizations would be under no pressure to be responsive to Trust management.

Forest policy and management would be the trust's responsibility, including raising enough money to meet its costs. User fees of many kinds would likely be major income sources. In trusts with large memberships, volunteers often provide considerable resources as well, as they do now for the Nature Conservancy and similar organizations. Private and foundation donations and grants may also prove important sources of support.

Lack of access to tax monies eliminates any incentive to subsidize extractive industries or other private interests, as is unfortunately currently the case. Nor could Congress or Parliament use financial threats to interfere with forest policies. The forest would become protected from political intervention by parties unconcerned with its long-term well-being.

Court cases involving American state legislature's attempts to overrule state trusts are suggestive. The Washington state legislature passed a bill to absolve timber companies from a contract they signed with state forests obligating them to pay what, in retrospect, was an overly high price per thousand board feet. Skamania County and other beneficiaries of trust funds sued to over turn the legislative bailout. The State Supreme Court supported the plaintiffs on several grounds, one being the trustee's duty of "undivided loyalty." The trust was obligated to serve the interests of its beneficiaries over any other set of interests, private or public. The court wrote "To our knowledge, every case that has considered similar issues has held that the state as trustee may not use trust assets to pursue other state goals."[27]

Trust status would be further buttressed by there being thousands, perhaps millions, of citizen members who would oppose legislative overruling of trust self-governance. Member support would address one of the weaknesses in O'Toole's approach by creating a sizeable organized constituency that would strongly oppose outside political intervention in their affairs. Both these forms of protection are largely absent in the public forests today.

While having to meet its overhead expenses, the forest would be under no institutional pressure to make a significant profit. Decisions would remain influenced by economic opportunities and constraints, but because members' votes are apportioned democratically, economic values become only one among many influences, rather than the guiding principle in deciding policy, as with privatization or marketization.

This kind of forest trust will represent a true public interest. It is open to all citizens concerned with a public forest's well-being. Such a trust employs modern society's capacity for enabling even widely dispersed people with common interests to organize effectively for their own purposes. It is difficult to imagine representatives and management becoming divorced from their public constituency under such circumstances, because some individuals and organizations will always monitor policy and implementation. People using the forest can observe for themselves the impact of managerial decisions. Renewal of directors through public debate and elections, where contrasting visions compete for the allegiance of voters deeply concerned with the forest's fate, would inhibit the rise of self-serving elites and in-grown administrations.

DEMOCRACY AND SUSTAINABILITY

The land trust concept offers a basic institutional framework for managing forests, one harmonious with the systemic realities of political democracy. It offers an expansion of political democracy into areas where geographically defined conceptions of the public do not work. It provides a framework within which the competing values of different groups of citizens concerned with the fate of the forest can be effectively heard. Forest Trusts are also likely to be largely free from the two worst problems facing public management of forestlands today: intervention by representative bodies not particularly concerned with forest viability and institutional sclerosis within public bureaucracies.

The concept of the National Forest Trust developed in this chapter addresses the three basic requirements I listed for devising sustainable national forest institutions in the modern world. It creates organizations with institutional time horizons far in excess of either the market or traditional elected officials and bureaucracies in the public sphere. It creates a decentralized framework encouraging responsiveness, innovation, and organizational learning. Finally, in the context of forest policy, it solves a serious problem confronting complex liberal democracies: serving public interests when the relevant publics are not primarily geographically situated. For all except the most parasitic of groups, which take much and give little, it offers a potentially win-win framework for political action.

Time Horizons

The Forest Trust model resembles in crucial ways institutions that have an impressive record in looking to the long run. In Japan and Switzerland, where the relative absence of foreign invasion has made it possible for traditional institutional forms to survive for centuries, local cooperatives have managed to maintain community forest and grazing land for as long as 800 years. This is longer than it takes to establish an old growth forest.[28]

In these traditional village institutions the long-term perspective probably reflects both tradition and family loyalty across generations. Moderns do not share these values so strongly. However, alternative sources for similar commitments exist, and Forest Trusts can rely on them. Self-selection where individual economic pay off is usually far smaller than the personal time and money invested helps to keep the money realm a guide, and not a boss. There is little temptation to take a short run perspective. Under these circumstances we can reasonably expect many of the advantages of traditional forms of co-operative ownership to continue in a modern framework.

Learning and Adaptation

Because there would be many trusts, each with responsibility for only one forest, membership in each would be focused in its interests. Requirements for informed voter knowledge would be reasonable. Local knowledge would be as accessible as more general and abstract principles of forestry and ecosystem stewardship when determining policy options and value choices.

Inevitable errors in policy will usually be confined to a single area or forest. Over time, equally localized initial successes will often be copied or adapted elsewhere. This decentralization will also encourage the exposure and correction of errors and dissemination of successes as they are discovered.

Only in genuine crises would national intervention likely be tolerated. And in such crises (if they occur) the government probably should intervene. With respect to forest policy, the public good would almost certainly be far more consistently served than is the case today.

The democratic Forest Trust encourages an information rich environment, where the democratic process and laws requiring openness in the governance of trusts, combine to create a rich mix of insights and facts regarding actual and proposed policies.[29] These incentives are the opposite of those existing within hierarchical bureaucracies, where information is a resource and tool of power, most useful when it is controlled.

Such an institutional arrangement maximizes the advantages of having a multiplicity of decision-making centres, while using this same characteristic to minimize the impact of poorly chosen policies. It facilitates learning and adaptation. It is in harmony with the scientific community and the diversity of public perspectives.

Forest Trusts free protection of some public values from traditional political forms rendered less competent through globalization, market values, and complexity. They demonstrate that political democracy need not be confined solely to geographical boundaries when such boundaries undermine the vitality and value of the democratic process. As such, they broaden the horizon of democratic possibilities and create new spheres of active and responsible citizenship. They seek to make the fluidity and openness of democratic political boundaries sources of strength rather than weakness. Forest Trusts also suggest the political implications of the liberal democratic transformation of politics may have only just begun to be explored.

NOTES

1 Heclo (1978) pp. 94-5, 104.
2 Ibid., pp. 87-124
3 McConnell (1966); also Reisner, op. cit., p. 408.
4 Hirt (1994) pp. 78-9.
5 Ibid., p. 94-7.
6 See Wilkinson (1992) pp. 3-27.
7 Clary (1986) p. 196.
8 Kaufman (1978) p. 235n.
9 Hirt (1994); O'Toole (1988).
10 Hirt, p 31.
11 Gould (1990) pp. 15, 18.
12 Hull (1988); Polanyi (1969).
13 Maser (1988) pp. 80-82.
14 Langston (1995) pp. 297-8; see also Maser, p. 84.
15 May (1998) p. 11.
16 Ibid., p. 37
17 Ibid., p. 55.
18 O'Toole, p. 214.
19 Sagoff (1988) pp. 50-1.
20 Extensive discussion of the role of context in choice can be found in Rhoads (1985) pp. 143-78.
21 Souder and Fairfax (1995) pp. 44-53.
22 I take this term from Banighen (1990) pp. 4-6; see also Banighen (1997).
23 Among the organizations in the U.S. and Canada applying trust strategies to protecting natural land, see Forest Trust, P.O. Box 519, Santa fe, NM, U.S.A., 87504; Ecotrust, 1200 NW Front Ave., Portland, OR, U.S.A., 97209; Pacific Forest Trust, P. O. Box 879, Boonville, CA, U.S.A., 95419; and Turtle Island Earth Stewards, Box 3308, Salmon Arm, BC, Canada, V1E 4S1.
24 Dwyer and Hodge (1996) p. 84.
25 A price may not need to be very high to winnow out those who are not really concerned. One group of California Medicaid recipients was asked to pay one dollar for each of their first two visits to a doctor's office each month. Another group received these services free. Those paying a maximum of $2 per month reduced office visits by eight per cent, see Rhoads, p. 29.
26 For a number of studies illustrating this point in other resource areas, see Blomquist (n.d.); Ostrom (1990).
27 Souder and Fairfax, pp. 38, 46-7.
28 McKean (1992); Ostrom, pp. 58-69, 88-102.
29 I am grateful to Walter Hardwick for the felicitous term "information rich environment."

REFERENCES

Banighen, Tyhson. 1990. "Intentional Communities and Land Stewardship Trusts." *The Trumpeter: Journal of Ecosophy* (winter).

Banighen, Tyhson. 1997. "An Ecoforestry Land Stewardship Trust Model." In Alan Drengson and Duncan Taylor, eds., *Ecoforestry: The Art and Science of Sustainable Forest Use*. Gabriola Island, BC, Canada: New Society.

Blomquist, William. n.d. *Dividing the Waters: Governing the Groundwater in Southern California*. San Francisco: Institute of Contemporary Studies Press.
Clary, David A. 1986. *Timber and the Forest Service*. Lawrence, KS: University Press of Kansas.
Dwyer, Janet, and Ian Hodge. 1996. *Countryside in Trust: Land Management by Conservation, Recreation and Amenity Organizations*. Chichester, U.K. John Wiley and Sons.
Gould, Steven Jay. 1990. "The Horn of Triton." *Natural History* (December), pp. 15, 18.
Heclo, Hugh. 1978. "Issue Networks and the Executive Establishment." In *The New American Political System*. Washington, DC: American Enterprise Institute for Public Policy Research.
Hirt, Paul. 1994. *A Conspiracy of Optimism*. Lincoln: University of Nebraska Press.
Hull, David. 1988. *Science as a Process: An Evolutionary Account of the Social and Conceptual Development of Science*. Chicago: University of Chicago Press.
Kaufman, Herbert. 1978. *The Forest Ranger: A Study in Administrative Behavior*. Washington, DC: Resources for the Future.
Langston, Nancy. 1995. *Forest Dreams, Forest Nightmares: The Paradox of Old Growth in the Inland West*. Seattle: University of Washington Press.
Maser, Chris. 1988. *The Redesigned Forest*. San Pedro: R and E Miles.
May, Elizabeth. 1998. *At the Cutting Edge: The Crisis in Canada's Forests*. San Francisco: Sierra Club.
McConnell, Grant. 1966. *Private Power and American Democracy*. NY: Vintage.
McKean, Margaret A. 1992 "Management of Traditional Common Lands *(iriaichi)* in Japan." In Daniel W. Bromley, *Making the Commons Work: Theory, Practice, and Policy*. San Francisco: Institute of Contemporary Studies.
Ostrom, Elinor. 1990. *Governing the Commons: The Evolution of Institutions for Collective Action*. Cambridge: Cambridge University Press.
O'Toole, Randal. 1988. *Reforming the Forest Service*. Washington, DC: Island Press.
Polanyi, Michael. 1969. "The Republic of Science: Its Political and Economic Theory." In Marjorie Grene, ed., *Knowing and Being: Essays by Michael Polanyi*. Chicago: University of Chicago Press.
Rhoads, Steven. 1985. *The Economist's View of the World: Government, Markets, and Public Policy*. Cambridge: Cambridge University Press.
Sagoff, Mark. 1988. *The Economy of the Earth*. Cambridge: Cambridge University Press.
Souder, Jon, and Sally Fairfax. 1995. "Forestry on State Trust Lands." *Different Drummer* (summer).
Wilkinson, Charles. 1992. *Crossing the Next Meridian: Land, Water, and the Future of the* West. Washington, DC: Island Press.

Chapter 11

OLD WINE IN NEW BOTTLES? CIVIC REPUBLICANISM AND THE CHALLENGES OF THE GLOBAL ERA[1]

Laurent Dobuzinskis
Simon Fraser University

Modern liberal democracies have been shaped by several currents of thought. Since the fall of the Berlin Wall in 1989, it has become commonplace to underline the liberal half of the liberal democratic hybrid. The globalization of trade and financial transactions has superimposed upon political liberalism, with its emphasis on the discourse of rights, a neoliberal (i.e., market-oriented) economic dimension. However, the democratic half has also been the subject of much attention recently. In several countries, notably France and the United States, the democratic ideal has been reframed in explicitly republican terms. But civic republicanism is given a very prominent place in political and intellectual debates on the future of the nation-state taking place in several other countries, including Australia, Ireland, and Germany.[2] (The qualifier "civic" adds little to the meaning of republicanism but it distinguishes it from the ideology of today's Republican party in the United States with which it has little in common.) Republicanism is a somewhat elusive notion but it can be defined rather succinctly in terms of a commitment to the common good (res publica) and to a particular way of reaching that goal, namely, self-government. Self-government implies equal access by all citizens to public institutions, and participation in deliberative politics. However, these simple words are subject to a wide variety of interpretations, some of which reflect concerns with the effects of globalization.[3]

On the one hand, republicanism offers a set of reassuring certainties that seem to offer protection against the socio-economic transformations brought about by emerging global trends. But this protection will probably prove illusory. On the other hand, a rethinking of traditional republican ideals offers the promise of a new liberal democratic strategy for re-directing global

S. McBride et al. (eds.), Global Instability, 181–199.

trends. This would involve a more encompassing definition of the political obligations associated with the notion of citizenship – one that would aim at fostering a new awareness of the links between the local, national and global dimensions of traditional republican themes like civic engagement and non-domination.[4]

A brief synthetic overview of the history of the republican tradition, with particular references to France and the United States follows. Then the temptation to use republicanism as a rampart against globalization and a refuge for communitarians disillusioned by neoliberal individualism is confronted. Finally, a more forward looking perspective is proposed according to which republicanism is uniquely suited to transform the nation-state of yesterday into the political project of outward looking cosmopolitan citizens who are also actively involved in the construction of culturally pluralistic societies. However, my discussion of these two tendencies points toward a dialectical conclusion that underlines the practical difficulties involved in dividing the ideas and values constitutive of republicanism into a dichotomy of this kind; republicanism is a paradoxical ideology that simultaneously produces openness and closure, freedom and obligations, democratic empowerment and cultural dispossession, particularism and universalism.

REPUBLICANISM: WHAT'S IN A NAME?

The republican tradition reaches back to the Roman republic and Cicero's speeches. In early modern times, it was revived by Machiavelli, notably in his *Discourses*, then again adapted to the English political climate of Cromwell's England by James Harrington. It was further refined and modernized by the American founders, notably Thomas Jefferson and James Madison. But its appeal began to fade away in the later part of the nineteenth century. Historians of ideas have put it back on the intellectual map, inspiring political philosophers in the Anglo-American world to discuss its merits.[5] Outside of these academic circles, explicit allusions to civic republicanism are not very common in American politics. Yet many republican ideals resurface on the occasion of current policy debates, notably in relation to education, immigration and multiculturalism. One could reasonably argue that civic republican theorists indirectly influenced the ideological orientation adopted by the Democratic Party under Bill Clinton or, for that matter, of the British Labour Party under Tony Blair. In Australia, of course, republicanism is a more debated topic. The issue of the abolition of the monarchy is obviously crucial but the Australian republican tradition is not limited to the discussion of that institutional question alone.[6] There is also a parallel between civic republican ideas and the much debated notion of deliberative democracy[7] that is relevant to all contemporary western democracies, including those (e.g., Canada) where the vocabulary of republicanism is less current.

Americans are worried about two things: "the loss of self-government and the erosion of community."[8] Contemporary advocates of civic republicanism in the United States and beyond tend to agree about the centrality of the notion of self-government but interpret its moral implications differently. Thus R. Dagger[9] is on very solid ground when he defines republicanism in terms of self-government and "publicity," i.e., the idea that public life has a value in itself, in other words, that government is more than a necessary evil. But how far this point should be pushed is a matter of debate. Does it simply mean that republicanism complements liberalism – the two systems of ideas remaining compatible, which is Dagger's[10] position? This compatibility has been analyzed by Philip Pettit (1997) in the following terms: republicanism takes the liberal notion of non-interference in the lives of individuals one step farther by offering protections against all – even merely potential – instances where the freedom of citizens could be violated by powerful interests abusing their powers.[11] But Sandel proposes a more radical departure from contemporary liberalism (in both its more progressive and conservative forms); for him, public life is a way of life, a commitment to the creative search for the common good and the formation of a truly autonomous citizenry.[12]

The French republican tradition has followed a somewhat different course and uses distinctive symbols (*"liberté, égalité, fraternité"*). It claims to be largely *sui generis* and not to originate in what Pocock calls "the Atlantic republican tradition" but rather in Rousseau's political theory and the spirit of 1792.[13] That self-proclaimed identity is actually not unique or as distinct from the civic republican tradition described above. This is because the revolutionary and radical democratic dimensions of French republicanism were considerably toned down and re-cast in a far more liberal frame by the founders of the Third Republic who, in a less epic but far more effective way than the Jacobins, really created the republican institutions and principles that continue to undergird the French political system. Thus at least the first two elements of the French republican triptych have much in common with the civic republican understanding of liberty and equality in general. I am not implying that there are no difference at all between Anglo-American republicanism and French republicanism – that would be absurd; but, apart from the more typically French evocation of *Fraternité*, these differences have more to do with the historical events or the philosophical texts cited to illustrate or defend republican virtues than with these virtues themselves. In any event, I do not intend delve on these subtle differences but rather to analyze the relevance of the civic republican tradition broadly defined to the global era.

Indeed contemporary republicanism in France moved even further away from its Jacobin roots during the late 1970s and early 1980s. This occurred because of globalization that, in the case of France, produced two opposing ideological effects. To elaborate on this point, I must introduce the concept of "French exceptionalism." The French response to globalizing trends has at first consisted of a rejection of deeply rooted political beliefs and cleavages that made France appear exceptional among another modern democracies. These include the exceptionally fractured quality of French politics that, on several occasions throughout the nineteenths and twentieth century, led to revolutionary upheavals or other violent conflicts. The legacy of the French Revolution continued to be rejected on the right by a reactionary right while the defenders of the republican tradition were themselves divided among the liberal heirs of the spirit of the 1789 and the Rousseauean Jacobins, some of whom after 1917 espoused the new Marxist utopia. But by 1989, most of these differences had vanished and a new liberal republican consensus had replaced yesterday's divisions. Revolutionary utopian Marxism, in particular, was reduced to the same negligible role it had played in most other western democracies since the end of the war (with the possible exception of Italy). While this liberal democratic political consensus has not broken down yet, new divisions have emerged. The new French exceptionalism is marked by a rejection of the forces of cultural homogenization and neoliberal globalization; at first, this neo-nationalist consciousness was not explicitly partisan or, in any event, cut across party lines, but Le Pen's National Front has rather successfully capitalized on it. In this new fight, republican symbols are often mobilized in the defence of the uniqueness of the French national heritage by both *bona fide* republican mavericks within established parties and by the National Front – a party, ironically, whose ideological discourse often sounds decidedly anti-republican. Whereas traditional republican nationalism has tended to paint France as a civilizational model for the world, Le Pen's more frankly xenophobic discourse rejects most of the tenets of the Enlightenment.

Nostalgic Republicanism

The rediscovery of liberal values and a remarkable acceptance of the institutions of the Fifth Republic formed the context within which a new discourse on republicanism evolved in France during the 1980s. However, that discourse has more recently been put to the service of more inward-looking, nostalgic nationalist causes. (Even in the eighteenth century, republicanism was already an odd mixture of antiquarian symbols and modern concepts, such as representative democracy.) The meshing of republican ideas and values expressed in universalistic terms ("the rights of man and the citizen") and of nationalistic rhetoric has a long history, of course, and is not limited to France.[14] In the French case, this ambiguity can be traced back to the dilemmas faced by the first revolutionary government dedicated, as it was, to a universalizable emancipatory agenda but surrounded by foreign enemies. Even during the Napoleonic era, when the republican aspirations to autonomy and self-government were all but smothered by the personal ambitions of Napoleon himself and of his entourage, it could still be argued that the Grande Armée was helping to defeat the forces of reaction and to spread the message of the Enlightenment. But the return to nationalist republicanism has become even more ambiguous in recent years because it is far more difficult to discern its progressive import, even if it is proudly asserted by its proponents on the left side of the political spectrum.

Nationalist republicanism in contemporary France is strongly associated with certain segments of the political left, but it is by no means limited to the left. This current cannot be said to be typical of the French left as a whole, however. Its electoral appeal is confined to groups and individuals who feel threatened by globalizing trends and/or by the de facto transformation of French society into a multicultural society; these trends in fact divide both the left and the right.

To probe a little deeper into the current tensions within French republicanism around the issues of national sovereignty and citizenship, it is necessary to look at both practical politics and theoretical reflections. French politicians do not simply take their cues from public intellectuals but intellectuals often frame political discourse in ways that have no parallels in America.

At the risk of being unfair to several other authors, I would suggest that two French scholars stand out for having most forcefully brought back the notion of republicanism on the intellectual scene in the 1980s and 1990s: the historian Claude Nicolet (1982, 2000) and the philosopher Blandine Kriegel (1995, 1998). While one can find many common themes in their works (e.g., the importance of the rule of law), they have chosen to outline two different dimensions of French republicanism; one is more retrogressive, the other more forward-looking. Kriegel insists on the uniqueness of the French political tradition, which she contrasts with the German tradition. In her view, the German conception of political authority never took a radical turn away from the ideal embodied in feudalism and the Holy Roman Empire; more specifically, in that tradition the Roman law tradition was never developed in a close relation with state sovereignty – an ideal that remained elusive through much of German history. Therefore, while the notion of the rule of law (Rechststaat) was not unknown to German thinkers (Kant being, of course, a good example), its occasional practice was not firmly rooted in any kind of historical reality. In contrast, countries, like France or Britain very early on established their own sovereignty, centred on the person of their own monarch whose legislative powers gradually were themselves subordinated to the supremacy of law. The rule of law is the necessary condition for republican or liberal-democratic citizenship. It is an assurance against the arguably more German conception of an autonomous subject whose romantic aspirations to authenticity are fulfilled outside of the legal and political institutions of a government of laws (Etat de droit, Rechststaat). The notion of citizenship in itself, however, cannot be separated from its historical context. The history of French republican regimes from the Third to the Fifth Republic have undeniably left a legacy that clearly distinguishes the French republican discourse on citizenship. But if Kriegel insists on the specificity of the French republican vision, she does not maintain that the fundamental principles of republicanism are uniquely French. Indeed, she looks forward to the establishment, on that basis, of a European republic – a point to be taken up in a subsequent section.

For his part, and in contrast with Kriegel, Nicolet[15] has chosen to emphasize the rootedness of the republic in the national history of France rather than the more abstract symbols it stands for (the common good, political virtue, and so on). Nicolet is not alone. Indeed, his approach is generally more subtle and moderate than that followed by such well known intellectual personalities as Régis Debray, Max Gallo, Pierre-André Taguieff, or Paul Thiebaud.[16] French neo-republicanism is far from being a purely intellectual movement. Prominent politicians have made extensive use of republican rhetoric and symbols. They can be found on the right (e.g., C. Pasqua and even further toward the extreme right, P. de Villiers), the centre-right (e.g., P. Seguin) or the left (e.g., J.-P. Chevènement) of the political spectrum. Chevènement's numerous crusades against what he perceived as deviations from sound republican principles by his colleagues within prime Minister Jospin's cabinet, notably on the question of the status of Corsica (see below), have done much to identify his dogmatic and traditionalist republicanism with the Left. Some currents within the French intellectual Left have rallied behind him. They constituted a minority within the coalition of political forces and intellectual movements that supported the Jospin government. But the reasonably strong score achieved by Chevènement during the first round of the 2002 presidential elections prevented Jospin from competing in the run-off election between the first two best placed candidates (in this instance, J. Chirac and J.-M. Le Pen).

The themes that these republican activists have been most clearly associated with in recent years include: the threat posed by globalization in general and by European integration to France's political and cultural sovereignty; opposition to demands by Corsican nationalists for a devolution of legislative and administrative powers, and to the Jospin government's willingness to accommodate these demands;[17] the rejection of any move toward the official recognition of minority language rights (as contemplated in the European convention on minority languages); and the refusal to grant any legitimacy to the very idea of multiculturalism. All these themes, in sense, allude to the disappearance of a political settlement that is more than a hundred years old. In recent years, this sense that the old order is vanishing has been refocused on more concrete issues having to do with law and order and "insecurity," i.e., the alarming rise in criminality and petty vandalism attributable in large measure to youth gangs that have sprung up in the suburban ghettos populated mostly by North African immigrants and their families. This problem ironically speaks to the failure of the republican model of assimilation.

Some of these attitudes are anchored firmly in the French historical memory. Regional and other subnational identities have been judged incompatible with the preservation of the unity of the republic ever since the harsh repression of the insurrection of 1793 in Vendée. But today these themes also serve to express deep suspicions about the effects of globalization, especially in the context of European integration. Regionalism is perceived as the Trojan horse of transnational interests, undermining the democratic central state from within, leaving it too weak to mobilize all citizens around some common project.

The issues of multiculturalism and the increasing marginalization of North Africans, however, deserves special attention because it has different implications for France in comparison with most other European countries where the influx of immigrants is a rather new phenomenon. By contrast, since the middle of the 19th century, waves after waves of immigrants from southern Europe, eastern Europe and the French colonies – now independent countries, of course, but still, indeed even more so than before, a source of immigration – have settled in France. (The only difference that globalization has made is that during the last decade many more recent migrants have come from non-traditional origins, e.g., Turkey, China.) For more than a century, immigrants have been able to settle permanently and to obtain French citizenship that is automatically granted to their children born in France. Republican institutions founded on the principles of universalism and equality – in particular the public school system and military conscription – very efficiently moulded generations after generations of French citizens with foreign-sounding names whose self-identity owed little to the culture of their parents. The mastery of the French language and academic achievements almost always guaranteed social acceptance. But the French republican melting pot has been working much less well since the 1970s for two reasons.

The first is that the ethnic and cultural mix of immigrants began to tilt more decisively toward migrants from non-European origins, a fact that brought about more overt racist reactions. The second was that many immigrants themselves began to resist cultural assimilation, notably because Islam does not accept the very literal and rigid separation of church and state that is central to the French republican tradition. It is to accommodate these new circumstances that various groups and political currents began to articulate a multicultural project whose goal would be to celebrate rather than to stamp out difference. This is what traditionalist French republicans strongly object to, while at the same time asserting their opposition to discrimination and racism. In their view, citizens leave behind themselves all their religious, cultural or other social differences before entering the public sphere. Thus it is not the specific goals and values of multiculturalism they reject as the particularism they entail.

Critics of this discourse have coined the phrase "national republicanism" to describe it with the deliberate intent to draw attention to its latent or imagined fascistic connotations. This is somewhat unfair insofar as the French republican notion of an ideal citizenship that transcends all cultural, ethnic or religious particularisms, and refuses to cede ground to consumerism by asserting that freedom cannot be reduced to the choices that economic agents make, is a progressive one. The real question, however, is how such a transcendence is to be achieved; there is a way to acknowledge "difference" that does not magnify or exacerbate divisions but signifies an acceptance of diversity as a prelude to a more balanced and reciprocal form of integration. But dogmatic republicans are not interested in pursuing that option. Ironically, the recent adoption of the label "Mouvement National Républicain" by a new extreme right, avowedly racist, anti-immigration party led by B. Megret which split from J.-M. Le Pen's National Front both confirms the fascistic connotation of the phrase and its inapplicability to traditionalist republicans whose rhetorical excesses do not betray the same sort of atavistic intolerance. Le Pen's unexpected score in 2002 brings out more ironies. On the one hand, it is clear that all the racist and fascistic causes that Le Pen has espoused during his long political career clearly put him on the ideological spectrum far beyond even the republican right, a fact which was evidenced by the impressive "republican" mobilization of most political parties and personalities behind the moderate conservative Chirac in the run-off election. On the other hand, Le Pen actually ran a rather clever campaign by toning down his usual rhetoric and echoing many of the arguments about "insecurity" and loss of sovereignty voiced by traditionalist republicans in recent years.[18]

The return to civic republicanism in Anglo-American political discourse is less evidently related to globalization. According to John Gray Pope,[19] there have been many "republican moments" in American history when citizens have engaged "in serious political discourse"; when "their arguments [have been] couched primarily in moral rather than pecuniary terms"; and when "the subjects of debate [have included] fundamental aspects of the social, political or economic order." While the present moment shares some of the last two characteristics, it appears to be more the product of discussions among political philosophers or legal theorists than of ordinary citizens breaking away from apathy, even if this discourse has made voters' apathy, the erosion of social capital and the capacity of the voluntary sector topics of much concern in the media and among political activists. Anglo-American republicanism also tends to put more emphasis on the local civic scene than the French do, although there is some degree of disagreement over the extent to which the American republican tradition is rooted in local politics.[20] Moreover, in the wake of the events of 11 September 2001 one can speak of a new climate of civic friendship on a national scale in the United States. At the same time, this patriotic fervour also reveals latent fears about the dangers inherent in a globalized world. In this climate, civic republicanism, whether it is practiced at the local or national level, might turn out to be another element in the development of an inward-looking public discourse that would if not preclude, at least hamper the possibility of launching a serious debate about both the role and responsibilities of the American civil society – as distinct from the government of the United States or corporate elites – in global affairs.

To a considerable extent, contemporary civic republicanism in the United States takes the form of a critical discourse on constitutional law and the role of the courts in the political and social life of the country,[21] with very few ramifications for areas such as global trade or human rights. It tends to reinforce the view that if the central political problem is a lack of civic engagement, the solution to that problem must be worked out at the level of domestic politics first. Considering the extraordinarily important role of the U.S. Supreme Court in American politics, there is a certain logic to that singular focus on constitutional law, even if it takes the form of a paradox. A recourse to the courts can be viewed as a way out of the interest-based politics that seems to have swayed political parties and the legislative branch – a style of politics that hides behind a discourse of procedural neutrality and that cannot pose problems in terms of a search for the common good. This seems to underline much of Sandel's (1996) analysis, although he insists that the problem also rests with the courts themselves since they have shied away from addressing the issues before them in explicitly moral terms.

Other republican theorists, however, argue that by refusing to defer to the authority of the elected branches, the courts have weakened the political institutions where a serious debate about the nature of the common good could – and should – take place.[22] Setting aside these controversies, it is clear much of the civic republican discourse in the Anglo-American world – and in the United States in particular – echoes in some ways the critique of individualistic neoliberalism that anti-globalization activists have also voiced. Many civic republicans, however, seek solution to this woe by advocating a return to more robust styles of political commitment at the local and national levels and/or judicial activism with little or no regard for other international or global forums. They give the definite impression that something important has been lost and must be recovered, but pay far less attention to emerging realities that may render a project of that nature futile. Next, I discuss the views of some civic republican theorists who have shown a greater interest in global issues.

Toward a Universal Republic?

Immanuel Kant attempted to prove that "republicanism... is the only constitution that can lead to a perpetual peace."[23] Indeed the idea that genuine democracies – a phrase that necessarily entails respect for such republican principles as the rule of law and an understanding of self-government as something more complex than mere majoritarian government – do not go to war has come to be rather widely accepted. From that standpoint, even the most inward looking and nostalgically nationalist republicanism could, in the (very) long term help to bring about a more peaceful world in which republican virtues would become universal in their reach, ultimately leading, as Kant himself thought, to the creation of a universal confederation of republics.[24] In the mean time, however, the question that matters is to what extent do republican principles facilitate or hinder the efforts of citizens to take advantage of the emerging global markets without losing their ability to resist domination at the hands of either international or domestic economic interests, or to fall prey to new forms of global lawlessness (e.g., terrorism, transnational organized crime, etc.). Insofar as the nation-state may have become obsolete to deal with such problems, does the strong association of republicanism with national sovereignty (and, a fortiori, its defence of popular sovereignty at the local level) condemn it to remain an ideological remnant of a by-gone era? Questions of this sort are frequently raised by political theorists concerned with the future of the idea of democratic citizenship.[25]

For one thing, the core principles of modern republicanism have often typically been formulated in universalist terms. R. Kearney[26] is right to point out that, historically, republicanism has veered often toward sectarian nationalism, as the example of Irish republicanism reminds us; French republicanism has not itself always been able to resist that pull either. Nevertheless, Kearney still thinks that the authentic legacy of republicanism consists of universal principles originating in the Enlightenment.[27] Modern republicanism is indeed a child of the Enlightenment and one of the most succinct and compelling statement of the synthesis of universalism and republicanism remains the French Déclaration des droits de l'homme et du citoyen; that document was definitely not meant to describe only the rights of Frenchmen at a particular juncture of French history.[28] In spite of the nostalgic motivations that, as we have seen, also inspire the present wave of republican sentiments, it is its universalist implications that deserve the most attention.

It is clear that the scale and scope of what republican theorists call "domination" – recall Pettit's definition of republican freedom as "non-domination" – have changed significantly in recent decades. This is a challenge for republicanism that, until recently, has been concerned primarily with the dynamic interaction of local and national institutions, legal norms and identities but has not paid as much attention to the international scene, except when it was perceived as a threat to national autonomy. But today "non-domination" cannot always be achieved at the national level. Transnational corporations as well as less than fully "public" institutions like the International Monetary Fund (IMF) or the World Trade Organization (WTO) operate beyond the normal range of the legal instruments that citizens can use to hold political authorities and private interests accountable or liable. Considering the central importance of the notion of the rule of law in republican theory, the still imperfect development of international law, and the fact that the meaningful practice of self-government rarely extends to the formulation of rules that can be enforced internationally pose a fundamental challenge to republicanism. One can discern two types of strategic responses to that challenge.

One approach looks forward to the inclusion of existing republican nation-states into larger ensembles within which some of the functions they carry out at present would be taken over by new institutional mechanisms more adapted to the challenges of the global era, but without giving up the fundamental principles of self-government and publicity. In other words, the republican nation-state has not become fully dysfunctional or obsolete; even if various kinds of international regimes and networks have more or less spontaneously emerged, from a republican standpoint they cannot yet replace the existing international system because they still are not sufficiently responsive to "expectations of national sovereignty and human rights."[29] Thus the republican state must not be abandoned but transformed in ways that allow for a new forms of legitimation and integration in its relations, externally to supranational institutions and, internally, to multicultural communities. Pursuing this line of reasoning a little further, James Bohman acknowledges that republicanism posits a "thicker" notion of citizenship than one usually associates with cosmopolitanism, but he denies that republican citizenship can only be achieved within territorially bound communities.[30] Bohman argues that in the global era an argument in favour of cosmopolitanism has to be recast as an argument in favour of "cosmopolitan republicanism"; a purely liberal approach would be inadequate. Two tactics can be followed to bring about cosmopolitan republicanism, according to Bohman.

Protest campaigns, such as those we have become familiar with since the 1999 demonstrations against the WTO meeting in Seattle, constitute one way in which groups can engage in new forms of transnational politics. From

Bohman's standpoint, such tactics could contribute to the globalization of republican values by making it more difficult for governments to avoid their responsibilities to the international community; in other words, one of the justifications for the global contestation is that it might help to establish a regime of international obligations. This would be a significant move both in terms of the public character of the new global responsibilities incumbent on governments, and in terms of their effects on the corporations and international organizations with which they have tended to interact until now in a typically ad hoc manner. Bohman,[31] however, argues that cosmopolitan republicanism must go beyond contestation in order to bring about "directly deliberative forms of cosmopolitan democracy." There is little doubt that the technocratic nature of newly empowered international organizations like the WTO or the IMF is worrisome to those who believe in the principles of civic republicanism and, in particular, to the ideal of self-government. Any progress toward that goal will depend on how political activists, governments, legal scholars, and so on, can resolve the daunting complexities inherent in transforming citizenship into a transnational reality.

The possibility of becoming a "citizen of the world" is not exactly a new idea but recent scholarship has taken it seriously again.[32] Kriegel (1998) argues that one must always take care not to confuse the four different sets of legal and moral rights[33] upon which the philosophy of republicanism rests: public law, human rights, citizenship rights, and the law of nations. It is equally important to try to find ways of reconciling their different logics but it is not established for all times that the nation-state provides the only framework for such reconciliation. In other words, because citizenship and national legislation are conceptually distinct, it is possible to separate the locus of citizenship from the state, even if, in practice, domestic laws may need to be used to give expression to transnational citizenship rights (e.g., the laws of the member states of the European Union now authorize local residents to vote in municipal elections, whether or not they are citizens of the country in which they reside, provided that they are citizens of a member state). Indeed Kriegel considers the project of building a united republican Europe entirely feasible and, of course, desirable for, as she exclaims in an almost lyrical voice, "the world needs a democratic and republican Europe."[34]

While the preceding remarks offered a brief sketch of various reflections on ways to move republican politics onto a new transnational plane, the alternative strategy is a variation on the old chestnut: "Think globally, act locally," or, as Archon Fuchs (2001) puts it, "act locally, deliberate globally." From this standpoint, citizens are more likely to move in the direction of civic cosmopolitanism if they can be convinced that international commitments follow logically from their practice of civic virtues in their national or local communities, and within the institutions to which they are accustomed. International solidarity cannot be created instantaneously. Advocates of this more prudent approach believe that a global outlook must be built gradually upon more familiar experiences. Thus Dagger (2001) argues that while cosmopolitanism may be desirable, it is only when it is supplemented by civic virtues rooted in "a sense of place" that progress can be made toward some sort of genuine cosmopolitan morality.[35]

In Dagger's case, the opposition between the two strategies I am contrasting here may simply be due to the fact that his definition of cosmopolitanism makes no room for the kind of participatory politics envisioned by Bohman. In other words, they start from different premises about what cosmopolitanism means today and yet they may be following parallel routes toward the future goal of cosmopolitan citizenship. But, in general, one can still think of two possible attitudes toward the very possibility of achieving self-government and publicity at the global level; one seeks to transcend national boundaries that are perceived as porous, the other considers that the root of civic virtues cannot easily be transplanted, that international engagement is desirable but not sustainable on its own. Indeed globalization brings about a clearer realization that what has usually been taken for granted, namely, the existence of a place and a context familiar to all participants in democratic debates, is not only important but perhaps at risk.[36] In the end, though, it is clear that civic republicanism must find a balance between local and global concerns, and the problem of how to re-position civic engagement at the local level within a global perspective is the challenge that neo-republicans must confront if they have any hope of deflecting the criticism that they are merely cultivating nostalgia.

Even if cosmopolitanism and a more "bottom-up" approach can be mutually reinforcing, there is no consensus about the future prospects of international citizenship and solidarity. The same sort of disagreement among both groups of republican theorists extends to the issue of how republican regimes in the twenty first century should address the politics of identity in increasingly diverse societies. Partisans of an "open republic" may be more likely to argue in favour of more international integration and the recognition of diversity in domestic politics;[37] Dagger,[38] on the other hand, approaches multiculturalism with the same scepticism with which he treats cosmopolitanism – a scepticism, however, that ought not to be confused with outright rejection.

If global cosmopolitanism is to be achieved through a gradual transformation of national and local politics, the question of the prospects for the gradual propagation of the republican ideal throughout the world must be raised., It is may be comforting for republican theorists to note that their ideas are spreading throughout much of western Europe, including – and perhaps especially – Germany where, republican values had fallen on a very infertile ground in earlier times. Elsewhere, however, the picture is far less clear.

As Brugger[39] points out, the combined effects of colonialism, religious fundamentalism, authoritarianism and ideological dogmatism create formidable obstacles to the progression of the republican ethos in much of Africa and Asia. Brugger nevertheless suggests that we should not be content with a superficial view. When one looks more attentively at the cultural and institutional contexts within which the problems of democratic reform are posed, it appears that there can be a variety of ways in which the republican idea can be adapted to a whole range of circumstances. His analysis is far too detailed to do justice to it here, but a couple of examples may illustrate the reasons for this guarded optimism. Brugger, for instance, notes that the artificial character of the borders drawn in colonial times between African countries is not a problem from a republican standpoint since republicanism does not pre-suppose, and in fact, runs counter to ethno-cultural homogeneity. Or, to give another example, Confucianism, which is strong throughout much of East Asia, constitutes a set of remarkably flexible and adaptable values that are entirely compatible with the republican insistence on the need to separate civic virtues from moral and religious precepts. The point is not that republicanism can be easily transplanted everywhere, nor that Kant's vision can be realized in the very near future, but simply that "[r]epublicanism... is only one of several streams of thought which attempt [the] task [of achieving a more harmonious balancing of the universal and the particular] but... the modesty of its universals is such that it can escape the charge of cultural imperialism better than most other streams of thought."[40]

The time has come to soften the contrast I have drawn so far between self-proclaimed republicans who strongly believe in cosmopolitan and universal values, and others who, as I argued in the previous section, are less enthusiastic about such prospects. In reality, most republicans – especially political activists and opinion leaders for whom civic republicanism is a source of inspiration rather than a clear theoretical framework – are sitting uncomfortably on the metaphorical fence. It is indeed in the very nature of liberal republicanism to occupy a median position between a variety of more radical solutions. In its defence of representative government, publicity and civic virtues against populists, and radical democrats, on the one hand, and Churchillian democrats for whom democracy is no more than a necessary evil, on the other, it seeks to revitalize traditional liberal democratic institutions rather than to subvert them or let them decline. In its defence of personal autonomy and responsibility, it stands mid-way between free market libertarians and partisans of the endless expansion of the meliorist welfare state. In its opposition to both sectarianism and cultural or moral relativism, its stands somewhere between ethnic nationalism and unbridled pluralism. By the same token, in the face of strong currents undermining the nation-states, republicanism is torn between the preservation of the old rules and the promotion of new ones. In part this is due to the eminent reasonableness of the republican ethos – the common good being ill-served by utopian or doctrinaire projects. This prudent attitude, however, may prove extremely difficult to hold on to in a rapidly changing world. The question that must be addressed as a priority is whether the ambiguities surrounding the notion of citizenship at the moment can be transformed into a renewed republican project. Such a project could speak to the concerns of a wide range of individual and groups who may have different views about the advantages and disadvantages of economic and cultural globalization but are nevertheless united in their desire to rule out emerging forms of domination that could replace those than the republican ideal had successfully brought under control. Alternatively, these ambiguities may be so intractable that they may derail the project altogether.

CONCLUSION

Civic republicanism is an ideal that appeals to many critics of interest-based politics and the seemingly a-moral individualistic consumerism that accompanies the turn to global markets. I have tried to show that these critics have either used republican themes as a way to satisfy their nostalgia for a heroic age when strong ties of citizenship used to unite self-governing political communities, or a springboard for a new and virtuous cosmopolitanism. Insofar as the former is fraught with the always present danger of being re-cast into an authoritarian nationalism and/or xenophobic paranoia,[41] the latter is the obvious choice for liberals, social democrats and sceptical conservatives[42] alike for whom some balance must always be maintained between liberty, equality and fraternity.

In trying to articulate a new cosmopolitanism, republican theorists may inadvertently encourage the sort of illiberal tendencies I have just hinted at. However it is one thing to acknowledge one's debt to republican ideals when looking back at the formative process through which the United States, France and other liberal democracies have established the foundations of their civil societies and political regimes; it is another to argue that these ideals provide the best responses to the challenges they are facing at present. The contrast between universalism and sectarianism plays itself out in ever more complex and changing ways. It is becoming increasingly difficult to separate the local and global, national and international dimensions of every issue. Moreover, the contrast between interest and virtue no longer appears evident. In a knowledge economy, powerful professional interests (e.g., health specialists; ethics counselors; and so on) authoritatively determine what counts as virtuous; the virtues of reputedly disinterested advocates of social and political equality, on the other hand, have become increasingly disruptive and sectarian in their rigid pursuit of unalienable and one-sided rights defined without reference to obligations of civility. Besides, in spite of the disconcerting aspects of the postmodern discourse on difference and recognition, and in spite of the corrosive nature of the libertarian cult of individualism, both of these tendencies embody profound socio-psychological currents that cannot simply swept under the rug. The very notion of self-government through deliberation, mutual respect and compromise, however, is threatened by these combined developments. Republicanism can perhaps be reinvented in a manner that would recast non-domination in terms that could protect the citizens of future democracies against the dangers posed by the dilapidation of social capital, a perceived trend toward cultural homogenization,[43] paternalistic statist interventionism, corporate recklessness and a new religion of human rights, among other topical issues; but if that immensely complicated task is to succeed, resolving the opposition between cosmopolitanism and nostalgic communitarianism may turn out not to be the most pressing or difficult problem. Redefining the notion of citizenship – finding new ways of making this concept meaningful again instead of invoking it as a mantra against complex transformations and the turbulence they occasion – here, is the real challenge.

NOTES

1. This chapter constitutes the first installment of a more extensive comparative project that I have undertaken on the parallels and differences between Anglo-American and French republicanism.
2. In the German context, see, for example, Habermas (1998), Delbrück (1994) and Hagedorn (2000).
3. For example, see Dagger (2001); Habermas (1998).
4. According to Philip Pettit, non-domination is a central feature of republicanism; it is equivalent neither to negative freedom or non-interference alone, nor to positive liberty, but combines features of both. Liberty as non-domination is liberty from unwelcome interference by others but also protection against potential interference by more powerful interests, see Pettit (1997) p. 27.
5. Sullivan (1986); Sandel (1996); Pettit, (1997); Dagger (1997); Brugger (1999).
6. Indeed the defeat of the referendum of 1999 had much to do with the fact that the proposed constitutional reform was too exclusively centred on that question alone.
7. Gutmann and Thompson (1996).
8. Sandel (1996) p. 3.
9. Dagger (2001) p. 159.
10. Dagger (1997) p. 12.
11. In the French tradition, that line of thinking can be traced back to Rousseau; on Rousseau and republicanism, see Spitz (1995) pp. 271-466. On the origins of the idea of non-domination in the Anglo-American tradition, see Bailyn (1992) and Pettit (1997).
12. However, Kymlicka (1998) argues that Sandel's goals can all be met without giving up the tenets of progressive liberalism.

13 For a critical examination of this thesis, see Larrère (2000).

14 Habermas (1998) pp. 114-17. Not only does the history of republicanism in France and the in United States illustrate this tension between the universal and the particular, but Irish republicanism offers another example, see Kearney (1997); McGovern (2000).

15 Nicolet (2000) p. 97.

16 See Debray (1998); Gallo (1998); see also Barreau (1999). Debray, for example, has formulated a rather farfetched comparison between what he regards as the "Anglo-Saxon" idea of pluralist democracy in which civil society plays an important part and the French republican tradition rooted in Rousseau's rather ill-fated contrast between the "will of all" and the "General Will":

> Republic stands for equality, rewarding merit, secularism (*laïcité*), popular sovereignty, the General Will, and the nation-state... Democracy is almost the opposite: the right to difference, everyone for themselves, federalism and intermediary bodies (Debray, 1998, p. 64).

17 A law passed by the National Assembly in December or 2001 grants to the Corsican regional assembly the power to adjust the implementation of national laws to the local circumstances. But even this very modest step toward the decentralization of political responsibilities (as opposed to administrative responsibilities which have been rather extensively decentralized beginning in the 1980s) has been fiercely resisted by the centre-right opposition and by all republican nationalists.

18 Le Pen's relative success has parallels in the growing support for law and order, nationalist, anti-immigrant parties in Austria, Italy, Holland and Denmark. At least in continental Europe, it turns out that anti-globalization has been co-opted by the least progressive political forces.

19 Pope (1990) p. 312.

20 Brinkley (1996).

21 As Brest puts it, "it is at least ironic that much of the legal scholarship of the republican revival, rather than to promote participation and discourse... is as court-centred as the pluralist scholarship from which it distinguishes itself," cited by Pope (1990) n.66.

22 For example, see Sunstein (1996).

23 Kant [1795] (1983) p. 112.

24 For a critique of the limitations and inconsistencies of the Kantian project, see Habermas (1998) pp. 165-201.

25 For example, see Dagger (2001); Habermas (1998); Kriegel (1998).

26 Kearney (1997) p. 25-38.

27 It must be remembered that Cicero, the great classical republican theorist, already remarked (in Book I of his *The Laws*) that the human mind can think of itself as "a citizen of the whole universe."

28 Jefferson's republicanism is a more complicated case since his universalist vision did not seem to include slaves but this paradox was probably not as obvious in his times as it strikes us today.

29 Habermas (1998) p. 125.

30 Bohman (2001) p. 3.

31 Ibid., p. 16.

32 Cohen (1996); Bosniak (2000).

33 In French, "droit" means both a right and a system of laws; Kriegel has both meanings in mind when she employs that term which she often uses in the plural, seemingly meaning rights ("*les droits*" usually means rights rather than laws) but can

also refer collectively to the various types of laws that embody these rights and which, she claims, are irreducible to each other.

34 Kriegel (1998) p. 307.

35 While also stressing the benefits of localism, Fuchs (2001) is more attentive to the risks attendant to such a strategy and insists on the need to put in place strong institutional safeguards against parochialism.

36 See, for example, the Symposium on "The Politics of Place in a Globalizing Era" (2001).

37 For example, see Delbrück (1994).

38 Dagger (1997), p. 180.

39 Brugger (1999) pp. 153-180.

40 Ibid., p. 178.

41 As diZerega (2000) puts it, "[t]hose desiring a national political life of high intensity seek something best unsought" (p. 351). It may be a little unfair on my part to imply that this rather harsh judgment can be applied to contemporary civic republicans without any further distinction since many of them are well aware of the dangers that diZerega has in mind (and this is most particularly evident in the case of most American theorists discussed above, for they tend to be more liberal than republican after all) but, by the same token, there is an even greater danger in minimizing these dangers.

42 A term by which I wish to distinguish people who feel closer to a Michael Oakeshott than to a Milton Friedman.

43 This phrase is meant to allude to both intra- and international relations between unequal cultures, e.g., cultural minorities within an organized political community, and the fate of languages other than English in a world where English has become the *lingua franca*.

REFERENCES

Bailyn, Bernard. [1967] 1992. *The Ideological Origins of the American Revolution*. Enl. ed. Cambridge, Mass: Harvard University Press.

Barreau, J.-C. 1999. *Le coup d'Etat invisible.* Paris: Albin Michel.

Bohman, James. 2001. "Cosmopolitan Republicanism: Citizenship, Freedom and Global Political Authority." *The Monist*, 84, no. 1, pp. 3-22.

Bosniak, Linda. 2000. "Citizenship Denationalized." *Indiana Journal of Global Legal Studies*, 7, pp. 447-508.

Brinkley, Alan. 1996. "Liberty, Community, and the National Idea." *The American Prospect*, 7, no. 29.

Brugger, Bill. 1999. *Republican Theory in Political Thought.* London: Macmillan Press.

Cohen, Joshua, ed. 1996. *For Love of Country: Debating the Limits of Patriotism.* Boston: Beacon Press.

Dagger, Richard. 1997. *Civic virtues: Rights, Citizenship, and Republican Liberalism.* New York: Oxford University Press.

Dagger, Richard. 2001. "Republicanism and the Politics of Space." *Philosophical Explorations*, no. 3 (September), pp. 157-173.

Debray, Régis. 1998. *La République expliquée à ma fille.* Paris: Seuil.

Delbrück, Jost. 1994. "Global Migration-Immigration-Multiethnicity: Challenges to the Concept of the Nation-State." *Indiana Journal of Global Legal Studies*, 2, no. 1, pp. 45-65.

diZerega, Gus. 2000. *Persuasion, Power and Polity.* Cresskill, NJ: Hampton Press.

Fink, Zera. [1945] 1962. *The Classical Republicans*, 2nd ed. Evanston, Ill.: Northwestern University Press.
Fung, Archon. 2001. "Act Locally, Deliberate Globally." *The Good Society*, 10, no. 2, pp. 4-7.
Gallo, Max. 1998. *La France expliquée à mon fils*. Paris: Le Seuil.
Gutmann, Amy, and Dennis Thompson. 1996. *Democracy and Disagreement*. Cambridge, Mass.: Harvard University Press.
Habermas, Jürgen. 1998. *The Inclusion of the Other*. Cambridge, Mass.: MIT Press.
Hagedorn, Heike. 2000. "Republicanism and the Politics of Citizenship in Germany and France: Convergence or Divergence?" *German Policy Studies*, 1, no. 3.
Kant, Immanuel. [1795] 1983. *Perpetual Peace and Other Essays on Politics, History and Morals*. Ted Humphrey, ed. Indianapolis: Hackett.
Kearney, Richard. 1997. *Postnationalist Ireland: Politics, Culture and Philosophy*. London: Routledge.
Kriegel, Blandine. 1995. *The State and the Rule of Law*. Trans. M.A. LePain and J.C. Cohen. Princeton: Princeton University Press.
Kriegel, Blandine. 1998. *La philosophie de la république*. Paris: Plon.
Kymlicka, Will. 1998. "Liberal Egalitarianism and Civic Republicanism: Friends or Enemies?" In *Debating Democracy's Discontent*, A.L. Allan and M.C. Reagan, Jr., eds. Oxford: Oxford University Press.
Larrère, Catherine. 2000. "Libéralisme et républicanisme: Y-a-til une exception française?" *Cahiers de philosophie de l'université de Caen*, 34, pp. 127-46.
McGovern, Mark. 2000. "Irish Republicanism and the Potential Pitfalls of Pluralism." *Capital and Class*, 71 (summer), pp. 133-161.
Nicolet, Claude. 1982. *L'Idée républicaine en France*. Paris: Galimard.
Nicolet, Claude. 2000. *Histoire, nation et république*. Paris: Odile Jacob.
Pettit, Philip. 1997. *Republicanism: A Theory of Freedom and Government*. Oxford: Clarendon Press.
Pocock, John G.A. 1975. *The Machiavellian Moment*. Princeton: Princeton University Press.
Pope, James Gray. 1990. "Republican Moments: The Role of Direct Popular Power in the American Constitutional Order." *University of Pennsylvania Law Review*, 139, no. 2, pp. 287-368.
Sandel, Michael. 1996. *Democracy's Discontent: America's Search of a Public Philosophy*. Cambridge, Mass.: Harvard University Press.
Skinner, Quentin. 1981. *Machiavelli*. Oxford: Oxford University Press.
Skinner, Quentin. 1998. *Liberty Before Liberalism*. Cambridge: Cambridge University Press.
Spitz, Jean-Fabien. 1995. *La liberté politique*. Paris: P.U.F.
Sunstein, Cass. 1996. *Legal Reasoning and Political Conflict*. New York: Oxford University Press.
Symposium: The Politics of Place in a Globalizing Era. 2001. *The Good Society*, 10, no. 2, pp. 1-35.

Chapter 12

DIMENSIONS OF GLOBALIZATION: CULTURAL AND INSTITUTIONAL NOVELTIES, ETHICAL NEEDS

Andrea Migone
Simon Fraser University

INTRODUCTION

Globalization has become a buzzword for the social sciences. Nonetheless this concept has a dual problem: on the one hand its definition lacks precision, on the other it is, mostly, devoid of any moral or ethical prescriptions. These problems are intertwined and help to explain conflict regarding the goals, processes and effects of globalization.

Without a precise (or at least comprehensive) definition of the phenomenon debate and participation about globalization are stunted; without an ethical reference they are, *per force*, limited and incomplete. In this chapter I endeavour to render a definition of globalization in line with its complex nature and to introduce some ethical elements related to Economic Personalism. This approach represents the re-emerging of the Catholic ethical tradition in economics while distancing itself from the clumsiness of past attempts that ended up superimposing ethics on economics without taking into account economic realities.

The fusion of moral and ethical principles with the understanding of free-market rules and operating principles allows Economic Personalism to inject deeper and wider ethical elements into the current process of globalization by offering realistic values and processes to implement those values. In particular, the notion of human dignity and the anthropological level of analysis that are associated with Economic Personalism is helpful in analyzing globalization.

First, I shall deal with redefining the concept of globalization so that it matches its multifaceted and interconnected nature. Then I examine the contested nature of globalization, and, finally the notion of Economic Personalism is introduced and ways in which it may be beneficial to the development of a truly inclusive globalization are suggested.

S. McBride et al. (eds.), Global Instability, 201–218.

WHICH GLOBALIZATION?

Scholars use the term globalization variously: from increasingly interdependent and wide-ranging patterns of trade, to patterns of Foreign Direct Investment, to uniformity in financial regulations, and from the spreading of a capitalist mode of production to an increasing number of economic units at a worldwide level. Consequently the analytical power of the term, and its usefulness, are in doubt.

Here a definition of globalization is proposed that brings together economic and technological, but also cultural and institutional explanatory variables. It is only by recognizing that globalization is a complex and multifaceted phenomenon that we can properly deal with its effects and devise strategies to build accountability and democratic control into its development. I believe that it is time for an alternative concept of globalization, a concept that captures the complexity of the phenomenon while remaining a useful analytical tool.

At the same time we need a concept that discriminates between "globalizing" phenomena and "global" ones. A phenomenon is global when it is embedded in a socio-economic system that makes it available to consumers on a worldwide scale.[1] In this sense, images, culture and symbols are consumed just as goods are: ideas like western canons of beauty, images like the CNN logo, and goods like a can of Coca Cola fall into this category. They are readily available throughout the world in a relatively homogenized form and can be accessed and consumed easily by the masses.

Globalizing phenomena undergo a process of meaning attribution that spans the global system. When this happens, these values, images, symbols or goods acquire a special position in the process of creolization and/or of homogenization of the world system.[2] Marshall McLuhan's concept of "global village" is not globalizing unless it becomes a prevailing interpretation for a majority of the world. A CNN image is global insofar as it is available throughout the world; it is globalizing only if a shared meaning becomes attached to it. Arguably few concepts enjoy a globalizing character; yet we should not underestimate their ability to homogenize culture in the global arena.

To be able to deal in a coherent manner with the idea of globalization scholarly accounts of the subject are summarized. Various options are open at this point; one could group writers according to their commitment to the process of globalization dividing them, as Held and McGrew[3] do, in the categories of "hyperglobalist," "skeptical" and "transformationalist," or we could approach the problem by looking at the position the authors occupy in the political arena.

Sklair[4] identifies four fields in which we can subdivide globalization studies: the world-system school, the capitalist model, the global culture one and the global society approach.

The world-system school is premised on Wallerstein's work[5] and still relies on the classical division of the world in socio-political and economic dimensions in the well-known tiers of the core, periphery and semi-periphery. While there are merits to the world-system theorists' integrated approach, especially when it underlines the processes of *long dureé* and the historical nature of the world-economy, it retains an economic flavour, the nation-state is still the crucial actor, and too often cultural elements are added almost as an afterthought.

Another model of globalization has at its core the increased relevance of the capitalist mode of production as the (pre)dominant organizational structure for nearly all economies in the world. Authors in this category share little beyond the general understanding that capitalist forces have become crucial in organizing our world. There are at least three main ideological camps that can be delineated here. At one end of the spectrum, we find historical-structuralist explanations of globalization.[6] These narratives to stress the political nature of globalization, making it rather more the brainchild of national and supra-national political institutions and elites than the natural evolution of the market. Alongside the historical-structuralists, are those nationalists who believe that globalization reduces the individuality of national cultural and economic traits to a homogenized state, and that such a trend should be opposed.

On the opposite side, at least as far as the mechanics of globalization are concerned, we find true believers in the power of the hidden hand of the market. They believe that the current economic trends towards more integration, increased mobility of financial instruments and higher levels of regulative convergence are a natural and inevitable evolution of our market system. Any policy attempt at countering these changes is bound to have detrimental effects and the only viable solution is to eliminate the shackles that immobilize market forces. These authors tend to be ideologically libertarian and embrace this school's tenets of minimal state and place efficiency before redistribution.

In between these two currents is the neoliberal one. Proponents of this brand of political economy believe that economic globalization has such an inertial power that it cannot be stopped or reversed by any one state or coalition of states. Governments, though, can use policy to reduce the negative impacts that economic globalization is likely to inflict on the polity. It is in this context that we can explain the programs aimed at retraining low-skilled workers and incentives for hi-tech companies to invest in a certain area.

While the two schools that we have looked at use economic forces as their main explanatory variable, the next two look more to the cultural and sociological areas of the social sciences. The third "vision" of globalization is called the global culture approach by Sklair.[7] Featherstone, Robertson and Appadurai also fall in this category.[8] Their work has been very influential, especially in sociology, in hinting at the possibility of establishing a global culture. Concepts of hybridization and creolization of cultural elements have emerged in an attempt to deal with the processes of interaction that have become more common in the recent years.

This group of scholars hardly constitutes a school proper. The variance among the arguments used in approaching the subject of globalization and culture is too great. Authors' interests range from the analysis of what happens to local cultures in the face of an advancing "global culture" to the issue of globalscapes and the role of the state in filtering global trends.[9]

The global society model is closely related to the global culture model.[10] Proponents of this model look at sociological elements to support their arguments and focus on the current viability of the notion of global society. They argue that recent changes in science, industry, and technology have made universal values increasingly viable and attractive. This approach looks at modernity and at the disrupting effects that global forces seem to impose onto local realities and particularistic loyalties. One of its most interesting contributions concerns the ethical dimension that needs to be appended to economic and technological globalization if we really desire a viable global society that will not be synonymous with the global exploitation of human and natural resources.[11]

The problem with all these approaches is that they tend to focus overwhelmingly on a single dimension. World-Systems theory tends to be economistic, the global capitalism model is focused on market forces and their impact on the economy and, through this lens, on society to the detriment of cultural and sociological variables that are instead captured by the global culture and global society approaches.

A more varied and multi-layered approach is necessary. David Held has conducted some of this analysis.[12] These models are sophisticated in that they attempt to bring together the variables already discussed. Globalization, according to these authors, exists in dynamic relation with regionalization, localization, and internationalization. It should then be possible for the researcher measure it by assessing the relative weight of four elements: first, the extent of political and economic activity across borders; second, the growing intensity of what are regular, interconnected patterns of activity among nations; third, the growing speed at which these relations occur; and fourth, the increased importance that distant events have for the local activity. The patterns of globalization in our time trace a watershed in human history not only because of convergence at an unprecedented rate in the political, economic and cultural spheres; but also because they are supported by a novel set of powerful institutional constraints both at the national and international level that have forced a new set of values and ideas onto the world stage.

THE CONTESTED GLOBAL ORDER

There are four equally relevant elements involved in the globalization process of the latter part of the century: economic, technological, cultural, and institutional. The economic element comprises the increased convergence of financial and industrial sectors across the world economy, along with the increased relevance of MNCs in the new economic order. The technological element consists of the revolution in the communication and information sectors and the radical changes that these new technologies have brought to our society.

These two elements are quite commonly dealt with in most of the relevant literature. However, it is important to stress that, whereas there have been periods during which economic and technological patterns closely resembled those that we see today,[13] and while empires spanned vast regions of the world providing regular long-distance commercial ties,[14] the nature of the current phase of globalization is novel in a few crucial ways.

The nature of economic convergence that we see today is different from convergence in the nineteenth century, the time period that is most quoted by those who believe globalization to be an ongoing historical process. Nineteenth century commodity market integration depended on falling transportation costs, but in the modern era, after 1950, a crucial role was played by liberal trade policies. International organizations and multilateral agreements were fundamental in strengthening these policies. The second difference is the nature of the technological revolution that is taking place today. It is not possible to compare the technological changes in transportation and communication of the late 1800s and early 1900s (refrigeration for naval transports, transatlantic telegraph cables, falling costs for rail transport) with the current revolution in information technology. The latter has changed our capacity to move, and use wealth, information and goods well beyond what our grandfathers experienced. But more importantly, it has changed our very notion of goods, information and culture, as we have been socialized to consume and use virtual goods and identities.

The cultural element of globalization is a crucial one. Cultural identities, symbols and ideas used to be less contested: national roots were more important than they are today and information and communication was much more strictly controlled by national actors. While it is true that around the world there are still strong nationalistic feelings, the West has declared nationalism to be a bankrupt ideology, something upon which modern capitalist democracies could not, and would not, build their political systems. The concepts of liberal democracy and of capitalistic development have become the new anchoring values.

In the 1980s and 1990s the relevance of liberal individualism, as it is applied in economics, has become ever more crucial in defining the identity of most individuals in the industrialized world. The main effects of this philosophical approach are an increased tendency towards individualistic behaviour, a shift in the way we construct our identity both in relation with ourselves and in relation with others. More and more we are defined and classified according to our consumption patterns, and a change in what determines social membership; this latter becoming coterminous with membership in the market.

The most striking element of the cultural influxes of globalization resides not so much in the possibility of creating a global culture or a global society, but in the current reality of the creation of an accepted image of the world market. According to this image, we all share an economic-based identity and economic-driven goals and only on a secondary level do we share other commonalities.

While concerns over the hybridization/hegemonization of culture are important and worth pursuing, most people do not give a second thought to the division of labour that has occurred at a global level and that is truly having globalizing effects. It has become very difficult, today, to frame any discourse regarding national economic policy outside of the global market paradigm. It is almost impossible to challenge this socio-economic paradigm outside of its own language, symbolism and ideology.

Not only has the liberal economic paradigm become hegemonic in the realm of market exchanges, but it has become central to our political and social exchanges too. Examine, for example, the seemingly harmless and certainly widely accepted notion that nations should be competitive to succeed in the world market. The truth is that competitiveness is a concept that pertains to firms rather than to nations because the two entities are premised on radically different needs, constituting parts and goals. Yet, very few people challenge this vision. Socialization and cultural growth have also changed because of this new philosophy and because of the technological revolution in which we are steeped.

Western societies are shaped more and more obviously by consumption patterns. At the same time the state, which has been the guardian of national cultures, is now forced to bow to global economic concerns and allow consumption and behavioural messages to enter national borders and influence citizens. In this context, while some ideas and symbols may undergo creolization processes, the greatest majority of goods have homogenized characteristics and flow from a few cultural and industrial centres. The state retains the ability of filtering some of these messages, but even here the latitude that is allowed to the individual state is limited.

The nature of the information technology revolution has also been crucial in increasing the number and type of goods readily available for consumption and in modifying the patterns of production and consumption themselves by introducing virtual goods and increasing the consumption of cultural and recreational goods and services.

This process of deep change in the way we organize our socio-economic world has also had a deep impact on the ethical and moral values that support, justify and help reproduce.

Because we model our interactions on market-type exchange and we define and evaluate ourselves in relation with our consumption we have tended to focus on an individualistic morality that has marginalized social ethics and solidarity. There is, though, a more worrisome element in this transition from a societal and political culture to one premised on economic individualism. Because neoclassical economics is premised on the concepts of efficiency and profit, rather than on solidarity and redistribution, states and groups have less room for developing social policies. Similarly, accountability and democratic control have often given way to efficiency and technocratic control.[15]

An essential part of these processes has been devised, implemented and sustained through international organizations that have become more and more relevant in brokering and enforcing agreements.[16] There is no doubt that the institutions that originated from the Bretton Woods Agreement have been very successful in establishing a cohesive epistemic elite within their top management. They have also achieved staggering results as far as opening new markets both for goods and investments, reducing tariffs and barriers to trade and increasing the free circulation of capitals.

They have played the pivotal role of imposing and legitimizing the new global "economic" world vision that we have delineated above. In their interaction with nation-states, they have been instrumental in fostering and supporting the shifting focus of the state from redistribution to efficiency.

While international and supranational organizations have grown and expanded their reach, nation-states have transferred many powers to the International Monetary Fund (IMF), the Organisation for Economic Co-operation and Development (OECD), the World Trade Organization (WTO), the European Union (EU) and so forth. While this is not necessarily the end of the nation-state, it represents a change in its focus. This change, while ensuring a degree of cohesiveness in economic and trade policy, increases the distance between rulers and ruled and makes the process of accountability less straightforward.

The concept of globalization seems often to be shaped and developed in the ivory towers of the international financial and trade organizations, away from the input of grass-root and opposition groups and, sometimes, away from the reach of any but the most powerful governments. Globalization is a process of dynamic interrelations, among unequal actors, premised on a system of exchanges that functions at the economic, technological, cultural, and institutional levels. This process of dynamic interrelations may lead to interdependence, creolization, or homogenization.

The meaning of globalization is strongly restricted, leaving little room for true creolization and negotiation. The following section proposes that we utilize some of the concepts developed by Economic Personalism to attach a different ethical dimension to the current wave of globalization so to render it more inclusive.

Drawing from Economic Personalism: A Suggested Ethical Blueprint for Globalization

Globalization needs to be comprehensive and complex because of the varied impacts that it bestows upon societies and economies. However, the neoliberal concepts that fuel much of the economic processes have slowly spilled over in the cultural and social realms, changing deeply our notion of ethics by pushing it in a utilitarian and individualistic direction.

While economics is a moral science, the type of moral ethics that have emerged from the diffusion of the neoliberal economic paradigm are insufficient and poorly adapted to the current wave of globalization. Just like industries, activists, labourers, and governments had to adapt to the sweeping social, technological, economic, political, and cultural changes wrought by globalization, so our ethical framework should be amended.

A useful set of general principles may be found by looking at Economic Personalism. In the past few years the debate between market economists and moral philosophers and theologians (especially from the Catholic area) has been interesting. The scholars who have been part of this process have tried to develop an anthropological understanding of the human person and to weave the moral elements of persons into their economic behaviour as opposed to earlier attempts at simply superimposing a religious ethic onto the economic sphere, thus ignoring basic economic laws and realities.

The origins of Economic Personalism are to be found in the evolution of personalism, as it was defined by Mounier,[17] along lines of intellectual development pioneered by Karol Wojtyla,[18] and later developed by Novack, O'Boyle, Gronbacher and Rush Finn among others.[19] In Mounier, the anthropological outlook of philosophical research and the social and dynamic nature of the person are juxtaposed to the closed and limited notion of an individualistic or economist reading of society. In Economic Personalism these notions are retained: personalists talk of persons rather then of individuals; in their view the former is a complex construction of social, religious, physical, economic and cultural elements. Persons live in an interconnected society, rich with groups and relationships that encompass, but go well beyond the restrictive boundaries of economic behaviour. It is only in recognizing this complexity and in accounting for the natural tensions and by grounding our work in a full understanding of the human person that we can hope to speak to, and try to resolve, the problems of our society.

Economic Personalism does not assume to be the final answer to the issue of morality in the economic realm but the scholars who embrace its vision are aware of the fact that this is the first coherent synthesis of Catholic moral ethics and economic realities. In the past both Catholic and Protestant writers tried, with varying degrees of success, to do the same. In the Catholic tradition, modern economic reflection started in 1891 with the encyclical *Rerum Novarum.* The focus on property rights and on the conditions of worker after massive industrialization contained in the encyclical brought many to theorize that a better distribution of wealth would benefit the world. The idea of *distributism*, though, led more to the nostalgic idealization of a lost agrarian community than to real life solutions.[20] By assuming the stock of wealth to be fixed and by working only on the modes of its distribution, the authors discounted the study of production and generated, at best, a limited analysis of economic reality.

In 1931 Pius XI wrote the encyclical *Quadragesimo Anno*. This work contained another important principle of Catholic economic thought: the notion of solidarity. Pius XI was concerned by the trends economicism that he saw in both the capitalist and socialist regimes, at the same time he was wary of excessive state intervention in the market because he believed it would limit individual freedom and choices. In response to these dual needs he envisioned a society in which voluntary, non-governmental associations would set rules for moral conduct and behaviour that would safeguard human dignity and freedom of activity by inspiring a moral environment. With the publication of the encyclical a Solidarist movement developed.

Solidarism was deeply connected with the German Historical School and shared with it the organic vision of society and the search for specific economic principles to apply to specific economic and historical situations. Notwithstanding the good intentions, this approach still relied primarily on a very crude economic model and, ultimately, its unsophisticated nature sapped its usefulness.

Outside of the realm of religious writers there are other moral discourses such as those of the Postmodernist, Neo-Marxist and Liberal theories. However, they are not as useful as Economic Personalism for the analysis of the current wave of globalization. Neo-Marxist writers often tend to assume too much about the substantive content of their moral position, Post-Modernists seldom go beyond a general critique of the bonds and limitations imposed by knowledge meta-narratives to spell out a well defined set of moral rules,[21] and Liberalism, at least in the format that most impacts on globalization (the philosophy of the international financial and economic organizations), developed into a mainly individualist philosophy.

Postmodernist analysis, in its most general terms, is based on the opposition to the impositions of meta-narrative categories that constrain and label what is an otherwise individual landscape, and on relativism. Postmodern analyses have traditionally been interested in the processes and effects of globalization because these technological, economic, and cultural processes mark the end of the modern organization of societies,[22] developing a new mode of capitalist development and the reactions it met.[23]

While the postmodernist field is composed by a variety of eclectic authors from a variety of different disciplines, all share the rejection of any claim to truth as an undue constraint on the freedom and creativity of individuals. Based on a deeply relativist premise, postmodernism argues that our perception and codification of the attributes of an object generates the reality of that object. The problem is that just as there are infinite possible attributes for an object, so there are infinite possible ways of codifying and perceiving those attributes. It follows that infinite realities are possible and that no universal reference can ever be established.[24]

Suspicious of those who would impose a framework of thought through theory, postmodernist authors strive for the creative redefinition of the systems of signification that emerge from the epistemic hegemony of the state. They do so by refusing the constraints of theory and by embracing an ever-shifting system of creative analysis premised and built on the moral priority of the creativity and freedom of the individual (Lindholm, 1997). Much like the Romantic vision by which it is inspired, postmodernism runs the risk of slipping into a morally suspicious area; caught between the Scylla of an extremely individualized approach that refuses all theoretical references, and the Charybdis of a very low tolerance for those who, instead, would wish to propose these references.

While the moral relevance of the individual is a positive trait of Postmodernism, its refusal to engage in positive analysis and concrete suggestions as to the minimal moral basis of the process of globalization makes it a somehow second choice as a model for a humane economy.

Marxist and Neomarxist authors share with Postmodernists the idea that the power structures that depend on the capitalist mode of production, be they the political, social, or economic expression of the economic structure of the world. In this approach the process of globalization is inherently political and the changes we observe depend on the needs of the capitalist world system and on its requirements of consistent, unchecked expansion. Marx's theory of ethics is part of his general social theory. This is that economic forces determine the course of history: the whole superstructure of society (politics, ideas, legislation, art, religion and, morals) is determined by the material conditions of production. The morality that prevails in any society is premised on the need of the ruling class.[25] Most examples of Neomarxist approaches, as noted above, are heavily critical of the established economic order and very suspicious of the redistribution of wealth that it generates. While we should be careful not to discount these questions because they are central to the discussion of a fair society we should also be careful of the alternative most often put forward by these authors, i.e., a heavy external intervention in the market. The assumption that state control or direction in the economic realm is a better choice than freedom of choice by the individual has been often proven wrong, sadly, by left wing governments.

Liberalism has a tradition of generating debate about ethics and freedom,[26] and their relationship with the market.[27] Liberal theories of justice tend to stress the principles of equality and freedom of the individual, are generally couched in terms of objectivity and impartiality, and, in their market approaches, strongly rely on the notion of the hidden hand to support the claims of efficiency and impersonality.[28] Liberal moral theory has tended to hinge much of its power on the claim that by refusing to find its roots in a parochial or local ideology, it instead, relies on general concepts. This would allow Liberal moral theory to gain a measure of distance from the various competing social groups, to reduce to a minimum internal friction, and to achieve, as a result, an impartial social agreement based on justice as in Rawls Political Liberalism. Various critiques have been levelled against these statements. The more forceful are the Postmodernist and Neomarxist claim that many of the key tenets of Liberal moral theory can be traced back to Liberal economic theory, by no means a value free enterprise, and the Communitarian position that criticizes the Liberal attempt at achieving impartiality by distancing morals from the local and personal as a "view from nowhere."[29]

From the point of view of morals and the economy Liberal theorists have a varied approach but share the common trait that high priority is given to individual freedom as a necessary premise to free activity and the impartial role of free market mechanisms in allocating resources.

While it is certainly true that the market is the best allocative system at our disposal, the issue that is most disturbing in the dominant liberal thought is the underlying idea that the workings of the Hidden Hand, as described by Adam Smith and as it is championed by all liberal thinkers, is the close similarity between the process of market allocation and the Darwinian process of natural selection.[30] In the current individualist climate this process has the potential to degenerate into a forced race to the bottom and inherently denies the moral primacy of the individual independently of his/her material contribution to society. Because of these shortcomings liberal moral theory is, like the postmodern and Marxist ones, not quite what we are looking for.

None of the approaches seen above seems satisfying in assisting in the development of a moral outlook for the globalizing world. Economic Personalism holds a better chance of succeeding where these other authors failed because it is based on a sophisticated anthropological analysis of both the human being and the economy. The following tenets are the result of this analysis.

The Centrality of the Person. It is imperative that the affirmation of every person in each circumstance be at the centre of personalist behaviour;

Subjectivity and Autonomy. Persons are both unique in their being and autonomous. Persons are subjects *sui juris* enjoying selfmastery. This freedom comes with the limitation of proper exercise of freedom.

Human Dignity. Every human person deserves affirmation and respect irrespectively of their talents or contributions to society.

Social Nature of the Person. Persons can only truly blossom and affirm themselves in a social setting. Relational ties with others are crucial in building a true community where people work and live together rejecting individualism.

Participation and Solidarity. Persons operate together demonstrating solidarity towards one another.

Fundamental to the whole theoretical and moral construction of Personalism is the recognition that human beings, ontologically, exist before society or the economy or the state, and that they operate in a social context, meaning that they cannot be dealt with as separate from their familial, social, associational, and political ties to other human beings.

Economic Personalism firmly believes that a free market economy is the best possible way of organizing the exchange and production of goods and services. Premised on the Catholic economic doctrine, this position notes that economic freedom, premised on the respect of private property, is a necessary element of human freedom given that its lack often leads to the impossibility of reaching other forms of freedom.

Nonetheless economic freedom should be properly mitigated by moral concerns for the welfare of others and by the notion of universal destination of goods.[31] This means respect for human capital, stewardship of resources, and complete support for the poor. The society that emerges from these premises is caring, moral, and lively. At its centre is a responsible citizen, both from a social and a corporate point of view, who respects human dignity and recognizes the need of the person to be affirmed in her/his own right independently of circumstances. In embracing the free market as the best way to organize economic exchange these authors do not automatically accept it in its current neoliberal structure. Rather there is the recognition that a free-market approach is the least constraining of all the system of economic exchange, but that an explicit set of moral tenets must be incorporated into the system.

Economic Personalism is a concept based on individual freedom and responsibility. The individual is at its centre but this same individual rejects individualist and needlessly egoistic behaviour, recognizes the role that social agencies and groups (families, parties, associations, the state) can play and participates in their activities. In this context even methodological individualism, if properly understood, can be fruitfully incorporated in the personalist economy. This means understanding methodological individualism as expressing the ontological priority of the individual over society or the state and the unique individuality and autonomy of each human being, but not as representing moral individualism in its retreat from the social nature of human beings into a selfish world.

Economic Personalism is very keen on asserting the freedom and individuality of each and every person. In doing so it limits but does not reject the state. The central role of the state in economics is the creation of legislative frameworks for the market without unduly restricting the flow of free economic transactions. The concept of *subsidiarity* as developed in the encyclical *Quadragesimo Anno* (1931) is crucial in this context. Helping others (the Latin *subsidium*) does not always mean direct intervention; rather it is the art of facilitating the ability of persons to choose for themselves. As it applies to the state, *subsidiarity* translates in the allocation of policy-making functions to those institutions that can perform them most efficiently, generally those institutions that directly supervises those who will feel the effects of the decision most keenly.

In such a context the state is a decentralized structure thriving on the feedback of the citizenry and the latter participates in the policy-making process ultimately making the state its own voice.

Of the precepts noted above two hold particular interest for anyone who is interested in a more inclusive approach for globalization: these are the centrality of the human person as an autonomous and unique being, and the need for participation. The centrality of the human person is not a particularly new concept or even a solely Catholic concept. A lay notion of this respect can easily be traced to the Kantian notion that no human being can ever be reduced to means to and end. Respect of the dignity of persons and an interest in allowing for the affirmation of all human beings must naturally pass through the process of participation.

It is one of the tenets of liberal thought that the individuals are best positioned to understand and articulate their interests and goals. In the current period of globalization more than before, we have a moral duty to facilitate this process and we should expand this notion from the realm of economic behaviour to all the spheres of human relations.

This process must be implemented through the tools of participation and consultation. The minimum required ethical standard that we must meet in a global society is consultation. When the decisions we take have global-reaching social, economic, cultural and technological effects, they must be dealt with through a process that assures open and effective consultation, maximum participation and the willingness to listen, debate and allow for different views and principles. Ideally this process should lead to a process of creolization, to a truly global result stemming from the fact that the symbols, goods and ideas that undergo this process are the product of human interaction rather than the product of cultural, economic of political homogenization.

If the preservation and enhancement of human dignity, and the achievement of the affirmation of the human person are our ultimate goals, then a corollary of this goal is that to maximize this effort we should use a Pareto-efficient mechanism. This is a further case in which the articulation of goals, interests, and desires would be immensely aided by a meaningful process of consultation and participation the like of which the current system, based on technocracy and elite decision-making, does not seem able to produce.

Globalization has deep economic, technological, cultural, and institutional effects on our world. None of these effects is, per se, negative or positive. Their evaluation must depend on whether they contribute to or counter the dignity and affirmation of those they touch. In this sense this last wave of globalization has an edge on previous ones in that its novel institutional setting can be fruitfully used to generate the needed level of dialogue and interaction that we described above. To some extent the notion of interaction and creolization is already present in the system. Multilateralism is a process of interaction and modification of trade policies and economic processes aimed at capturing as much assent as possible.

It will be fundamental for the future of globalization to take to heart the need for human dignity and effective participation and dialogue, and to make the necessary corrections to the institutional framework that supports, validates, and replicates the elements of globalization so that they can allow for meaningful and inclusive debate.

The price to pay for failing to do so would be staggeringly high. The ethical foundations of the current system do not match the scope and reach of its impact on other societies and economies around the world often making the process of globalization needlessly difficult, painful and skewed.

NOTES

1 The notion of consumption and its socializing effect in our society would deserve a whole new study, let me stress here that it is my position that much of our socialization is achieved through either the act of consumption or through the actual consumption of goods, services, images and symbols.
While the consumption (and the production) of images and art in a market-like fashion is nothing new (Jardine, 1996), our current system has attributed unprecedented importance to this type of consumption.

2 By homogenization here we intend a process through which a certain image or product is provided to international consumers in much the same way and form in which it provided to national consumers. Creolization, instead, is a process of hybridization that modifies the original image, idea, product or symbol through the contact it has with other images, ideas, products and symbols. It is a more balanced process, in which the elements of the exchange are negotiated and modified.

3 David Held et al. (2000) pp. 54-60.

4 Sklair (1999) pp. 143-162.

5 Wallerstein (1979); Shannon (1989).

6 For example Hirst and Thompson (1996).

7 Leslie Sklair (1999) pp. 143-162.

8 Featherstone (1995) (1990) pp. 1-14; Robertson (1992) pp. 295-310; Appadurai (1990) pp. 295-310.

9 Appadurai (1990) pp. 295-310.

10 Giddens (1991); Robertson (1992).

11 Held (1995).

12 Held et al (2000) pp. 54-60; Held et al (1999) pp. 7-13.

13 O'Rourke (1999).

14 Abu-Lughod (1989).

15 While there is no reason to believe that the state could be a better moral paragon than the economic agent socially inclined states were often more responsive and more accountable to the voters at large than the current neoliberal economies.

16 Cohn (2000); Longman (1984).

17 Mounier (1970) [1952].

18 Wojtyla (1975).

19 Rush Finn (1999); Gronbacher (1998); Gronbacher (1999); Novack (1993); Novak (1982); O'Boyle (1998).

20 For distributism, see, among the rest, Dale (1982); Chesterton (1910); Belloc (1912).

21 Lindholm (1997); Wyschogrod (1990).

22 Sarup (1993).

23 Burbach et al. (2001); Elazar (1998); Jameson (1991): Harvey (1989); Gottdiener (1995).

24 See, for example, Shweder (1984) (1991).

25 Thomas (1997); Hazlitt (1964).

26 Rawls (1993); Rawls (1999); Kelly (2001); Neal (2000).

27 Buchanan (1975); Gauthier (1986) (1990) (1993); Hayek (1962); Lund (1996); Torek (1994).

28 Kessler (2000).

29 Nagel (1986); Strike (2000).

30 Kauffman (1995); Kelly (1994).

31 In Catholic economic doctrine the notion of "universal destination of goods" refers to the proper use of the goods and resources that are available to us. Given that God has

created the universe with all that it contains and that God's aim is to allow for the harmonious development of humanity Catholics have two duties when utilizing these resources: on the one hand they must see to the needs of themselves and of their families, on the other, once the former needs are satisfied, they have a stewardship role to play making sure that what is in surplus for them reaches those in need.

REFERENCES

Abu-Lughod, Janet. 1989. *Before European Hegemony*. Oxford: Oxford University Press.

Appadurai, Arjun. 1990. "Disjuncture and Difference in the Global Cultural Economy." *Theory, Culture And Society*, 7, pp. 295-310.

Belloc, Hilaire. 1912. *The Servile State*. London: T.N. Foulis.

Buchanan, James M. 1975. *The Limits of Liberty: Between Anarchy and Leviathan*. Chicago: University of Chicago Press.

Burbach, Roger et al. 2001. *Globalization and Postmodern Politics: From Zapatistas to High-Tech Robber Barons*. London: Arawak Publications.

Chesterton, Gilbert Keith. 1910. *What's Wrong with the World*. London: Cassell and Co.

Cohn, Theodore H. 2000. *Global Political Economy: Theory and Practice*. New York: Longman.

Dale, Alzina Stone. 1982. *The Outline of Sanity: A Biography of G.K. Chesterton*. Grand Rapids: Eerdmans.

Elazar, Daniel Judah. 1998. *Constitutionalizing Globalization: The Postmodern Revival of Confederal Arrangements*. Lanham: Rowman & Littlefield Publishers.

Featherstone, Mike. 1990. "Global Culture: An Introduction." *Theory, Culture And Society*, 7.

Featherstone, Mike. 1995. *Undoing Culture: Globalization, Postmoderism and Identity*. London: Sage Publications.

Gauthier, David P. 1986. *Morals by Agreement*. Oxford: Oxford University Press.

Gauthier, David P. 1990. *Moral Dealing: Contract, Ethics, and Reason*. Ithaca: Cornell University Press.

Gauthier, David P., and Robert Sugden, eds. 1993. *Rationality, Justice and the Social Contract: Themes from Morals by Agreement*. New York: Harvester Wheatsheaf.

Giddens, Anthony. 1991. *The Consequences Of Modernity*. Cambridge: Polity Press.

Gottdiener, Mark. 1995. *Postmodern Semiotics: Material Culture and the Forms of Postmodern Life*. Cambridge: Blackwell.

Gronbacher, Gregory. 1998. "The Need for Economic Personalism." *Journal of Markets and Morality*, 1, no. 1.

Gronbacher, Gregory. 1999. "The Humane Economy: Neither Right nor Left. A Response to Daniel Finn." *Journal of Markets and Morality*, 2, no. 2.

Harvey, D. 1989. *The Condition of Postmodernity*. London: Blackwell.

Hayek, F. B. 1962. *The Road to Serfdom*. London: Routledge and Kegan Paul.

Hazlitt, Henry. 1964. *The Foundations of Morality*. New York: Van Nostrand.

Held, David. 1995. *Democracy and the Global Order*. Cambridge: Polity Press.

Held, David, and Anthony McGrew. 1999. "Global Transformations." *ReVisions*, 22, no. 2, pp. 7-13.

Held, David, Anthony McGrew, D. Goldblatt, and J. Perraton. 2000. "Rethinking Globalization." In David Held, and Anthony McGrew (eds.), *The Global Transformation Reader*. Cambridge: Polity Press.

Hirst, P., and G. Thompson. 1996. *Globalization in Question: The International Economy and the Possibilities of Governance*. Cambridge: Polity Press.

Jacobson, H.K. 1984. *Networks of Interdependence*. Second Ed. New York: McGraw-Hill.

Jameson, F. 1991. *Postmodernism, or, the Cultural Logic of Late Capitalism*. Durham, Duke University Press.

Kauffman, S. 1995. *At Home in The Universe: The Search for the Laws of Self-Organization and Complexity*. New York: Oxford University Press.

Kelly, Erin, ed. 2001. *Justice as Fairness: A Restatement*. Cambridge: Harvard University Press.

Kelly, K., 1994. *Out of Control: The New Biology of Machines, Social Systems, and the Economic World*. New York: Addison-Wesley.

Kessler, Clive. 2000. "Globalization: Another False Universalism?" *Third World Quarterly*, 21, no. 6, pp. 931-942.

Lindholm, Charles. 1997. "Logical and Moral Dilemmas of Postmodernism." *Journal of the Royal Anthropological Institute*, 3, no. 4, pp. 747-760.

Lund, Brian. 1996. "Robert Nozick and the Politics of Social Welfare." *Political Studies*, 44, no. 1, pp. 115-122.

Mounier, Emmanuel. 1970. [1952] *Personalism*. Notre Dame: University of Notre Dame Press.

Nagel, T., 1986. *The View from Nowhere*. New York: Oxford University Press.

Neal, Patrick. 2000. "Three Readings of Political Liberalism: Rawls, Maritain, and Crick." *Journal of Political Ideologies*, 5, no. 2, pp. 225-246.

Novak, Michael. 1982. *The Spirit of Democratic Capitalism*. New York: Simon and Schuster.

Novak, Michael. 1993. *The Catholic Ethic and the Spirit of Capitalism*. New York: Free Press.

O'Boyle, Edward J. 1998. *Personalist Economics: Moral Convictions, Economic Realities, and Social Action*. Boston: Kluwer Academic.

O'Rourke, K.H., and J.G. Williamson. 1999. *Globalization and History, The Evolution of a Nineteenth Century Atlantic Economy*. Cambridge: MIT Press.

Rawls, John. 1993. *Political Liberalism*. New York: Columbia University Press.

Rawls, John. 1999. *A Theory Of Justice*. Cambridge: Belknap Press of Harvard University Press.

Robertson, R. 1992. *Globalization: Social Theory and Global Culture*. London: Sage.

Rush Finn, Daniel. 1999. "The Economic Personalism of John Paul II: Neither Right nor Left." *Journal of Markets and Morality*, 2, no. 1.

Sarup, Madan. 1993. *An Introductory Guide to Post-Structuralism and Postmodernism*. Atlanta: University of Georgia Press.

Sklair, Leslie. 1999. "Competing Concepts of Globalization." *Journal of World-Systems Research*, 5, no. 2.

Shannon, T.H. 1989. *An Introduction to the World-Systems Perspective*. Boulder: Westview Press.

Shweder, R. 1984. "Anthropology's Romantic Rebellion Against the Enlightenment: or There's More to Thinking than Reason and Evidence." In Shweder, R., and Levine R. eds. *Culture Theory: Essays on Mind*. Cambridge: Cambridge University Press.

Shweder, R. ed. 1991 *Thinking Through Cultures: Expeditions in Cultural Psychology*. Cambridge: Harvard University Press.

Strike, Kenneth A. 2000. "Liberalism, Communitarianism and the Space Between: In Praise of Kindness." *Journal of Moral Education*, 29, no. 2, pp. 133-147.

Thomas, Robert Murray. 1997. *Moral Development Theories - Secular and Religious: A Comparative Study*. Westport: Greenwood Press.

Torek, Paul. 1994. "Liberties, Not Rights: Gauthier and Nozick on Property." *Social Theory and Practice*, 20, no. 3, pp. 343-361.
Wesley, John. 1999 [Feb. 17, 1744]. "The Use Of Money." Wesley Center for Applied Theology: Wesley Center at Northwest Nazarene University, Nampa, ID.
Wojtyla, Karol. 1975. "Rodzicielstow'a *Communis Personarum* [Parenthood and the *Communis Personarum*]." *Ateneum Kaplanokie*, 84, no. 1.
Wyschogrod, Edith. 1990. *Saints and Postmodernism: Revisioning Moral Philosophy*. Chicago: Chicago University Press.

Chapter 13

QUASI DEMOCRACY

Duncan Cameron
University of Ottawa

Politics is about property, and about property rights.[1] In Canada, and other OECD industrialized countries, this is clearly the case; and it is largely true for non-OECD countries as well. Other issues are also important, politics is not exclusively about the rights to property, but these rights are central, crucial even to the nature of the political process generally described as liberal democracy. It is one of the great qualities of C.B. Macpherson as a political scientist that he saw this so clearly and was able through his talent for clear exposition to help others to understand it as well.[2] In his works property rights played a role, from his first book on Social Credit in Alberta,[3] to his powerful short work *The Life and Times of Liberal Democracy*.[4] He also edited a collection of texts called simply *Property*, perhaps so that it would be clear to all what he thought was important.[5]

Pierre Bourdieu, the French sociologist has recently described social science as being charged with making visible what many would prefer remained invisible.[6] In this sense Macpherson was a great social scientist, serving as an example to emulate. But sadly much of what he had to say about property rights and democracy seems to have been obscured despite the flourishing of political theory writing. In a sense Macpherson anticipated this. He wrote, "the predictable result is increasing obfuscation" referring to the failure of theorists to see the role of property accumulation in our societies. He saw that some theorists might be "unaware of the restraint imposed by the accumulation factor." [7] By this reasoning it is less easy to excuse Canadian theorists who presumably are familiar with his main ideas.[8]

In what follows I bring some of the analytical categories developed by Macpherson to bear on the need to revisit and update our conceptual thinking in the light of "global turbulence." In Macpherson's *Life and Times*, he points to the link between liberal democracy and class. It is the attempt to reconcile a society built around the class relations of market capitalism with liberal democratic values that characterizes the beginnings of liberal democracy that Macpherson dates to Bentham and James Mill. He called this period protective democracy where a limited franchise would protect the

S. McBride et al. (eds.), Global Instability, 219–231.

governed from the governors. It was model one in a series of historical evolutions of liberal democracy. Model three depicted contemporary liberal democracy as equilibrium democracy. The main influence was the work of Schumpeter. Writing in the mid-1970s, Macpherson found this version of liberal democracy to be less inspiring than the ethical conception of liberal democracy favoured by John Stuart Mill and described in model two as developmental democracy, and less satisfying than what Macpherson saw on the horizon, participatory democracy.

My argument here is that in Canada, at least, we have retreated from the democratic ideals of model two put forward by J.S. Mill. In model three the idea that democracy was about the nature of society, its ethical underpinnings, was already absent. But by the end of the 20th century the ideas that gave model three its legitimacy have gone missing as well. Macpherson's model three was a competitive market model where political entrepreneurs (parties) chased individual voters (consumers). The two were connected by an electoral system about which Macpherson made little comment. What caught his attention was that the competitive market was in fact more like an oligopoly. Voters were not sovereign anymore than consumers were sovereign in an economic oligopoly market. Just as the choices before voters were limited by the structure of the party system, choices in the market were governed by the emergence of giant firms that dominated production and distribution.

Macpherson called model three equilibrium democracy for an important reason. In an essay first published in 1961 he explained how the term "equilibrium" linked thinking about political science to economics.[9] In the world of the economy autonomous consumers buy and sell the products produced by enterprises. The choices made by each independently of the other, when aggregated, constitute the general equilibrium of the productive forces in society. With no one setting out to do anything more than express their personal preferences, and without conscious design, especially not by government, society has established a pattern of economic relationships that can lead to growth, full employment and low inflation if allowed to operate freely. Without anyone being compelled "to perform social functions," but rather by their buying cheap and selling dear, they allocate resources productively. Similarly, voters expressing their individual preferences end up electing a government. Irrespective of what motives compel people to enter politics, the need to seek voter support forces the parties to supply the demanded political goods to the electorate or face expulsion from elective office. In both cases the "equilibrium" occurs in the abstract. It is outside the influence of history, institutions, social class, international relations of dominance and control.

I suggest that when we set the workings of the early 21st century party system against the principles of equilibrium democracy we get a new category. I call it (inspired again by Macpherson, this time in his discussion of the party system in Alberta) quasi democracy, "quasi" in the sense of "not real" or "almost" democracy. Rather than moving ahead towards participatory democracy, as Macpherson wanted to see, we have moved away from liberal democratic values. In addition to the failings in contemporary liberal democracy identified by Macpherson, those similar to a market system dominated by few "sellers," our society has experienced new weaknesses. Most importantly by the end of the century the option of removing the government from power seemed to have disappeared so that Canada no longer qualified as an equilibrium democracy, one where voters can choose to change the government. Surprisingly, it is open to question whether Canada deserves to be called liberal democratic at all.[10] Why may Canada not be a full-fledged liberal democracy? Because it fails to meet the criteria generally accepted by political science: majority rule, government by discussion and debate, and respect for minority rights.[11]

Though saying that Canada has now become a mere quasi democracy may seem an audacious claim, I do not think that it is all that out of line with what is being said by some others. Indeed what theorists call a crisis of legitimacy is much about us.[12] Public recognition of the failings of our political institutions and leadership was expressed to the Spicer Commission, for instance.[13] Professor Donald Savoie has come close to saying something similar in his recent book and his CPSA presidential address looking at Prime Ministerial power.[14] The political columnist of the *Globe and Mail*, Jeffrey Simpson has entitled his book about the Chrétien government *The Friendly Dictatorship*.[15] And while it has always been easy to exaggerate the democratic nature of Canadian politics, I do see a significant deterioration from the textbook descriptions of liberal democracy as representative government and parliamentary democracy.

This is not to say that Canada is now a tyranny. Most of the elements of formal liberal democracy remain intact; the secret ballot for example, and constitutionally mandated elections. It is more that the tendency to govern by oligarchy has overrun the democratic character of our politics. What Macpherson alluded to as "pluralist elitist" politics and government in his discussion of model three has deteriorated into a sort of self-perpetuating oligarchy. The oligarchy in question is made up of those with large scale property holdings that they are determined to protect and enrich, or what is called in every day language, large investors.

The chapter is divided into two parts. The decline of liberal democracy in Canada and its eventual replacement by a quasi-democracy is the subject of the first part; the reasons for this substitution are essayed in the second part. The argument will be made that the Canadian democratic gap can be traced to the reassertion of property rights to the point that the effective control of the political system has ceased to lie with the people of Canada. Political power now rests with large property owners to a degree that is incompatible with the basic principles of liberal democracy. The conclusion follows: Canada needs a democratic revolution. Such an event can only occur if and when a mass movement of citizens decides to use the democratic franchise to implant majority rule.

THE DEMOCRATIC GAP

It will easily be agreed that majority rule is a basic element of democracy. Of course in a Westminster model, using a first past the post electoral system, once there are more than two parties it is possible to have a majority government with less than majority support. Following the 2000 election Canada had a majority government; the Liberals held about 60 per cent of the seats in parliament. Yet only about five million of the about 20 million eligible voters turned out to vote for them in that 2000 election. With nearly 40 per cent of our citizenry deciding not to vote, it left the Liberals holding a comfortable parliamentary majority with the support of about 25 per cent of eligible voters.[16] We had moved a long way away from majority rule, further away than ever before, so far away that it was hard not miss that something was amiss.

Perhaps the first quality of a democratic society is that has the means of renewing itself. Through a change in government when something needs to be done it can be done. But it is not apparent that Canada can fix our electoral system. What clearly needs to be done to reverse the situation is first to recognize there is a problem. But that requires a commitment to majority rule. And, unfortunately we can no longer assume we have the mechanism – liberal democracy – to change the system.

The obvious way to fix the most glaring electoral inequities of the first past the post system is to follow the rest of the world and adopt proportional representation (PR). This has been advocated by the NDP for some time. As the erstwhile third party they would have benefited, obviously, but they are no longer so alone in addressing the issue. It has become a research question for the IRPP (now headed by Hugh Segal a prominent Conservative). It published a paper by a leading electoral studies scholar, Richard Johnston, which concluded this is the way to go, and organized a conference to discuss the idea more completely.[17] Unfortunately for PR supporters the way ahead to PR is far from clear. Few believe that the current government would introduce measures to eliminate its own standing in the country. It is not likely that a coalition of parties can be brought together to defeat the government around the PR issue.

Professor Johnston (among others) sees the principle of political alternance, a government in waiting ready to replace the ruling party, as now lacking in our current multi-party incarnation of the Westminster model. If Canada looks like a one party state to an authority on electoral politics this is prima facie evidence that something is amiss with Canadian equilibrium democracy. It will be recalled that Macpherson drew on the seminal work of Joseph Schumpeter to characterize the role of this model that is "to choose the men who will do the deciding." [18] When there is no meaningful choice for government except the leading party, the model no long carries out its main function.

Some maintain that pure or partial PR leaves countries with majority rule but may also brings ineffective government. Rather than debate this point, or debate the idea that one party states can be democratic, I prefer to take the absence of majority rule as a starting point for a description of other ways in which Canada falls short of the democratic mark. These will be presented, and then briefly discussed, but none of the characteristics stands alone, and each is linked to others. It should be added that I would not maintain that these anti-democratic features could be removed or modified by the institution of PR. But I do see the current electoral system as making things less democratic than they could be under PR.

Macpherson pointed out that a competitive market did imply that consumers could choose between competing baskets from producers of different goods. Today this proposition seems to fail in three related ways. First, sometimes it seems opposition parties offer the same electoral goods as governments are providing, irrespective of the differences they claim to represent. This absence of "product differentiation" is more than a problem of political marketing. It represents an unwillingness to break ranks with the dominant class interests represented by business. An example would be the Ontario Liberal party. It has not attempted to contrast its tax policies with those defended by the Harris government. Yet tax cuts make up the central substantive changes introduced by the Harris regime with the strong support of business groups. Instead the Liberals offer different packaging.

Second, when voters believe they are choosing one set of policies, they may find themselves getting for their vote another set of policies they did not vote for, and may even have voted against. This represents a lack of transparency and reflects an absence of authenticity in political life; it has widespread consequences for democratic legitimacy. For instance, the federal Liberals won the 1993 election promising to fight unemployment and protect government spending. By 1995 they were going further in implementing spending cutbacks than the two parties rejected by voters in 1993 had proposed . In short the clear choice turned out to be largely illusionary. Cutbacks were the outcome even though more people voted for the party that won by promising not to cutback. Liberals wanted to preempt any resurgence of business interest and support for the two parties likely to be the beneficiaries of business financial support in the event the Liberals were found wanting on the deficit issue. In effect the political system had no mechanism to make the party in power accountable to anybody other than its financial backers. Eventually the economy did recover, once the Canadian dollar underwent what was in effect a competitive devaluation of close to 20 per cent. But as was shown by the annual CHO!CES/CCPA Alternative Federal Budgets it need not to have taken so long if reducing unemployment had been the goal.[19]

I take this second feature to be a violation of a general principle associated with democracy at least since the Athenian polis: government by discussion and debate. In effect our system no longer functions through open discussion and debate. Behind the scenes pressure was exerted on the Liberals by a business coalition that favoured cuts to government spending (and a neoliberal package of privatization, de-regulation, and expanded rights for corporations through international trade agreements). The financial backers of the government were determined to get their way. In the debate over economic policy, secrecy and "behind closed doors" decision-making pushed open politics aside. Without open politics democracy becomes a self-parody.

The third way in which voter choices were reduced was through the policy package associated with neoliberalism that favoured investor rights over citizen rights. In fact the choices made by the Liberal government amounted to a reduction in options open to citizens. This can be seen through a series of policy changes. Pressure to maintain low wages was one result of the social cuts of the 1995 budget. When it came to making its spending choices the Liberals abolished the Canada Assistance Plan, which was the federal government's commitment to alleviate poverty, and further reduced unemployment benefits while tightening eligibility. In effect parliament reduced the choices available to the unemployed in order to reduce the cost of labour to business. For much of the 1990s when employment creation did take place it was short-term, part-time, poor quality jobs and so-called self-employment that prevailed.

The gamut of neoliberal policies including privatization, de-regulation, and so-called free trade had the effect of taking issues out of the public sphere and putting them into the hands of private-for-profit operations. As more and more rules and regulations are made by private business, the amount of public space diminishes and so does the democratic potential of a society.

Where this becomes most clear is with the exercise of monopoly rights by corporations that are akin to taxation powers, supposedly reserved for democratic bodies, legislatures and parliament. Those who must deal with the banks, and that is most people, pay the equivalent of a tax, called a service charge, every time they undertake a transaction. Banks profits are underwritten by the privileges granted them by parliamentary charter. Yet the parliament no long exercises regulatory control over bank charges, credit card interest rates, or lending practices. Until 1967 there was an effective parliamentary regulatory ceiling of six per cent on bank loans. It was removed to "foster competition." Bank oligopolies increased their dominance of the financial industry by taking over the independent brokerage firms. As Eric Kierans has argued, these provided an alternative avenue for domestic Canadian business to seek to expand.[20] The Canadian banks now have acquired the equivalent of taxation powers along with their monopoly position in consumer and business finance.

In other industries such as scheduled domestic airline service, cable television, or residential telephone service, effective monopoly positions have been acquired by privately owned corporations such as Air Canada, Rogers, Bell Canada and Telus. The loss of public ownership over vital infrastructure leaves the public interest to be defended by regulatory bodies that have a history of being captured by the industries they are supposed to be controlling.

The role played in the democratic process by institutions that are secretive and difficult to make accountable to parliament or even to cabinet is not limited to regulatory bodies. This has been evident also with the Bank of Canada. The Bank is independent of government but ultimately its governor is answerable to the Minister of Finance. However, since the advent of floating exchange rates internationally, after the American President ended the Bretton Woods system in 1971, the Bank of Canada slowly gained the upper hand over the government in economic policy. Until it over-played its hand in the early 1990s, it was in effective control of the direction of economic policy. Those who realize and knew about this largely thought it was a good thing. Mostly it went unnoticed and unreported. The Bank's power has been somewhat more restrained in the late 1990s since it has, by and large, accomplished its major objectives. However, the power of the central bank to get its way in the context of an eventual international crisis should not be underestimated.[21]

A central bank issues currency; and it is the lender of last resort to the banking system in the event of a crisis. Recently the C.D. Howe Institute has been promoting the idea of a Canada adopting a common currency with the U.S. or a NAFTA dollar. In effect, Canada would give up the sovereign function of central banking. It would adopt the U.S. dollar, eliminating the foreign exchange risk in the process. This could be done through a currency board as in Argentina. But events early in the new century in that country show that a currency board (which acts as borrower of last resort to eliminate the foreign currency risk) can endanger the national credit altogether.

Neither an autocratic central bank operating outside public scrutiny, or a central bank without the power to issue currency are likely to promote democracy. Indeed operating otherwise is perhaps a precondition for democracy, though it is not self-evident how a democratic monetary policy can be organized. The Bank of Canada has made some small steps to open its process to public scrutiny. And more measures would be welcome.

Among other undemocratic features of our politics there is the well-known role of corporations in financing political parties. Less well recognized and documented is the influence peddling that goes on as the parties sell access to cabinet ministers in return for membership fees in the Laurier Club (Liberals) or its Tory equivalent. It is standard practice for corporate lobbyists to have their clients ante up and pursue their goals through the Laurier Club. It holds meetings for its sponsors with politicians that take place safely away from the public domain or convenes dinners featuring the Prime Minister where tables are sold to corporate sponsors.

The parliamentary tax credit was to be a mechanism for bringing individual donors into a more important role. But thanks to the Laurier Club the role of independent donors has not increased markedly. In fact the importance of corporate money has if anything increased since the inception of the political tax credit. This is particularly the case for leadership races as they fall outside the purview of party finance legislation.

The control of the parliamentary process by the Liberals and the decline in resources allotted to parliamentary journalism has meant that the parliamentary committee process is less open and less frequently the subject of reports. Even printed records have been suppressed. Together these measures reduce the role of parliament to the point that we have less credible parliamentary democracy than in any period in recent history.

Perhaps the most openly undemocratic feature of the Canadian political system is the role now played by international agreements in limiting the sovereignty of our representative bodies. The FTA of 1988 – described by the then U.S. president as a new economic constitution for North America – and now its successor accord, NAFTA, set clear limits on the role of government, and give new rights to corporations. The potential of a trade deal to act as a corporate charter of rights was first revealed to others and me through our examination of the interim agreement that preceded that final text of the FTA.[22] This characterization has stood up through examinations of the legal text of the FTA, the NAFTA, the MAI draft text, the WTO agreements and now the FTAA draft. This aspect of the agreements is routinely denied by ministers and by academics favourable to the deals yet is obvious to thousands of anti-free trade activists.

Irony of ironies, international agreements were widely understood in postwar Canada as enhancing sovereignty. Smaller states gained when rules tied down the capacity of larger states to exact advantage in bilateral "negotiations." The Bretton Woods system was deemed important to Canadian autonomy to the extent that it succeeded in bringing the actions of the U.S. under international control. But the movement towards continental integration by the Canadian authorities and the demise of the multilateral system of payments with the Europeans establishing first the EMS and now the Euro have left Canada in a more exposed position *vis à vis* the U.S. In effect, as is increasingly clear, the U.S. leverage over Canada has increased to the point where Canada is stuck defending or not opposing U.S. action however reprehensible that action appears to others. The new openness to a continental energy pact and the reluctance of Canada to stand firm on the Kyoto accord once the U.S. withdrew its support contributes to what supporters of a common or human security agenda must see as an international embarrassment for their goals.

A less well understood aspect of our public life is the role played by intellectuals. I would argue that despite the emergence of independent thinkers associated with social movements – where there are some strong minds and articulate voices that deserve more public space than they get – on balance intellectuals have been an active force promoting and assisting democratic decline. The idea that thinkers and writers on the corporate payroll enhance business capacity to secure public policy outcomes favourable to corporate objectives is hardly an exceptional argument. The extension of this mercenary principle to corporate support for research and publication by so-called think tanks means that in the U.S. alone, in the 1990s, about one billion dollars was "invested" in this fashion with most of this output spilling over into Canada. The perceived worth of these investments is signaled by their expansion.

What has been more significant in Canada is that the independent role of University research has been seriously comprised by the corporatization of University based intellectual life. In the context of public sector cutbacks which, as shall be discussed further below, threaten the social and economic equality needed for a democratic society, by and large the University moved to have corporate money (and student tuition hikes) replace public money. Students take part-time jobs to pay inflated tuition (and thus avoid the worst aspects of personal debt). As a result the Universities not only reduced the amount of time students could devote to course work, they limited student access to extracurricular intellectual activity, thus diminishing the quality of post-secondary education, especially for undergraduates.

The direct corporate sponsorship of University research through grants, consulting contracts, and even the naming of faculties and the creation of chairs with corporate funding, undermines scholarly independence. Few serious people doubt this.

Encouraged by University leaders fully beholden to big business and reluctant to criticize government, the search for truth has become the quest for funding. Training students for roles in government and corporations replaces education of future citizens in the virtues of independent thought and analysis. The cost to democratic life is significant.

WHY IS CANADA NOW ONLY A QUASI-DEMOCRACY?

A country that is far from respecting the principle of majority rule, has thwarted government by discussion and debate, and suspended respect for an economic minority, namely the poor, no longer qualifies as a full democracy in the eyes of a political scientist. Our arrival in the category quasi democracy is not an act of god, an accident or something outside our power to remedy. But as we act it is useful to try and understand what has led to this retrogression. From the heady days when Pierre Trudeau, echoing Frank Scott, called for Canada to become a just society, or when he asked fellow Liberals to embrace participatory democracy, what has happened? [23]

A basic understanding of Canada requires that our politics be seen as being about more than the Westminster model of parliamentary democracy.

As is well understood Canada has a written constitution and a federal structure so that its political life includes constitutional politics in addition to parliamentary democracy. But it is important as well to recognize that Canada is a post-colonial state. This is where the political economy perspective becomes essential to understanding political life. In fact I attribute the deterioration in Canadian democracy to a dynamic whereby the desire of owners of capital to protect the accumulation process has led to basic political rights of representation being overwhelmed by the combined political intervention of foreign and domestic investors to protect their perceived interests. Our postcolonial state facilitates the operation of outside forces, perhaps because it was largely created to respond to events overseas. The weight of corporate interests in public life reflects strategic cross-border alliances and new ways of doing politics.

What we have seen in contemporary politics with the ascendancy of neoliberalism is the extension of investor's rights to the point they now trump civic rights. Neoliberalism itself posits that there is no common good other than private gain. In this sense neoliberalism is the ideology of the investor, an investor who serves all by seeking to maximize profit. But what happens when the investor enters in conflict with workers and with the rest of society over the distribution of wealth and income? Does the greatest number win out through democratic government in action? Neoliberalism holds that only the market is productive, and that the public sector represents a burden on society. From there it is just a short step to urging the elimination of public services and arguing for tax cuts. But this is being done on behalf of property rights and accumulation, understood by, say, Hayek or Friedman, as the basis of freedom. Democracy is no guarantee of freedom; only the protection of property rights assures freedom.

To this neoliberal answer, the question is what about people who have no property or very little property? What exactly does freedom mean when it is exercised primarily for property holders? Freedom for whom, freedom for what ends?

There is yet a third way to see our world, call it the "basic needs" model of political economy or the democratic model. In this perspective, the economy is about people working together to meet each other's needs.

I would argue that human rights are founded on satisfying basic needs. The right to food, shelter and clothing means (in Canada and other OECD nations) the right to basic incomes. Access to education, leisure, recreation and cultural products requires public investment. Identity rights mean the right to citizenship and to exercise civic rights. The accumulation of *personal* property for private pleasure and enjoyment is not at odds with this perspective, but neoliberalism is inimical to it.

"Global turbulence" today features the clash of human rights against property rights. A new set of ecological concerns about clean water, safe food, atmospheric pollution and global warming are tied closely to human basic needs. When formulated as such it is readily apparent they are directly opposed to corporate property rights. Corporations want to use competitive industrial practices even if it means polluting ground water, they see profits in patenting plant life, and shareholder value in increasing the rate of exploitation of natural resources to maintain and export the American lifestyle.

The outcome of battles over water safety, food, and the atmosphere turns on the political process itself. Democracy is one of the tools for dealing with these issues. It is much easier to get legislative action through corporate donations to political parties, lobbying leaders, advertising budgets that keep investigative reporters away, research contracts with Universities, and international trade agreements than it is to win a public debate.

The power of politics is such that corporate property rights depend on favourable political outcomes. Changing the rules of the political system to provide for proportional representation, more open debate and informed discussion, and protection of the poor does not appeal to corporate leaders. Indeed much effort has been expended to ensure precisely the opposite. While Canadian business has proved mediocre at business, they have proven themselves highly skilled at the arts of politics. In essence they have succeeding in taking the equilibrium out of equilibrium democracy, leaving us with a political life so heavily balanced towards corporate interests that it no longer is democratic.

The conclusion is surely that Canada needs a democratic revolution. This is Canada so it should be peaceful. It can be based on the existing near universal franchise. Indeed the fight for the vote by women and by working people has yet to fulfill the hopes and aspirations of those who led the struggle. The potential power of the franchise should not be underestimated however. If electoral politics were unimportant would corporations spend so much time and effort in affecting the outcome? A citizen's movement, a Citizens party if you wish, has the potential to overcome the gap between our political system and a thorough going democracy.

NOTES

1 It is obviously possible to envisage a pre-historical time when "everything was *res nulllius* (a thing belonging to no one)." See Benn (1967) pp. 491-494.

2 He is perhaps best know for: Macpherson (1962).

3 Macpherson (1953).

4 Macpherson (1977).

5 Macpherson (1978).

6 Recently he has called for "scholarship with commitment" (using the English expression), see Bourdieu (2001).

7 Macpherson (1985) p. 91.

8 Canadian theorists such as Frank Cunningham, Phillip Resnick and David Shugarman owe an obvious debt to Macpherson. His work seems to have had little influence on Will Kymlicka. James Tully, who like Macpherson engaged with Locke seems to have been unimpressed by what Macpherson had to say.

9 The 1961 essay "Market Concepts in Political Science" first appeared in the *Canadian Journal of Economics and Political Science* and was reprinted in Machperon (1971) Chapter X.

10 Macpherson saw theories of equilibrium democracy as being both a description and a justification, see Macpherson (1977) p. 22, pp. 80-90.

11 Discussion of whether or not a particular action is democratic is traditional in partisan politics, its an element of party competition. Similarly observers of politics use non-democratic as a criticism of policies. In what follows something else is being attempted. The paper argues that the shortcomings of the political system itself are now so great that it can no longer be considered liberal democratic, even by those who are partisans of that system. In other words, by the terms of the equilibrium model, whether one is a partisan of that model or not, Canada no longer qualifies.

12 For a major summary statement, see Wolfe (1977).

13 Formally known as the *Citizen's Forum on Canada's Future* it was established by the Prime Minister in 1990 following the failure of the Meech Lake Accord. It was headed by Keith Spicer then editor of the *Ottawa Citizen.*

14 Savoie (1999).

15 Simpson (2001).

16 Complete results are available from Elections Canada Internet web site.

17 Johnston (2000).

18 Macpherson (1977) p. 78.

19 See, for instance, Canadian Centre for Policy Alternatives and Choices: A Coalition for Social Justice (1997).

20 Kierans (2001) pp. 60-5.

21 On the relationship between the Bank and the government, see McQuaig (1998) pp. 102-38.

22 Cameron (1988).

23 McCall and Clarkson (1990) p. 115.

REFERENCES

Benn, S. I. 1967. "Property." In *The Encyclopedia of Philosophy*, Vol. 5 & 6. London and New York: Macmillan, pp. 491-494.

Bourdieu, Pierre. 2001. "Pour un savoir e engagé." In Contre-feux 2. Paris: Editions Raisons d'Agir.

Cameron, Duncan, ed. (1988). *The Free Trade Deal.* Toronto: Lorimer.

Canadian Centre for Policy Alternatives and Choices: A Coalition for Social Justice. 1997. *Alternative Federal Budget Papers 1997.* Ottawa: CCPA.

Johnston, Richard. 2000. "Canadian Elections at the Millennium." *Choices*, 6, no. 6 (September).

Kierans, Eric (with Walter Stewart). 2001. *Remembering.* Toronto: Stoddart.

Macpherson, C.B. 1953. *Democracy in Alberta: Social Credit and the Party System.* Toronto: University of Toronto Press.

Macpherson, C.B. 1962. *The Political Theory of Possessive Individualism: Hobbes to Locke.* Oxford: Oxford University Press.

Machperon, C.B. 1971. *Democratic Theory.* Oxford: Oxford University Press, ch. 10.

Macpherson, C.B. 1977. *The Life and Times of Liberal Democracy.* Oxford: Oxford University Press.

Macpherson, C.B., ed. 1978. *Property: Mainstream and Critical Positions.* Toronto: University of Toronto Press.

Macpherson, C.B. 1985. "Property as a Means or End." In *The Rise and Fall of Economic Justice and Other Essays.* Oxford: Oxford University Press.

McCall, Christina, and Stephen Clarkson. (1990). *Trudeau and Our Times Volume 1: The Magnificent Obsession.* Toronto: McClelland & Stewart.
McQuaig, Linda. (1998). *The Cult of Impotence.* Toronto: Viking Penguin.
Savoie, Donald. 1999. *Governing From the Centre: The Concentration of Power in Canadian Politics.* Toronto: University of Toronto Press.
Simpson, Jeffrey. 2001. *The Friendly Dictatorship.* Toronto: McClelland & Stewart.
Wolfe, Allan. 1977. *The Limits of Legitimacy.* New York: The Free Press.

Index

S. McBride et al. (eds.), Global Instability, 233–237.

Social Indicators Research Series

1. V. Møller (ed.): *Quality of Life in South Africa.* 1997 ISBN 0-7923-4797-8
2. G. Baechler: *Violence Through Environmental Discrimination.* Causes, Rwanda Arena, and Conflict Model. 1999 ISBN 0-7923-5495-8
3. P. Bowles and L.T. Woods (eds.): *Japan after the Economic Miracle.* In Search of New Directories. 1999 ISBN 0-7923-6031-1
4. E. Diener and D.R. Rahtz (eds.): *Advances in Quality of Life Theory and Research.* Volume I. 1999 ISBN 0-7923-6060-5
5. Kwong-leung Tang (ed.): *Social Development in Asia.* 2000 ISBN 0-7923-6256-X
6. M.M. Beyerlein (ed.): *Work Teams: Past, Present and Future.* 2000 ISBN 0-7923-6699-9
7. A. Ben-Arieh, N.H. Kaufman, A.B. Andrews, R. Goerge, B.J. Lee, J.L. Aber (eds.): *Measuring and Monitoring Children's Well-Being.* 2001 ISBN 0-7923-6789-8
8. M.J. Sirgy: *Handbook of Quality-of-Life Research. An Ethical Marketing Perspective.* 2001 ISBN 1-4020-0172-X
9. G. Preyer and M. Bös (eds.): *Borderlines in a Globalized World.* New Perspectives in a Sociology of the World-System. 2002 ISBN 1-4020-0515-6
10. V. Nikolic-Ristanovic: *Social Change, Gender and Violence: Post-communist and war affected societies.* 2002 ISBN 1-4020-0726-4
11. M.R. Hagerty, J. Vogel and V. Møller: *Assessing Quality of Life and Living Conditions to Guide National Policy.* 2002 ISBN 1-4020-0727-2
12. M.J. Sirgy: *The Psychology of Quality of Life.* 2002 ISBN 1-4020-0800-7
13. S. McBride, L. Dobuzinskis, M. Griffin Cohen and J. Busumtwi-Sam (eds.): *Global Instability.* Uncertainty and new visions in political economy. 2002 ISBN 1-4020-0946-1

KLUWER ACADEMIC PUBLISHERS – DORDRECHT / LONDON / BOSTON

MIX
Papier aus verantwortungsvollen Quellen
Paper from responsible sources
FSC® C105338

If you have any concerns about our products,
you can contact us on
ProductSafety@springernature.com

In case Publisher is established outside the EU,
the EU authorized representative is:
Springer Nature Customer Service Center GmbH
Europaplatz 3, 69115 Heidelberg, Germany

Printed by Libri Plureos GmbH
in Hamburg, Germany